Quest For
World Monetary Order

A Twentieth Century Fund Study

The Twentieth Century Fund is an independent research foundation which undertakes policy studies of economic, political, and social institutions and issues. The Fund was founded in 1919 and endowed by Edward A. Filene.

Errata

The names of August Heckscher and Arthur M. Schlesinger, Jr., were inadvertently omitted from the list of the Board of Trustees of the Twentieth Century Fund, whose chairman is Don K. Price.

Published by John Wiley & Sons, Inc.

Copyright ©1980 by the Twentieth Century Fund

This publication is designed to provide accurate and
authoritative information in regard to the subject
matter covered. It is sold with the understanding that
the publisher is not engaged in rendering legal, accounting,
or other professional service. If legal advice or other
expert assistance is required, the services of a competent
professional person should be sought. *From a Declaration
of Principles jointly adopted by a Committee of the
American Bar Association and a Committee of Publishers.*

Library of Congress Cataloging in Publication Data:
Gilbert, Milton, 1909-1979.
   Quest For World Monetary Order.

   "A Twentieth Century Fund study."
   "A Wiley-Interscience publication."
   Includes bibliographical references and index.
   1. International finance. I. Title.

HG3881.G55   332.4'566   80-17865
ISBN 0-471-07998-7

Printed in the United States of America

10 9 8 7 6 5 4 3 2 1

. . . greatness thrust upon them

To Murray

Foreword

In the early 1970s, Milton Gilbert approached me with the notion of undertaking a study of the international monetary system under the auspices of the Twentieth Century Fund. I was at once receptive, partly because international monetary affairs were then undergoing great changes due to the recent move to floating exchange rates following the breakdown of the fixed exchange rate system set at Bretton Woods, partly because of my regard for Gilbert's intellectual grasp and independence. He was at that time the economic advisor to the Bank for International Settlements (BIS) in Basel, Switzerland, and from that position, where he had to cope with institutional inhibitions, he nevertheless commented so trenchantly on monetary developments that the BIS annual review was required reading for international bankers. In that first conversation with me at the Fund, he was so troubled by the conventional wisdom among economists—and what he considered to be the misjudgments and mistakes of policymakers in economic and monetary affairs—that he wanted to write, under his own name, a critical analysis of economic events from the beginning of the postwar period and to use that analysis as a means of formulating effective policy recommendations for the future.

Since Gilbert had been an informed and interested observer as far back as Bretton Woods and subsequently had been close to the center of events, first at the Organization for Economic Cooperation and later at the BIS, he seemed ideally suited to carry out this formidable task. Although I encouraged him to set to work on a proposal that could pass muster with the Fund's Board of Trustees, he did not submit his proposal for almost a year because of the press of his BIS responsibilities. Then, following the Board's approval, Gilbert had to postpone the start of his project for the Fund as one crisis after another, beginning with the recycling problem that followed the rise in petroleum prices, held him to his official responsibilities.

As one year passed, then two, I sometimes began to doubt Gilbert's intentions. More than once I suggested to him that his study would be overtaken by events. Yet he kept assuring me that he was committed to the project, and on each such occasion he argued that he could not desert the BIS at so critical a juncture; he would then go on to predict, with considerable prescience, a series of economic upheavals that he believed had to take place before there was any hope of reform. My patience was often tried, but I never quite lost faith that Gilbert would eventually meet his commitment.

My faith was based largely on a fairly long acquaintance with Gilbert. As a financial writer, I had always sought him out on trips to Europe because he was so informed and interesting a source. I do not mean to imply that Gilbert leaked information. He was, as his loyalty to the BIS attests, a remarkably conscientious civil servant who was always discreet about anything that demanded discretion. But although, for almost three decades, he worked abroad in international organizations where his words represented his own viewpoints and were not those of an official representative of the United States, he remained a concerned American rather than an expatriate, eager to discuss economic and political happenings and to provide his own spirited, often caustic views on the shortcomings of specific policies. It was only after Gilbert left the BIS and began work in earnest on his project that our relationship grew much more intimate. He had a diversity of interests, ranging from music to carpentry, from antiques to "whodunits," but our conversations inevitably returned to economic and monetary matters, particularly the American economy and the dollar—and to his manuscript.

Gilbert cared about language and writing, a comparatively rare trait among economists. He was a slow, even painstaking writer, who sought brevity sometimes at the expense of comprehension. Once he had begun to submit draft manuscript, we had many long arguments; often I wanted him to elaborate points to make his account more accessible to the nonexpert, whereas he, claiming that he had devoted a lot of time and effort to give the reader only what was essential, resisted. In the end, he agreed to make revisions and even additions, provided he found something to delete. He would fuss over a word, changing it to obtain a more precise meaning, and grumble about the insertion or addition of a paragraph. After the manuscript was in good enough shape to submit to publishers, and even after it was accepted by John Wiley and Sons, Gilbert continued his revisions. I remember an exhausting debate over the telephone concerning some suggested changes that he thought unnecessary; but he finally yielded when I pointed out that writing a few more pages would enable him to cut out a lengthy section with which he had been unhappy. He was working on the new material as well as some significant changes in the concluding chapter when, three days later, he died.

The loss of a friend, and I had come to know Milton Gilbert as a good and close friend, is always a shock. It was doubly so in this case because his was a sudden death that came when he was still not finished with his book. Indisputably, it was his book, but it still called for changes that Gilbert, who was something of a perfectionist, was intent on carrying out. Thus, after consulting with his wife, Ruth Gilbert, I asked Peter Oppenheimer and Michael Dealtry, both of whom had been friends and associates of Gilbert, to serve as editors of his manuscript. In addition, Edward M. Bernstein, an old friend and colleague who had commented on Gilbert's first draft, took time from a busy schedule to provide Oppenheimer and Dealtry with added comments.

All of us at the Fund are indebted to Gilbert's surrogates for their swift and smooth collaboration. Oppenheimer, who worked at Christ Church in Oxford, and Dealtry, who is still at the BIS in Basel, deliberately chose to refrain from impinging their own views on Gilbert's. And though they can rightly claim a thorough knowledge of Gilbert's position, they carefully avoided trying to capture the subtleties and nuances—and Gilbert was a man of nuance—of his thinking when they were at all in doubt. The result is a book faithful to Gilbert's work and a tribute to his memory. He was, as one friend has said, a man who "was sometimes wrong about little things, but always right about the big things." I can add only that while Gilbert could be distracted by a Chinese vase, a pretty girl, or a game of golf, he always kept his eye on the big things.

Anyone who knew Gilbert will acknowledge that he would have liked nothing better than to provoke debate and to respond to criticism. He had a zest for intellectual combat, which he was less than diplomatic about, despite all his experience in international negotiations. But that was a measure of his honesty. He also was fair, never engaging in personal attacks. I am sure that his book will be considered controversial, and more than anything else, I regret that he will not have the pleasure of answering his critics.

M.J. ROSSANT

Editors' Introduction

Milton Gilbert was working on the final stages of this book when he died on September 28, 1979. At the request of Murray J. Rossant, director of the Twentieth Century Fund, and with the agreement of Mrs. Ruth Gilbert, we have undertaken the tasks of editing the manuscript for publication and contributing this introduction.

Gilbert was with the Organization for European Economic Cooperation (OEEC) from 1950-60, first as Director of Statistics and subsequently also as Director of Economics. From 1960-75, he served as Economic Advisor of the Bank for International Settlements (BIS). His book is at once a personal memoir and an analytical history of the international monetary system from the Bretton Woods Agreement of 1944 to the late 1970s. His purpose in writing it was twofold: to present his view of events in which he had participated or whose consequences he had observed at close quarters and also to criticize what he saw as erroneous or misleading arguments of others, whether policymakers or academics. The criticism is, for the most part, mildly expressed; if an aggressive note sometimes creeps in, it is essentially in response to U.S. policies toward the dollar after 1960, policies that Gilbert believed to be fundamentally wrong and that he sought, in vain, to change. His efforts in this respect were based on his own contribution to the analysis of the monetary system, an absolutely central contribution that stands out from the mass of economic writing devoted to this area since 1960.

Gilbert first formulated his ideas on the subject in a long essay written in the mid-1960s, which was subsequently published in two parts: the first as Princeton Essay in International Finance No. 70, *The Gold-Dollar System: Conditions of Equilibrium and the Price of Gold,* and the second as a Charles C. Moskowitz lecture, "The Discipline of the Balance of Payments and the Design of the International Monetary System" (in *Inflation: The Charles C. Moskowitz Lectures for 1970*, New York University Press). The present posthumous book owes much to that earlier essay, although it ranges far more widely.

Gilbert's contribution was to fill an important gap in the analysis begun by Robert Triffin in *Gold and the Dollar Crisis* (Yale University Press, 1960) of the relationship between the U.S. balance of payments and the condition of the international monetary system as a whole. Triffin had noted that, by running an overall deficit in its balance of payments, the United States was acting as a net supplier of foreign-exchange reserves to the rest of the world. The "Triffin dilemma" focused on the fact that this process was weakening the external liquidity position of the United States and could not continue indefinitely without calling into question the dollar's convertibility into gold at $35 an ounce. Hence, it was argued, the United States would sooner or later have to take steps to eliminate its external deficit; the world would thereupon face a shortage of international liquidity and accordingly would have to choose among a higher gold price, abandonment of fixed exchange rates in favor of floating ones, and an increasingly centralized system controlled by an International Monetary Fund (IMF) with greatly extended powers over the policies of its member countries.

This account, impressive though it was, had little to say about the *causes* of the U.S. deficit or whether the causal mechanism was important for the system's future development. Was it deliberate philanthropy on the part of the United States, a kind of extension of Marshall Plan aid? Or a fortunate accident? Or was the dollar basically overvalued in some long-run sense? And if it was, in what sense? Gilbert provided the main outlines of an answer to these questions. The roots of the U.S. deficit lay neither in philanthropy nor in coincidence but in the condition of the international monetary system itself, and specifically in the deficient inflow of new monetary gold at the prevailing official price, coupled with the world's reliance on gold and dollars to provide for the expansion of international reserves. To satisfy the demand of the rest of the world for increments in reserves, the United States was not only bound, if it failed to run a payments deficit of its own accord, to be pushed into deficit by the policies of other countries; in addition, at the existing price of gold, this deficit was bound to involve a persistent drain on the U.S. gold reserve because the U.S. Treasury, by standing ready to sell gold to foreign monetary authorities against dollars, was acting in effect as buffer-stock manager for the underpriced gold reserves of the world as a whole. In this respect, the dollar's problems arose from its overvaluation—but overvaluation, in common with all other currencies, vis-à-vis gold, not overvaluation vis-à-vis other major currencies.

The picture was complicated by the fact that in the late 1960s, as a consequence of the war in Vietnam and other factors, the dollar also gradually became overvalued in relation to other currencies. The two causative elements in the U.S. deficit were difficult to disentangle—especially, of course, by those who refused to recognize that gold had played any part in the first place. The IMF Articles had used the term "fundamental disequilibrium" to denote a situation in which a change in the exchange parity of an individual currency was appropriate. Gilbert's insight was to see that this term also could be applied by analogy to the monetary system as a whole, to denote a situation in which a change in the gold value of all currencies, as opposed to the parity of a single currency, was appropriate. Such a situation affected the United States in a unique way because of the dollar's central role in the system. But just as the IMF Articles provided for alteration of the par value of a single currency (including the par value of the dollar) if that currency was in fundamental disequilibrium, so they also provided for a "uniform change in par values," that is, for a general rise in the price of gold, to remedy what Gilbert called a fundamental disequilibrium of the system itself.

It followed from this analysis that Triffin was mistaken in his conception of a world not having to choose its future monetary constitution until the U.S. external deficit had been corrected. The choice would be essentially preempted by the United States itself in deciding what to do, or not to do, about its deficit—that is, whether to devalue the dollar against gold or to abrogate its convertibility into gold (it was evident that Triffin's third option, centralized management of the world monetary system, was not a practical possibility since it would require a large step in the direction of world government).

Gilbert had much more than an academic's concern with the balance-of-payments adjustment mechanism for the United States. Throughout his years spent abroad as an international official, he never ceased to be a devoted American. And he perceived that an adamant refusal to raise the dollar price of gold would not merely render the fixed-rate system unworkable, but also would undermine the position of the U.S. dollar in particular, and was therefore contrary to the national interests of the United States. He received no thanks from U.S. officialdom for saying so, as he himself recalled at his farewell dinner at the BIS in 1975:

> When I look back now over fifteen years, I have to admit that in the main thing I tried to accomplish I failed. And that was to convince my own country to take the action necessary to maintain the status of the dollar, to correct the balance-of-payments deficit and to abide by the Bretton Woods system....It's not only that they did not want to follow me; they were so caught up by the political difficulty in the United States, they couldn't clear their minds enough to even understand me.... You know, they came to treat me not only as wrong, but as a kind of a half-traitor, lined up with Rueff and de Gaulle. Why? Just because I argued that we didn't have to sit on our hands and lose billions of dollars every year—to a total of over sixty-five billions, about five Marshall Plans.

Gilbert also was incensed by the acquiescence, or worse, in this process on the part of the great majority of his fellow American economists, an attitude that he felt reflected both intellectual and political shortcomings. Gold had long ceased to be a part of the domestic money supply, and the dollar was functioning as the principal intervention and reserve currency of the international system. In these circumstances, the idea that the character of the system still somehow hinged on gold was intellectually repugnant to most economists, who therefore did not take the trouble to try to understand it. Of course, the dollar's attraction as a currency was connected with its purchasing power in terms of U.S. goods and services, and also with the facilities offered by the New York money market for the investment of liquid funds. Gold, however, enabled the dollar to stand at the center of a fixed-rate system because, as an inherently scarce, real commodity alternative to the dollar, it provided the United States both with a criterion of balance-of-payments discipline (namely, the dollar's convertibility into gold), and with a vital instrument to help observe that discipline and keep the dollar strong (namely, a change in the dollar's par value).

Some commentators, both anti- and pro-gold, appeared to think that the discipline of gold was an all-or-nothing matter: either gold was the sole international reserve medium of any consequence and it had a price in terms of major currencies that never changed or it could play no monetary role whatever. This view may have been a tribute to folk-memories of the pre-1914 gold standard, but it showed little grasp of the foundations of the Bretton Woods system. A substantial change in the dollar price of gold was entirely consistent with—and in the end necessary for—maintaining the Bretton Woods system, provided only that such changes were not so frequent or so large that the gold market became continuously dominated by speculation about the next change.

With the abrogation of the dollar's convertibility into gold in 1971, the United States ceased to have a clear criterion of balance-of-payments discipline, a change reflected in the new presentation of U.S. balance-of-payments statistics after 1976 (see Chapter 9). Moreover, the U.S. authorities lost most of the power that the gold link had given them to manage the U.S. exchange rate and hence to maintain the strength of the dollar in the monetary system. Many academic economists welcomed the resulting move to floating exchange rates—and later added (as if it were self-evident) that the monetary consequences of higher oil prices after 1973 would have made floating inevitable anyhow. But there were also economists who argued that floating rates (and currency blocs) could have been avoided either by devising new options to the dollar in place of gold or by going over to a "dollar standard," in which all countries pegged on the dollar and the United States as the residual ("nth") country in the system would adopt a purely passive attitude to its exchange rate and balance of payments. This dollar standard was an armchair fantasy, particularly given the fact that a major spur to U.S. action on the balance of payments in 1971 was the urgent wish of the authorities in Washington to force a correction of the dollar's overvaluation vis-à-vis other currencies. A return to fixed rates on the basis of IMF Special Drawing Rights (SDRs)—with dollar and other currency reserves restricted in amount and possibly phased out altogether—is something vaguer than an armchair fantasy because its mode of operation cannot be clearly visualized. In the gold-dollar system, there was a strong and direct link between the exchange-rate policy and the international liquidity position of the United States; a reduction in the dollar's par value could always be made large enough to produce a decisive impact on U.S. reserves. To have any foreseeable prospect of viability, a fixed-rate system based on SDRs must reproduce this feature; and the fact that SDRs are a fiduciary asset and not a commodity means that any blueprint to date has been far from doing so.

Exactly how much a timely devaluation of the dollar in the 1960s would have contributed to world monetary stability in the 1970s and 1980s is open to debate. But the prolonged disequilibrium of the fixed-rate system, culminating in a massive flight from the dollar and a mushrooming of central-bank currency holdings, bears a considerable measure of responsibility for the inflationary outburst of the early 1970s—and, incidentally, for the extent of the subsequent increase in the market price of gold. In this connection, Gilbert's analysis also reconciles what were (and perhaps still are) often regarded as contradictory features of the international monetary scene: how could there be at one and the same time a shortage of international liquidity apparently requiring governments to search for new ways of creating reserves and an abundance of international liquidity permitting double-digit inflation by the early 1970s? The answer is that the shortage was never of total world liquidity but only of gold, and the gold shortage itself helped to produce a flow of dollars that ultimately became excessive not only from the standpoint of the U.S. balance of payments but also from that of global reserves and global price stability. By the same token, a deliberate and timely increase in the gold price, adequate to correct the disequilibrium in the gold-dollar system, would not have been inflationary.

Persistent worldwide inflation is the main economic reason why a return to a gold-based monetary system is ruled out for the foreseeable future. In the presence of two-digit inflation, gold cannot—any more than other commodities—be given a fixed price in terms of currencies. Attempts to restore gold's earlier monetary function would therefore have to be preceded by a return to price stability, not the other way around. Gold can help to maintain stability only when stability has been achieved. But questions of price stability apart, attempts to restore gold are ruled out by the political hostility of the United States and many other countries, particularly in the developing world. This hostility is reflected in the 1976 amendments to the IMF Articles of Agreement, which effectively abolished any role for gold in the working of the Fund.

Gilbert believed that exchange reserves are likely in the future to be a mixed bag. The question for the 1980s—just as for the 1960s—is not the volume but the composition of international reserves. Claims denominated in SDRs, and even SDRs themselves, may play a more prominent role than before, along with currencies other than the dollar, as well as dollars and gold. But all this will still be in the context of a floating-rate system among the major currencies. Moreover, under such a system stability is likely to prove an elusive goal for several reasons, not least because of the absence of satisfactory criteria for balance-of-payments policy. Under floating rates, "fundamental disequilibrium" has no clear meaning; the line between autonomous and compensating capital flows becomes even more blurred than before; and a significant element of unpredictability in exchange-rate movements, both short- and medium-term, is a fact of economic life. Yet a worldwide return to fixed rates among market economies is now difficult to envisage.

                              *   *   *

To assist the reader, we have grouped the chapters that follow into four parts. In the first part, which consists only of the first chapter, Gilbert sets forth the nature and causes of payments disequilibrium and the policy measures required to deal with different types of imbalance. The distinction between the two kinds of fundamental disequilibrium in a fixed-rate system— that of a single country's balance of payments and that of the system as a whole—receives primary emphasis, but attention also is paid to the distinction between nonfundamental and fundamental disequilibrium in the balance of payments of an individual country. The second part, which consists of Chapters 2-4, presents case studies of fundamental disequilibria in the balance of payments of individual countries—the United Kingdom, France, and the German Federal Republic—rather than in the system as a whole. At the same time, besides providing lessons in how to address, or not to address, external payments imbalances, the policies followed by these three major countries influenced the course of events in the monetary system. The third part, consisting of Chapters 5-9, focuses on the central issue of the dollar and the disequilibrium of the monetary system, and, in Chapter 8, covers the official negotiations on reform of the system that took place from 1963 to the beginning of 1976. The problems of international liquidity and of adjustment for the dollar were basically two sides of the same coin. Finally, the fourth part, again just one chapter, summarizes the main arguments that have been discussed and reflects briefly on the question of foreign-exchange reserves and international monetary cooperation in the years ahead.

In every chapter, we have corrected a number of obscurities in style or logic; these corrections, intended to improve the book's presentation, neither add to nor subtract from any of its arguments. In addition, we have made specific modifications in Chapter 2 and in the latter part of Chapter 10. Chapter 2 (on the pound sterling) has been somewhat shortened by the removal of secondary details about events in the 1950s and 1960s. At the same time, we did not think it appropriate to lengthen the later pages of the chapter by adding an account of events after March 1974. In the concluding chapter, the remarks on alternatives to the dollar as a reserve asset, which were left by the author in very terse form, have been spelled out at slightly greater length, and with some updating (particularly on gold) to the end of 1979. We removed a similarly terse comment on the desirability of some form of control over the Eurocurrency market. Although the comment itself was perfectly consistent with other parts of the argument, it was difficult to justify retaining it in the absence of any discussion or analysis of the Eurocurrency market earlier in the book. It had been suggested to Gilbert that he add a suitable section on the Euromarkets in the chapters about the dollar. He did not live long enough to do so, and we thought it inappropriate to try to construct what he might have written.

*   *   *

We are greatly indebted to Edward M. Bernstein for numerous comments on almost every chapter (many of which Milton Gilbert had already incorporated) and, in particular, for his remarks on the concluding pages. Gilbert also had received helpful comments from Christopher Dow on Chapter 2, Guillaume Guindey on Chapter 3, and Otmar Emminger on Chapter 4. Thanks are due to Paul Hümbelin and Robert von Werra of the BIS for extensive help with statistics, tables, and charts, and we should add that we have been responsible for the inclusion of all tables and charts. Most of the early drafts of the manuscript had been typed with great speed and efficiency by Gilbert's secretary, Margaret Roalefs.

In conclusion, we must emphasize our belief that the author, had he lived, would undoubtedly have made more substantial additions and alterations to the text of this book than we have felt it right to do. Nevertheless, we hope that the book may be seen as a worthy memorial to Milton Gilbert, who was not only a man of integrity, persistence, and profound insight into economic mechanisms, but also a much loved friend.

PETER OPPENHEIMER
MICHAEL DEALTRY

Oxford, England
Basel, Switzerland
May, 1980

Contents

List of Tables
and Figures

Part I

1

Balance-of-Payments Adjustment and the Gold-Dollar System

This study analyzes the evolution of the international monetary system over the period from the Bretton Woods Agreement to the mid-1970s and the balance-of-payments problems confronting the major industrial nations within the framework of the system. For most of this period, the rule of the system was fixed par values, defined in terms of the gold content of currencies, which were adhered to with but few changes by the industrialized nations from 1950 to 1970. Soon after, however, fixed exchange rates were abandoned in favor of floating rates. As this change was imposed by overwhelming market forces against last-ditch resistance of the authorities, the claim that floating was adopted as a "reform" is disingenuous. Christopher Fildes[1] put the case in better perspective by a quote from Fielding's *Jonathan Wilde:* "He would have ravished her, if she had not, by a timely compliance, prevented him."

An enormous literature has been devoted to the workings of the system, ranging from the books and articles of academic economists dealing with both theory and practice to the reports and statements from official sources. Added to this voluminous material is a mountain of statistics, laws, and regulations.

Yet the subject remains difficult to penetrate. The international monetary system abounds in technical details that must be assigned their appropriate significance. The state of the system changed drastically in the course of time, and traditions and problems differed from one country to another, all of which complicates the drawing of universal propositions. Then, too, the experts have been in rather bewildering disagreement, not only on theoretical issues and policy prescriptions, which is understandable enough, but also on what actually happened.

3

From my standpoint, however, the essential difficulty of a realistic appraisal of events lies elsewhere. Not only must the monetary and economic forces with which the authorities had to contend be taken into account, but the political and social considerations that influenced their attitudes and policy decisions as well. Because the political element was so important to the authorities, the motives for official action were often surrounded by secrecy and half-truths. For the same reason, official accounts of the situation frequently tried to put the best face on the policies and performance of government. An observation made in a quite different field is certainly applicable here: "Objectivity is a dearly bought intellectual commodity and what is unpleasant or distasteful or hurtful of national pride tends to be forgotten or distorted beyond hope of fair judgment."[2]

Because the authorities did not or could not deal forcefully with the balance-of-payments problems as they arose, the monetary system came apart. In some cases, contending with pressure groups proved beyond the strength that governments could muster. Moreover, conflicting advice and disputes over alternative courses of action left the top government policy-makers uncertain about the measures to take or even about the importance of taking them. But above all, governments and parliaments were hypersensitive to political risks and were loath to provoke them. As a result, they were inclined to attempt the art of the economically impossible (Lord Butler, drawing on Bismarck, entitled his political memoirs *The Art of the Possible*), so that the cost in terms of monetary disruption was all the greater.

The international payments problems that came about during the postwar years were of two distinct types. First, there were the situations that primarily involved individual currencies. Because external payments deficits and surpluses of individual nations are interrelated, the difficulties of a particular country may, of course, be influenced by developments in other countries. Excess demand in Italy or France, for example, may suck in imports from West Germany, creating an excessive surplus in West Germany's external accounts. Or Germany's superior competitiveness and consequent large trade surplus may create deficits for Britain and France. Hence, the authorities devoted a great deal of attention to apportioning responsibility for the imbalances between the deficit and surplus countries and to the corrective action that should be taken—with only limited success.

It was usually the case, however, that the problems of, say, sterling or the French franc stemmed mainly from internal developments in Britain or France and were recognized to be of primary concern to these countries. These problems called for national policy measures to bring about a process of adjustment of the country's deficit or surplus in its external accounts, and Chapters 2-4 are intended first and foremost as case studies of such problems and policies. The United States, of course, was also subject to this sort of balance-of-payments problem and was under the obligation to initiate an adjustment process by policy measures to correct its surplus or deficit. Currency difficulties of this type did not themselves jeopardize the stability of the system.

Second, problems arose involving the international monetary system as a whole, which finally led to the breakdown of stable exchange rates based on gold par values and the resort to exchange rates that floated. These problems inevitably involved the dollar. The dollar's involvement was not attributable solely to the weight of the United States in the world economy. The fundamental fact was that the dollar was the reserve currency of the system that commanded the confidence of central banks and of private portfolio managers by virtue of its gold convertibility. Since the system revolved around the dollar, confidence in the dollar and confidence in fixed exchange rates were one and the same. The dollar was the central pillar that held up the structure, and when the pillar was allowed to crumble, the house came down.

While not the exclusive concern of the United States, the problems of the international monetary system could not be solved without the United States. These problems had to do with the growth and composition of official reserves of convertible currencies and gold held by central banks for intervention in the exchange market to support the par values of their currencies. There was much futile wrangling about whether the key issue was the adjustment process or the adequacy of international liquidity (official reserves). In fact, both were involved, since a reasonably prompt adjustment was essential if excessive reserve growth was to be avoided.

I. THE NEW ECONOMIC ENVIRONMENT

The three decades following World War II constitute a unique period in economic and monetary history because of the new ideas and forces that took hold after peace was established. The contrast between the atmosphere of the Great Depression of the 1930s and that of the postwar period was exceptionally profound. Many political, scientific, and economic changes occurred that greatly altered the environment, such as the ending of colonialism, the development of nuclear energy, rocket missiles, space travel, and electronics and computers. But there were four changes critical to the management of external monetary relations.

The Keynesian Revolution

Perhaps the most pervasive change was the Keynesian revolution in economic thought. The practical importance of Keynes's ideas lay not so much in his policy prescriptions as such but in his conviction that through the deliberate management of total demand full employment could and should be a concrete objective of official policy. This objective was accepted by political leaders in almost all of the industrial countries. There was, in fact, such a remarkable success in meeting it that the rise and fall of business activity lost much of its former autonomous character and became rather a reflection of changes in official policy to stimulate the economy or to restrain inflation. It was only after the inflationary boom of 1973 and the impact of the large rise in the price of oil by the Organization of Petroleum Exporting Countries (OPEC) at the end of that year that the world economy suffered a relatively long and severe recession.

However, a consequence of the full-employment objective was that domestic and balance-of-payments requirements were at times in conflict, in the sense that demand policy appropriate to the former was not appropriate to the latter. A conflict of this kind became known in the trade as a "dilemma case." Furthermore, the role of government in economic affairs was thrust into the political arena to a far greater extent than ever before, and a high standard of performance in employment was demanded by the electorate. When the domestic economy was at a low ebb, governments were very reluctant to face an election year without making an effort at remedial action. In many cases, the business cycle became the election cycle—a policy of economic restraint was exercised when an election was sufficiently far off, but a policy of stimulus was followed when election time drew near.[3]

Expansion of the Public Sector

At the same time, the public sector of the national economy underwent a considerable further expansion, to the point where most Western developed countries came to be known as mixed rather than purely market economies. The development of the welfare state and, in countries such as France and the United Kingdom, the nationalization of sectors of the economy were largely responsible. While the various welfare programs reduced human misery, they were not easily contractable when the need for restraint arose, and they often tended to put an excessive strain on public finances, with inflationary consequences.

Increased Power of Labor Unions

The increased strength of organized labor was another important factor contributing to the new environment. Labor unions generally attained a monopolistic market power sanctioned by law in the sense that they were not subject to antimonopoly legislation. After being restrained by official controls during the war, unions were determined to improve the economic status of their members when peace was reestablished. The annual round of wage increases soon became a feature of economic life, with the size of the overall increase in wage levels frequently set by the successful demands of a strong labor organization. As the unions gained both strength at the bargaining table and staying power when the issue came to a strike, excessive wage demands were difficult to resist. The six-month-long strike in the U.S. steel industry in 1959 was only an extreme example of the general problem.

Compared with former times, the determination of wages became less a matter of demand and supply conditions in the labor market and more a sociopolitical phenomenon. In many cases, the unions were rather indifferent to the possible unemployment consequences of their wage demands, leaving it to government welfare programs to limit the damage. Wage policy and wage controls were frequently invoked, but governments were not strong enough to make them effective except over brief periods. In some countries, moreover, the strength of left-wing political parties inhibited official efforts to oppose the power of labor and hold down wage settlements to the size of the increase in productivity. Of course, the large degree of inflation over this period was not entirely the result of excessive wage demands, but this was the major factor. As wages could not be reduced in times of slack, most prices moved only in one direction. And prolonged anti-inflation policies were not practical because persistently high unemployment would have endangered political and social cohesion. The upshot of all this was that wage-push inflation became a force of frequent occurrence that added a new difficulty to the task of maintaining both domestic and external monetary stability.[4]

The Bretton Woods Agreement

The fourth major innovation was the Bretton Woods Agreement of July 1944. The balance-of-payments problems thrown up by the severe economic depression of the 1930s had forced currency depreciation on many countries, and the devaluation of the dollar by President Roosevelt had added to the chaotic international monetary situation, although it also initiated a general increase in the currency price of gold. Many countries had pursued narrowly nationalistic policies, imposing direct restrictions on trade and payments and in some cases joining currency blocs as they saw fit. Restrictions were vastly extended during World War II, partly because of economic rivalry, but mainly because of the pressing need to conserve limited foreign-exchange resources for the essential requirements of war. Hence, it was evident that the postwar period would start with most currencies inconvertible and with international trade and payments heavily constrained by bilateral agreements and other restrictions, many of them discriminatory. A principal motive behind the Bretton Woods Agreement was to commit countries to a return to freedom of trade and payments and convertibility of currencies, as well as to speed up the process of achieving these objectives. The United States, in particular, wanted to see an end to restrictions and discrimination.

At the same time, it was apparent that the war-torn countries would face overwhelming balance-of-payments problems both at the end of the war and in the years of transition to a viable peacetime economy. They would need help in meeting these problems, and the United States would have to be the major source of that help. In response to this need, the United States proposed the creation of the International Monetary Fund (IMF) and the International Bank for Reconstruction and Development (IBRD). Its quid pro quo for being the major supplier of financial resources to these institutions was the reestablishment of free trade and payments as rapidly as possible. With far-reaching vision, these institutions were established on a permanent basis. The Bretton Woods Agreement, concluded while the war was still going on, was an outstanding achievement of economic statesmanship.

It is often thought that Bretton Woods established a new, rigid monetary system based on fixed exchange rates. But this was not the case. The gold parity of the dollar, which was at the center of the system, already existed. The objectives of exchange stability and of cooperation to maintain it had been set forth years before in the Tripartite Agreement of 1936 between the United States, Britain, and France. Owing to the disturbed monetary situation at that time, the commitments undertaken by the three countries remained rather loose, but the basic ideas of exchange stability and cooperation were there.[5]

The Bretton Woods Agreement set up the IMF as the center of international monetary cooperation, declared the principles or objectives that the IMF and its member countries intended to promote, codified certain rules of behavior in monetary affairs, and provided a fund of resources to help members uphold the rules. This first international agreement looking forward to cooperation after the war was a great political achievement and was particularly important in promoting liberalization of international payments. But fixed exchange rates would have been the norm of the system even without Bretton Woods.

The plan submitted by Keynes to the Bretton Woods Conference offered an approach to a really new monetary system. He conceived of access to balance-of-payments credit in a clearing union as a matter of right, and his plan would have accommodated automatically and within large limits the financing needs of deficit countries. It was an idealistic conception, which assumed a world as rational and as high-principled as Keynes was himself. But the United States was skeptical of the plan because of the seemingly open-ended financing commitments that it proposed for surplus countries. Louis Rasminsky, the Canadian expert, criticized the Keynes plan on the grounds that it was not generally considered to be good banking to have the debtors control the bank. The United States clearly shared this view, and put forward the more conservative plan of Harry White of the U.S. Treasury, a plan built around a specified fund to which deficit countries would have access on condition that their policy programs gave reasonable assurance that the deficits would be corrected and the borrowings repaid.[6]

The high-minded intentions of the Bretton Woods negotiators were set forth in the Articles of Agreement of the IMF, which provided machinery for consultation and collaboration to carry out a number of interconnected objectives—to expand and equilibrate the growth of international trade, to promote exchange-rate stability, and to establish multilateral practices in international payments. The articles committed member countries to avoid competitive exchange-rate depreciation. In addition, they stated that the Fund's resources would be available to assist member countries in overcoming balance-of-payments difficulties without resorting to measures inimical to international prosperity. The Fund's role was subsequently reinforced by the new rules for the conduct of international trade set forth in the General Agreement on Tariffs and Trade (GATT).

The Bretton Woods Agreement was established before there was any clear idea of the problems that could arise from the effects of the other main features of the new economic environment. Yet the whole thrust of the agreement was that, after recovery from the war, a reasonable balance in international payments could be achieved in an environment of liberal trade and payments practices, by adequate policy actions. The architects of Bretton Woods were confident that equilibrium of the payments system could be reconciled with the deliberate pursuit of full employment, even though that had never before been tried. While they were too sophisticated in practical affairs to expect no difficulties to arise, they believed in their theoretical model of the world economy. Guided by some outstanding economists, they were on the frontiers of economic practice and much ahead of the textbooks. The suspense story during the years that followed was, therefore, whether the authorities would be able to cope with the various disruptive pressures that could threaten macroeconomic stability.

II. BALANCE-OF-PAYMENTS EQUILIBRIUM AND THE ADJUSTMENT PROCESS

The theory of trade and payments deals essentially with two questions: that of the basic economic forces that determine a country's volume of trade, services, and capital movements; and that of the adjustment process for correcting a country's balance-of-payments surplus or deficit. Such a theoretical framework is indispensable to the monetary authorities for treating the problems that confront them—although their views about it naturally tend to be less abstract, more eclectic, and more oriented to practical political choices than conclusions derived in pure theory.

The dollar was a unique currency in the monetary system, and the U.S. balance of payments was subject to forces that did not bear significantly on the payments problems of other countries. Much criticism of the United States was spurious because it gave little weight to the fact that the dollar was not just like other currencies. To grasp the peculiarities of the dollar, one must first review the general case of other countries, which was also in part— although only in part—applicable to the dollar.

To start with the exchange rate, the basic rule in the Bretton Woods Agreement was that the par value would be fixed and could be changed only in circumstances of "fundamental disequilibrium," after consultation with the IMF and with its approval. Each member country was to declare a par value for its currency expressed in terms of a weight of gold or in terms of the U.S. dollar of the gold weight in effect on July 1, 1944. Par values determined the cross-rates or parities among currencies. The acceptance of this rule imposed an obligation on countries to manage their affairs so as to maintain the market exchange rate within an allowed 1 percent margin on either side of the par value. And if the parity became unrealistic, because exports or imports got out of hand, countries were expected to shift to a new par value that could be maintained.

The question faced by the monetary authorities from time to time was whether, at the declared par value and consequent exchange rates against other currencies, the external payments position was in equilibrium. The conventional rule of thumb was that the payments position was in equilibrium when official reserves of short-term foreign-exchange assets and gold were approximately constant—with allowance being made for random movements. The change in reserves was taken net of reserve liabilities incurred for the purpose of compensatory financing. That is, if the central bank borrowed outside funds with which to intervene in the market to support the par value of its currency, it was recognized that net reserves had not remained constant since part of its assets were committed to repay these borrowings. But the precise significance of changes even in net reserves depended on circumstances.

Deficit Payments Positions

When net reserves declined appreciably because they were used by the central bank to buy its currency in the market in support of the par value, the payments position was considered in deficit. The question then arose whether the deficit was transitory and hence would correct itself or whether it was likely to persist and therefore required some adjustment action.

In practice, there were a number of cases in which a deficit was considered transitory. Most central banks, for example, looked upon a decline in official reserves that was accompanied by an increase in the net external assets of the commercial banking system as a transitory factor—unless there were specific reasons for a contrary view. They held this view because they could generally manage the position of the banks through direct controls or monetary measures. In some cases, the central bank placed foreign exchange with the commercial banks by way of short-term swaps[7] so as to mop up domestic liquidity or to allow the banks to make foreign-currency loans.

Another type of transitory factor was the relative state of economic activity at home and abroad. For example, a deficit in the balance of payments was more likely when there was strong expansion in the domestic economy while demand in the outside world was stagnating. The country's exports would then be limited by the slowdown of foreign demand while imports would be somewhat swollen by the high level of domestic requirements and by the extra effort of foreign producers to bolster output through exports. Recovery abroad could be expected to correct the situation. Such cases were discussed in official meetings, and the deficit countries did not hesitate to stress the responsibility of their trading partners to stimulate their stagnant economies. In the 1960s, it became customary to calculate the "full employment" balance-of-payments position of the major countries so as to clarify the basic position of their currencies and to evaluate the impact of the cyclical factors.

Still another type of transitory deficit arose as a result of unusually large exports of non-bank capital. Such capital exports could be stimulated by a temporary difference in short-term interest rates at home and abroad or by a temporary bulge in longer-term foreign investment.

Surplus Payments Positions

The opposite situation to a deficit is, of course, a surplus—marked by an increase in reserves bought in the market against domestic funds to keep the exchange value of the currency from rising by more than the permitted 1 percent above its par value. But the attitude of governments toward deficit and surplus positions was not parallel. In other words, the conventional rule of thumb about equilibrium positions noted above applied less on the surplus side. A surplus was a comfortable position to be in because it allowed the authorities to pursue domestic economic expansion with little concern for balance-of-payments difficulties. Hence, the amount of surplus that was considered acceptable was larger than the amount of deficit, and a country in surplus had a greater inclination to look upon its favorable position as transitory. Moreover, monetary authorities generally believed that it was right and proper for the official reserves to grow over time so as to keep pace with the expanding volume of domestic liquidity. In official discussions, it was not presumed that even a persistent surplus demanded corrective action unless it was an "extreme" surplus, as occurred several times in the case of Germany and later in the case of Japan.

In the case of surpluses of smaller countries, criticism was seldom aroused, even when the surplus was quite large relative to the size of the country. If the Dutch surplus, for example, rose from $50 million to $100 million, it hardly seemed worthwhile to the larger countries to raise objections because $50 million one way or the other would make so little difference to their own positions.

For all these reasons, responsibility for the adjustment of disequilibrium rested primarily on countries in deficit. They were seen to be the offenders— and that judgment was generally appropriate, with the special and partial exception of the United States. The Keynes plan at Bretton Woods contained several provisions designed to oblige surplus countries to share fully with deficit countries in the adjustment of imbalances. But these provisions were not acceptable to the United States, which expected to be a surplus country. Harry White said at the time that it would be more difficult for creditors to adjust their balance than for debtors, which was an accurate political judgment.[8]

Apart from their efforts to maintain equilibrium in the flow of external payments as a whole, the authorities were concerned about the structure of the balance of payments. Most industrial countries wanted the balance on current-account transactions (trade, invisibles, and unilateral transfers) to show a surplus, so as to provide a margin for foreign investment and for capital aid to poorer countries. When they were obliged by temporary difficulties to arrange for net capital imports, they took it as a disequilibrium. However, not all countries held this view. Several high-income industrial countries, such as Canada and Norway, believed they had large investment requirements that should be financed partly by borrowing from abroad. To some extent, certainly, net capital imports by industrial countries were a matter of attitude. An important aim also was for exports to show a healthy expansion since export growth indicated that the economy was maintaining its competitiveness and particularly since exports helped in the attainment of full employment. The idea, often expressed in economic literature, that the *raison d'être* of exports is to pay for imports and investment abroad was seldom heard in official circles. The jobs that arose from exports, however, were of great concern.

Causes of Disequilibrium

For several years after the war, the payments positions of many industrial countries were in large deficit, open or repressed, because of wartime dislocation and because of monetary inflation. These difficulties were gradually overcome as production recovered and inflation was brought under reasonable control. Economic aid under the Marshall Plan, the wave of currency devaluations in 1949, and the setting up of the European Payments Union (EPU) and the Organization for European Economic Cooperation (OEEC) Code of Liberalization of Trade were vital measures of international cooperation that assisted in the recovery process. In the subsequent period, various currencies got into difficulties at one time or another—most because of deficits, but some because of surpluses. The deficit episodes arose from a limited number of causes, acting singly or in combination—although outlandish reasons were given in some cases by the authorities concerned.

1. *Excess domestic demand.*   The orientation of government policy toward maintaining a full-employment level of economic activity and a strong expansion of output resulted at times in aggregate domestic demand becoming excessive—in the sense that it surpassed the available capacity of domestic productive resources to meet it. Imports would then tend to rise to fill the gap, and exports might be limited also by the demand pressure in the home market. Consequently, excess domestic demand produced a deficit in the balance of payments. The usual immediate cause of excess demand was an overly rapid increase in the money supply, arising from the financing of capital expenditures by business and buying on credit by consumers, or from a deficit in the accounts of the public sector financed through the banking system. In some cases, large wage increases were at the root of excessive aggregate demand; the central banks could not in practice fully withhold the increase in the money supply that might be required to implement the wage payments.

2. *Price-wage inflation.*   An external deficit could also result from a rate of inflation higher than that of other countries and hence liable to impair the competitive position of the economy. Excess demand usually had inflationary repercussions because it put pressure on prices and wages. But cost inflation, through high negotiated wage increases that exceeded the increase in productivity, pushed up prices even when demand was not excessive. Moreover, in the face of demand pressure on the labor market, the wage increases that emerged as a result of the bargaining process were, because of the monopolistic power of the unions, generally larger than would have come

from a free play of labor market forces. When the competitive position of the economy was weakened, a balance-of-payments deficit would develop because exports tended to become overpriced and imports became cheaper than domestically produced goods.

3. *Emergence of new foreign competition.*   In a few cases, the position of a country starting from reasonable balance in its external payments would worsen over time because its growth in output and productivity tended to lag behind the gains being made in competitor countries.[9] The more dynamic countries developed their export potential, which competed sharply with the goods of the lagging country in its domestic market as well as in foreign markets. This was not solely a matter of relative price changes; it also stemmed from lack of innovation in new industries and protection of declining industries, poorer styling and marketing efforts, or changes in tastes. It is theoretically possible for such nonprice factors to be offset by changes in relative prices, but in practice, this mechanism has proved hard to activate, not least because prices of manufactures tend to be inflexible on the down side. For example, U.S. auto manufacturers were unable to counteract the success of Volkswagens in the American market, and the hi-fi and television industries lost much of their market to the inventive and lower-cost Japanese producers.

4. *Increased capital exports.*   A deficit in the external balance came about in some instances through increased direct investment abroad and foreign lending. It was associated with a relatively easy stance in monetary policy and a reluctance to apply direct capital controls. An extreme example of this occurred in the United States in the late 1950s and early 1960s and ultimately led to the imposition of controls. When the state of the current account did not allow a high-income country to have an equilibrium with a reasonable volume of capital exports, questions about the competitive position of the economy and overvaluation of the exchange rate were liable to be raised. Again, an automatic adjustment through relative price changes was unlikely.

Political and social disturbances, such as the Suez crisis in 1956 or the student uprising in Paris in 1968, could also shift the payments balance into deficit by inducing a flight from the currency. But the effect was temporary unless the incident was followed by demand or wage-cost inflation. The prospect of a strongly left-wing government coming to power was likely, if it persisted, to cause a flight from the currency that could only be stopped by a resolution of the political uncertainty.

Naturally, the same four factors working in the opposite direction brought about periods of surplus in the balance of payments, reflected in increases of official reserves. Indeed, since deficits and surpluses are largely the counterpart of each other, it was not always apparent which was the initiating factor in the disequilibrium. Moreover, as already noted, a surplus situation was not generally taken to be a disequilibrium unless it became quite large and persistent.

Policy Instruments for the Adjustment of Disequilibrium

To some extent, the emergence of payments deficits and surpluses could set up forces that constituted an automatic mechanism of adjustment because money supplies and relative income levels between countries would be affected. International competition was also an active force. Many instances of payments balances shifting back and forth of their own accord were evidence of an automatic adjustment process at work. Automatic processes could not, however, be relied upon when an imbalance became sizable, particularly if the causes of disequilibrium were persistent.

A country in persistent deficit would be losing reserves and, as its reserves were limited, it would be under some compulsion to take measures to adjust the situation. This was particularly so because a continued loss of reserves would raise doubts about the authorities' ability to maintain the existing par value and would induce a protective and speculative flight from the currency. Adjustment could be delayed for a time by borrowing from abroad, including from the IMF. But credit resources also were limited so that, in the end, adjustment was a necessity. If the authorities did not have the political will or power to impose corrective measures on the economy, an adjustment would come about through a breakdown of the par value in the exchange market.

Prompt and forceful action to impose an adjustment process, which implies at least a measure of restraint on economic activity and the growth of money incomes, can seldom be expected to rally voters to the support of the government in office. Hence, some delay was usual, and in an election year a paralysis in policy was almost taken for granted. But to delay too long while reserves were draining away raised the risk of starting an exchange crisis and, even worse, threatened public confidence in the government.

The political obstacles that stood in the way of firm decisionmaking could in many cases be overcome only when the catalyst of a crisis atmosphere brought the matter to a head. Beforehand, spurious analyses of the situation, optimistic forecasts, fanciful theories of the adjustment process, and announcements of dubious policy measures were seldom lacking—although in some cases official news did present the difficulties of the situation clearly. The business and financial community learned that to examine official pronouncements with a skeptical eye was a wise precaution and that the announcement of policy objectives without adequate measures to support them was not to be taken seriously. Measures that produced no results was not really measures at all.

The corrective instruments used by the authorities varied considerably in technical detail. But considered from the standpoint of their normal impact, the kinds of actions available were relatively few, falling, as Harry Johnson described them, into measures that would reduce or increase domestic expenditures and measures that would switch expenditures between foreign and domestic markets.[10]

1. *Restrictive monetary and fiscal policies.* These are the classic instruments for acting against excess demand and demand inflation, and they were widely used to contain expansion of the money supply and disposable income. Monetary policy proved to be the more flexible instrument in practice, but there was no ideological bias in its favor. In fact, central banks often complained publicly or privately of the burden put upon them and urged elected government officials to take budgetary action.

When a central bank sells foreign exchange in the market, it receives domestic currency as the counterpart, which in itself restricts the money supply. Such restriction has sometimes been considered as an automatic adjustment mechanism. But central banks are not naive, and if they allow significant monetary restraint through this technical process, it is by deliberate policy decision.

In some cases, severe monetary restraint was subject to the limitation that high domestic interest rates, and the need of business for working capital in an inflationary situation, drew in funds from overseas through interest arbitrage by banks and through pushing firms to use their credit potential with financial institutions and businesses abroad. The inflow of foreign funds would at least delay the impact of monetary restraint by the central banks and could even frustrate it. This happened to a considerable degree at various times to the Bundesbank, the Netherlands Bank, and the Federal Reserve.

A further limitation on restrictive policies was political. In a situation in which an inflationary psychology had taken hold of labor and business, severe restraint on demand by fiscal and monetary measures needed to produce an economic recession in order to allow the charged atmosphere to subside. And the public knew whom to blame for the higher unemployment and the slack in business activity. In the inflationary boom in Italy in 1963-64, for example, the Bank of Italy succeeded in dampening the situation by restrictive monetary measures, with little help from the government. But its public relations suffered as a consequence. Governor Carli said afterward that, for political reasons, it was the last time the bank could use such drastic restraint. When a similar situation arose again in 1973-74, however, the bank had no option but to impose the same remedy. In the municipal elections that followed soon after, there was a decided swing to the left and an increase in the number of Communist party officeholders.

2. *Monetary measures to induce an inflow of funds from abroad or to reduce an outflow.* The inducement involved is, of course, higher interest rates, which may not be appropriate to the domestic economic situation. To some extent this dilemma can be managed by changing the mix between fiscal and monetary policy. On the external side, fiscal action works mainly on the current account; monetary policy works promptly on the capital account and with a lag on the current account. This difference is often a consideration in the policy mix. In 1977, for example, while President Carter was asking Congress to reduce taxes to stimulate the economy, the Federal Reserve, under Chairman Arthur Burns, increased the discount rate to help reduce the outflow of dollars. In the case of Britain, the balance-of-payments situation was so precarious over many years that monetary policy was dominated by external requirements; budgetary policy, which could be used more flexibly than in many other countries, was relied upon for the management of domestic demand.

3. *Direct controls on expenditures.* These are controls on the credit conditions for the purchase of consumer durable goods, for example, or on new housing construction. Larger down payments or a shortening of the repayment term were used to reduce borrowing and cut excess demand.

4. *Direct controls over domestic bank credit or over business borrowing from other sources.* Here too the objective was to dampen excess demand, but to do so more quickly than by general restraint on the money supply and without so large a rise in interest rates. A ceiling on the expansion of bank credit, for example, was a frequently used device that could be quite effective when not held so long as to create distortions and loopholes. General monetary restraint is not without problems in its effects on different types of financial institutions and different classes of borrowers. When the Federal Reserve imposed its severe monetary squeeze of 1969, its avowed intention was to cut down large corporate borrowing. But the large corporations were about the last to be squeezed because they generally had huge reserves and rated well with the banking community.

At an international gathering at Basel in the 1960s, Governor Holtrop of the Netherlands Bank was complaining that his policy of monetary restraint was being nullified by an inflow of money from abroad and by the ready access Dutch firms had to German banks. Governor Carli said: "Of course, you expect to achieve all your results by restriction on the supply side while you do nothing on the demand side. If I tried to do that in Italy I would have interest rates of 25 percent and contribute to inflation, instead of suppressing it." He was arguing, of course, for the utility of directly limiting the access of certain borrowers to additional funds, from whatever source. To employ such methods, the central bank had to be prepared to take the responsibility and to stand the gaff. But they could be effective. Governor Clappier said the Bank of France used every kind of control imaginable, and Carli replied that the Bank of Italy even had some that were not imaginable. In both countries, the inflation problem was acute.

5.   *Price and wage controls.*   These controls were used to interrupt a price-wage spiral and calm down wage-push inflation. The key was generally wage restraint, with price control added for political reasons.

6.   *Exchange restrictions on current transactions.*   These controls aimed to improve the external balance, although they often were imposed as a protective device for domestic business. Exchange restrictions on current account payments were contrary to the Fund's articles and were resorted to only reluctantly as a stopgap by the industrial countries. A special case of such controls was limitations on or reductions in the government's own expenditures abroad—defense expenditures being a primary target; another device was tying of aid to foreign countries to goods bought in the donor's domestic market. The Fund's rules did not attempt to tell governments how they should spend their own money, and balance-of-payments savings by such means were considered quite legitimate.

7.   *Exchange restrictions on capital flows.*   Such measures, which were also meant to improve the external balance, were freely allowed by the Fund's rules. A few countries shied away from their use because they adhered to a free-market ideology and argued that leakages in the controls would soon reduce their effectiveness. These countries also hesitated because of the strong opposition of their lending institutions. However, most countries believed that capital controls were essential to the management of the balance of payments. They found, in practice, that market forces alone would not keep net capital exports at a level appropriate to the current-account balance. Even the theory of how this is to be brought about with a fixed exchange rate is not very satisfactory—and it is more difficult in practice without some controls. The short-run alternatives are either simply to limit the creation of money or to combine this with restrictions on its outflow abroad. In the longer run, if money creation is not limited sufficiently, the currency will in any event have to be devalued.

Apart from the United States, Germany was the prime example of a country that opposed controls on capital flows. But, then, for many years it had relatively higher interest rates, and was continually in payments surplus. When it finally resorted to controls, it was to keep foreign money out. Holland, on the other hand, maintained controls over foreign borrowing on the new issues capital market, even though it was in external surplus. As the Dutch governor complained about imported inflation from the balance-of-payments surplus, I once asked him why he did not solve the problem by lifting the controls on the capital market. "If we did that," he said, "the first foreign bond issue would be by the city of Copenhagen to build a subway— just when we are preventing Rotterdam from building a subway so as not to add to excess demand." Central bankers have a hard life.

8. *Changes in par value.* According to the IMF Articles of Agreement, "a member shall not propose a change in the par value of its currency except to correct a fundamental disequilibrium." This rule was designed to prohibit competitive exchange depreciation. But a change in the par value was freely allowed when there was a *genuine* need for it, which was the meaning of "fundamental disequilibrium." The initiative for a change of parity, however, was left to the member country. Neither the IMF Executive Board[11] nor the Fund staff could formally propose such a change. The question of sovereignty was an important issue in the Bretton Woods negotiations, and the agreement was drafted so that there was no question but that sovereignty over par values was wholly in the hands of member countries. Faced with a case of fundamental disequilibrium, the Executive Board could protect the Fund's resources by refusing a member's request for a credit drawing on the country's quota if the needed devaluation was not among the corrective measures proposed by the country.

There was an apparent contradiction in this limitation on the Fund's freedom of discussion of needed par-value changes. Although the Fund was established as the center of cooperation to maintain stability of the monetary system, it was debarred from open consideration of an essential instrument of the adjustment process. But open discussion would have had to be cautious in any case because of probable repercussions on the exchange market, and the Fund staff was free to have private consultations with the monetary authorities involved. Needless to say, the Fund never opposed a country's proposal to devalue its currency in the interests of a necessary adjustment. It may be noted incidentally that when Pierre-Paul Schweitzer, the Fund's managing director, announced publicly that the United States should participate in the realignment of currencies in the second half of 1971 by accepting a devaluation of the dollar, he was exceeding his authority. While the United States was violating the Fund's rules, it had some reason to be angry.

Interestingly, the idea of fundamental disequilibrium was introduced into the Articles of Agreement at the suggestion of the legal experts, rather than by the economists, to create a basis for judging the appropriateness of a proposed change in a par value. The Fund's Executive Board, however, was never able to arrive at a definition of fundamental disequilibrium for the very reason that countries did not want to be committed to a precise formula that could entail political difficulties.

But the economic sense of the matter was easy enough to understand. The Fund was intended to favor economic expansion and high employment. But if a country's cost and price levels became uncompetitive, exports would be too low and imports too high to allow a balanced position in external payments at a full-employment level of economic activity—even though productive resources might not be under excessive demand pressure at the time and the situation not be inflationary.

Nonfundamental Disequilibrium and Its Correction

A country could seek to correct a deficit disequilibrium by suppressing expansion of the economy for a time, during which domestic prices and costs could be held down, while there was a price-cost rise in other countries. Some interesting cases of this actually arose. Belgium recovered very rapidly after the war because it had suffered little physical damage, it had a successful monetary reform, and foreign demand for its exports was very strong, particularly for steel. Having a surplus position, Belgium devalued only 12.3 percent in the widespread currency realignments of 1949, whereas many other countries followed Britain's devaluation of more than 30 percent. Because of the price-cost pressure of the previous boom, there was a threat to the Belgian payments position that lasted for several years in the first half of the 1950s. But the authorities respected balance-of-payments discipline and suppressed expansion of the economy to wait out a period of adjustment. While criticism was leveled against them in the OEEC for accepting a higher rate of unemployment, they were determined not to damage the image of the Belgian franc by a new devaluation. And after a few years, the inflation and expansion in other countries corrected the situation.

Another case occurred in Italy. The inflationary boom of 1963-64 produced a large increase in wages, which limited exports and sent the trade balance into a very substantial deficit. The currency was under grave suspicion, and a devaluation was expected by some competent observers. The Bank of Italy was strongly opposed to devaluation, believing that new wage increases would follow and that confidence in the lira would suffer for a long time. Hence, it held fast to a policy of monetary restraint and allowed the level of industrial employment to decline. Governor Carli went to Washington and obtained substantial support for maintaining confidence in the currency. While the exchange crisis was over quickly, industrial employment remained depressed through 1965 and 1966. And although minimum contractual wages rose a bit, overall wage costs were reduced by less overtime pay, improved productivity, and other influences. By 1967, the economy was on the upgrade with a strong export-led expansion. It is noteworthy that about three quarters of the increase of Italian exports in this expansion came from sectors of industry that had not even existed in 1950.

The United States in 1961-64 was another case of this kind, although, for reasons that will be taken up later, the improvement in this instance was confined to the current balance. Partly because of a recession in Europe, the U.S. trade surplus fell from the high level of $6.3 billion in 1957 caused by the Suez crisis to $1.1 billion in 1959. With the economy experiencing recession and slow recovery over the next few years, the trade surplus reached $6.8 billion in 1964, nonagricultural exports having risen from $13.5 to $20 billion. The enterprise of American firms in meeting foreign competition was essential in this gain, but a major reason for the improvement was the Kennedy administration's success in moderating wage increases.

Fundamental Disequilibrium Requires Devaluation

The difference between nonfundamental and fundamental disequilibrium was sometimes only a matter of degree. The foregoing cases have been cited to emphasize that balance-of-payments discipline could be effective without a change in par value if the authorities and the pressure groups gave it a chance to take effect. But if the authorities procrastinated and the disparity between different countries' price and cost levels became too large, this slow-acting corrective could not be expected to work. Disequilibrium then became fundamental, and a change in the par value was needed to restore a competitive level of prices and costs.

Devaluation would stimulate exports by reducing their prices in terms of foreign currencies, or increasing their profitability to domestic producers, or both, and would check imports by making them more costly to domestic buyers. In that way, the objectives of full employment and external equilibrium could again be achieved at the same time. By allowing for the adjustment of par values, the Bretton Woods Agreement assigned a lower priority to the goal of exchange-rate stability than to the pursuit of full employment; it was not expected that countries should sacrifice full employment to maintain an unrealistic exchange rate.

The devaluation instrument, however, was not without some practical difficulties. Secrecy was needed before the moment of announcing the decision, so as not to forewarn the foreign-exchange market and fuel speculation and hedging. Then, too, there could be a margin of uncertainty as to whether the disequilibrium was actually "fundamental." To be certain, it was necessary to appraise what the situation would be after any disturbing effects of excess demand and inflation had been eliminated. Hence, some time lag was needed—and bold denial of any intention to devalue in the interval.

There was also the problem of how much to devalue. This could not usually be determined by a simple calculation because econometric relationships were not so reliable and because the consequences of the devaluation itself had to be taken into account. Devaluation demanded a practical judgment also because it was essential not only that the computation be correct, but that the exchange market be convinced it was correct. And the market was not likely to be convinced unless the devaluation was accompanied by domestic stabilization measures that had a fairly immediate impact. But these difficulties were not formidable. The real obstacles to the adjustment process were political.

Although devaluation of the currency was the ultimate policy weapon to be called upon when needed, in practice governments were reluctant to resort to it because of its probable adverse political repercussions. Devaluation seemed to them like an open admission of monetary mismanagement, and in some cases they went to extreme lengths to delay it. Such delays were caused neither by any prohibition in the IMF Articles nor by pressure from the IMF staff. They were purely the political will of the government. Even in countries where the central bank had considerable power in the domestic monetary sphere, such as Germany, Belgium, the Netherlands, Italy, and the United States, the power to change the par value of the currency was reserved to the government. This division of responsibility had been established in the time of the gold standard, when the gold content of the currency was fixed by law.

*   *   *

With these various policy instruments at their disposal, the governmental authorities of an industrial country could correct a deficit disequilibrium in their balance of payments in reasonable time when they wanted to do so and were able to impose their will on the economy. Some time might be needed to diagnose the situation, to formulate a policy program, and to allow the measures to take effect. But the function of reserves was to provide that time and the Fund was there to supplement reserves when the authorities agreed to adopt a convincing program of adjustment.[12] Exception must be made for the immediate postwar years when a transitional period for reconstruction and stabilization was required. And, as will be discussed later, the considerable rise in the price of oil at the end of 1973 caused payments deficits for many oil-importing countries that could not be eliminated quickly by general restrictive measures.

The same kinds of measures, although pointed in the opposite direction, were available to deal with the cases of persistent surpluses. In brief, the authorities could push expansion of the economy to attract imports, allow some degree of domestic inflation to reduce the trade surplus, arrange more capital outflow, and revalue the parity of the currency. But the sense of compulsion that acted in cases of deficits was much less evident when it came to surpluses.

In order to give member countries some of the protection against persistent surpluses that Keynes had sought, the Fund Agreement had a specific rule (in Article VII) to enable it to find that there was a "general scarcity" of a particular currency, to issue a report on its causes, and to make recommendations for bringing it to an end. Although the Fund could not propose a revaluation, a finding of "scarcity" by it allowed countries to impose restrictions on exchange transactions in the scarce currency. These provisions, introduced at the time primarily as a protection against a dollar shortage, were never invoked against any surplus country.

The Official Preference for Fixed Exchange Rates

On a strict reading of the IMF's rules, the monetary authorities were to keep the exchange rate for each member's currency within a 1 percent margin on either side of its par value. And if the par value were changed, the new parity, in turn, was to be defended by central-bank intervention when necessary. Hence, it was a "fixed" rate system or, as it later came to be called, a "pegged" rate system. The Fund Agreement was drawn up at a time when it was evident that many countries would be faced with enormous problems of postwar reconstruction and adjustment. Moreover, there was a multitude of exchange controls and trade restrictions that would take a major effort to dismantle. It may seem surprising, therefore, that no explicit provision was made for the possible recourse to a floating exchange rate as a temporary expedient to facilitate the adjustment process and to speed up the removal of restrictions. Instead, the concessions made for the transition problem were that countries could change their initial par values cumulatively by up to 10 percent without objection by the Fund and that a grace period of five years was allowed for removing restrictions on trade and other current payments.

The official preference for fixed exchange rates was not arbitrary, but was grounded in the experience of the monetary breakdown in the 1930s. To abandon gold convertibility of the currency and to allow the exchange rate to float were taken as evidence of monetary mismanagement and a failure of discipline. While floating could clear the foreign-exchange market, various cases of floating during the 1930s, as in Britain, Australia, and Sweden, had shown that market forces would not necessarily produce a stable rate or one that could be considered satisfactory from the standpoint of trade. Floating often encouraged speculation and induced a flight of domestic savings abroad, depressing the exchange rate unnecessarily and worsening the terms of trade. For these reasons, fixed exchange rates that would be altered only by international agreement seemed an essential foundation for international monetary cooperation and liberal trading practices.

Apart from lending stability to foreign trade and the balance of payments, fixed exchange rates were considered essential to imposing discipline on domestic monetary affairs with respect to both the government budget and monetary policy. Too much creation of money in the domestic economy would soon show up in a payments deficit, which would help to enforce corrective action.

Paolo Baffi, then general manager of the Bank of Italy, presented a short paper to a meeting of the List Society in 1965 devoted to the pros and cons of floating exchange rates.[13] He avoided universal generalizations, confining his argument to the case of Italy. He recounted how the outburst of wage increases of 15 and 17 percent in 1962 and 1963 produced a considerable deterioration in the current external account and how the deficit itself and the restrictive action by the central bank developed a condition of monetary tightness that produced a dramatic reversal to a surplus position in 1964. In Italy, he argued, where a generalized system of (one-way) cost-of-living indexation clauses applies to wages, to have allowed the exchange rate to float down when the payments balance deteriorated would have implied continuing with the excessive rate of wage increases. By maintaining the exchange rate, the authorities made it the limiting factor to which their management of the rest of the economy had to be adjusted. Somewhat plaintively, Baffi added that the only members of the entrepreneurial class who really support the monetary authorities in fighting inflation are the exporters—insofar as they feel that changes in the exchange parity are out of the question. Under flexible exchange rates, he said, the support of business in fighting inflation would be close to nil.

This is the thesis of the advantage of balance-of-payments discipline that accounted for the wide preference for fixed exchange rates in the official world. Harry Johnson once put it to the central bankers at an international monetary conference that as countries had different rates of inflation, why not have floating exchange rates so that each country could have whatever rate of inflation it wanted? But the point was that the central bankers did not want inflation at all, and they wanted fixed exchange rates to help them combat it. Throughout the various difficulties encountered during the 1950s and 1960s, official opinion remained predominantly in favor of fixed exchange rates as the norm of the system, until floating was forced by the market itself after confidence had been destroyed by the vagaries of official policies.

Of course, many officials did not favor fixed exchange rates in all circumstances and, as will be seen, some supported a recourse to floating in special cases. No officials believed that the exchange rate could be allowed to float for any length of time without intervention by the central bank to steady the exchange market. Even with the floating of the Canadian dollar from 1950 to 1962, the Bank of Canada intervened in the market frequently for large amounts to maintain orderly conditions. In any case, the Canadian dollar was not a typical currency from the standpoint of floating because of the strong economic, monetary, and psychological links between Canada and the United States.

At the time of Bretton Woods, Keynes wanted the draft of the Articles of Agreement to reflect a country's right to greater flexibility of its exchange rate, and he foresaw frequent use of par-value changes as a policy instrument. But Harry White of the U.S. Treasury was unwilling to weaken the aim of exchange-rate stability and believed that par-value changes should occur rarely. I believe Keynes underestimated the problem of holding the sterling area together if Britain resorted to frequent changes of parity. In any case, the question of more or less ease in changing the par value had little influence on the functioning of the system. These were practical problems that the Bretton Woods Agreement could not resolve in advance. The Articles of Agreement were like a constitution, and the Fund's Executive Board would have to decide their application in specific cases.

Recourse to Floating

In practice, the Executive Board was not at all doctrinaire in applying the rule of fixed par values. In a fair number of difficult cases among the developing countries, it approved resort to floating, as it also did in the case of Canada. A rare case of an exchange-rate scheme being turned down by the Board was a proposal in 1948 regarding the French franc (see Chapter 3). And even in that instance, Edward Bernstein said that the par-value aspect of the French proposal could have been presented separately and would have been given approval by the Board. Temporary floating might have been a convenient tactical instrument in, for example, the case of Britain, and it was seriously considered by the authorities in 1951-52 (see Chapter 2). It was not the IMF rules that stopped them—it was just domestic politics and fear of the unknown.

Floating rates as a norm for the system were advocated by some academic economists, particularly as the monetary system deteriorated. What has often been called the classic case for floating was made by Milton Friedman in an article published in 1953.[14] He argued that fixed exchange rates were the primary cause of trade and exchange restrictions and that these could be wiped out while removing any burden on the reserves, by floating.

While Friedman made too light of the difficulties that could be encountered in floating—because of differences in the timing of the business cycle, for example—there were cases that justified the policy he advocated, particularly among the less developed countries. I had occasion to suggest this remedy in two cases in which trade and exchange restrictions were tying up the economy and were the cause of much corruption via the black market. But it was rejected out of hand in both cases as monetary (political?) suicide. As to the industrial countries, Friedman's article appeared when the postwar transition was largely over and the opposite course for removing restrictions had been decided upon—that is, fixed rates supported by the European Payments Union and the OEEC Code of Liberalization of Trade. Most countries did not then need to float their currencies, and few countries that did not need to ever floated. Certainly, the dollar did not need to float, and the dollar was the key case.

The Significance of Destabilizing Capital Flows

It is often said that the fixed-rate system became untenable because of "destabilizing capital flows." This phrase refers to international movements of money into surplus or out of deficit countries on such a scale that the authorities were not able to handle them within a fixed-rate framework. What has to be asked, however, is what caused the flights of money. I have mentioned earlier political or social disturbances as a cause in some cases, but these could be handled by using reserves and borrowing facilities in the IMF and elsewhere—provided the government did not resort to inflationary measures in attempting to settle the underlying problem.

Another cause that initiated such movements of money was extreme pressure of monetary restriction by the central bank, which induced large inflows of money from abroad and an increase in official reserves. If such restraint was long continued, the exchange rate might come under suspicion in the market, and a flight of money into the currency ensue, facilitated by the absence of direct controls over such inflows. In the case of Germany, the 1969 crisis in the exchange market precipitated a revaluation of the currency, while in the United States, the money inflow produced an artificial surplus on official settlements in 1968-69, which only aggravated the deficit when monetary policy was eased the following year and the money flowed out again.[15] As these repercussions were widely anticipated by experts, the basic fault lay with the central banks that pushed domestically oriented measures to excessive lengths before trying to protect the external accounts. It was well known that monetary policy in an open economy with a fixed exchange rate could not simply ignore the repercussions on the external account; economists of the monetarist school, who wanted monetary policy to be concentrated on domestic objectives, generally advocated a floating exchange rate to facilitate this concentration. In the cases mentioned, however, the monetary authorities wanted a fixed exchange rate, and their policy was not consistent with that aim.

By far the most important cause of flights of money was sheer neglect of the adjustment process when the existence of a large disequilibrium and the need for corrective action was clear to everyone—officials and the market alike. Of course, an adjustment of the parity of the currency, either by official action or by a breakdown in the market, was then anticipated. And of course, business firms, financial institutions, individuals, and even other central banks engaged in huge hedging operations in both the spot and the forward exchange markets to protect the value of their assets when devaluation was expected or to cover their liabilities when a revaluation was in view. In addition, pure speculation added to the so-called destabilizing capital flows. In the conspicuous cases of sterling, the deutsche mark, the yen, and the dollar, for example, it was hardly speculation; it was a free and riskless gift offered by the authorities through their hesitation to take appropriate action. It is difficult to understand why the United States, after an official settlements deficit of $10 billion in 1970, accepted a further deficit of $30 billion up to August 15, 1971, before acting to stop the rot.

Some observers seem to believe that the cause of these large capital flows was that money balances had grown enormously and that they were apt to move from one currency to another on a large scale at every minor scare or rumor. In fact, however, there was always an acute fundamental disequilibrium in the balance of payments underlying such cases, and forceful corrective measures were being avoided. There was not one example of "destabilizing capital flows" upsetting a currency without there having been a well-founded expectation of a change in parity. In minor cases, official reserves and borrowing facilities were adequate to tide over the flurry.

III. THE DOLLAR AND THE GOLD-DOLLAR SYSTEM

From the White House tapes, President Nixon is known to have said: "I don't give a [expletive deleted] about the lira." Presumably, he did give a [expletive deleted] about the dollar. Nonetheless, he and John Connally, his freewheeling secretary of the treasury, took the decision to declare the dollar inconvertible and thus disrupt the international monetary system. Nixon and Connally came into the game only toward its end. The three preceding administrations had followed the same course, by deciding what U.S. policy on the dollar should be and doggedly sticking to that policy in the face of an ever-mounting crisis. This rigid U.S. approach was contrary to the IMF rules, which were incorporated into U.S. law by the Bretton Woods Act of 1944. The crux of the matter was the absolute refusal to initiate an adjustment process in a situation of transparent fundamental disequilibrium. Of course, as the dollar was a unique currency in the system, its adjustment process had special features. But these were known and available. Pride goeth before a fall, the Bible tells us. Pride was certainly involved in this case, but to pretend that it was not, the fall has been called a reform of the international monetary system.

The monetary system in operation from 1946-71 is often designated the Bretton Woods system. But as already pointed out, the Bretton Woods Agreement inherited a good deal from earlier years and in any case covered only part of that system, the rest deriving from practices that monetary authorities chose to follow of their own volition. Thus, the system was more appropriately referred to as the gold-dollar system since it rested on the dollar being convertible into gold. The Bretton Woods Agreement did not enshrine the dollar and mentioned it only obliquely. The dollar existed and its existence was simply recognized by the Bretton Woods architects.

The Par Value of Currencies

The agreement prescribed that the "par value of the currency of each member shall be expressed in terms of gold as a common denominator or in terms of the United States dollar of the weight and fineness in effect on July 1, 1944." As there was no difference between gold and the gold-dollar of July 1944, the legal measuring rod or unit of account for currencies in the system was simply the weight of gold. There was no legal necessity for mentioning the gold-dollar at all; it was given as an alternative for countries that had political inhibitions about declaring a gold parity.

In a practical sense, however, it was very appropriate that the dollar be mentioned. The reason for this was that the operative unit of account for most countries was the dollar as such, and a fixed parity meant maintaining a pegged exchange rate on the dollar. The existing gold-dollar had to be specified because it was laid down that the gold value of the Fund's assets should be maintained, regardless of any changes in individual par values, including that of the dollar. Whenever the par value of a currency was reduced, the country was required to pay to the Fund an amount of its own currency equal to the reduction in the gold value of the Fund's holding of that currency. Likewise, if a par value was increased, the Fund would return to the member country an amount of its currency equal to the increased gold value of the Fund's holding of that currency.

The agreement further prescribed that foreign-exchange dealings in the spot market in each country "shall not differ from parity by more than one percent." This meant, of course, that the monetary authorities would intervene in the market—selling or buying foreign exchange as needed—to keep the market rates within the margins. But it also was specified that "a member whose monetary authorities, for the settlement of international transactions, in fact freely buy and sell gold within the limits prescribed by the Fund . . . shall be deemed to be fulfilling this undertaking." This provision again allowed for the unique position of the dollar in the system, as the United States was the only member that used this option. In principle, the United States left other central banks to maintain the dollar's cross rates with their currencies in the foreign-exchange market.

It is significant that no other country adopted this option as its technique for abiding by the par-value rule. One reason was that the gold reserves of other countries were not large enough. Switzerland, not a member of the IMF, was the only country that even considered at least partial use of this technique. The Swiss National Bank went so far as to mint a large volume of gold coins, which still remain in its vaults. But the Bank soon realized that the coins would just be gobbled up by gold hoarders and that it would, in any case, be left holding dollars.

For the United States, however, the gold technique was essential: first, because the United States was the last-resort seller of gold in the system; and second, because no other suitable reserve assets were available to it. The United States could not hold weak currencies without incurring an unacceptable exchange risk, and when in due course certain other currencies emerged as strong currencies, it could not acquire them in any significant amounts because they were in short supply on the exchange markets. It may be added that the central banks of the strong-currency countries did not want their currencies to become reserve currencies and would not open their money markets to central-bank placements of reserves. Another important point was that any working balances the United States might have held in certain foreign currencies were not usable in the way that dollars were usable by other countries—that is, for general or multilateral intervention in the foreign-exchange market—because central banks outside the United States in the main held only dollars as reserves. The dollar exchange market was in any case by far the largest, and the bulk of foreign-exchange transactions went through the dollar, including those between third countries that used the dollar as vehicle currency. Needless to add, the United States, at the start, had no interest in any other technique for maintaining its par value than buying gold from and selling gold to monetary authorities.

Official Reserves

The Fund's articles stated that "a member's monetary reserves means its net official holdings of gold, of convertible currencies of other members, and of the currencies of such nonmembers as the Fund may specify." This was simply an "explanation of terms," in accordance with current practice, and did not bind member countries in any way. The articles did not propose any rules for the holding of reserves or suggest anything about the composition of reserves. A few years after the Fund began large lending operations, the creditor balances of the countries whose currencies were drawn upon were also counted as reserves; they came to be called "reserve positions in the Fund."

The overwhelming bulk of foreign-exchange reserves was held in dollars and sterling. Holdings of sterling as an active reserve asset were confined largely to sterling-area countries. Other countries were not attracted to it because the risk of exchange loss on sterling was significant. Thus, sterling was a really regional reserve currency with the central reserves of the region held by the Bank of England largely in gold. Other currencies were held as reserves only in negligible amounts because, as noted previously, their monetary authorities did not accommodate such holdings. Reserves in deutsche marks and Swiss francs, for example, became significant only after the Euro-currency market developed in the 1960s and after the dollar became suspect.

In contrast, dollars could be freely held, since the United States traditionally placed no restrictions on foreign access to the U.S. money market. What induced foreign monetary authorities to hold reserves in dollars was that the money-market instruments yielded earnings of interest. It is of the first importance to an understanding of the system to appreciate this point. It was sometimes said that central banks maintained reserves in dollars because the dollars were readily available for market intervention. But this was the case also with gold held on earmark at the New York Federal Reserve Bank, which could be turned into cash dollars just as easily as could reserve holdings of U.S. Treasury bills. The proportions of dollars and gold in reserves differed widely among countries. Those that leaned very heavily toward dollars generally felt that they had a pressing need to earn interest in foreign currency to help their balance of payments. They were mostly smaller and less developed countries. Some central banks in poorer countries, which had little opportunity to realize earnings in the domestic economy, wanted earnings on their foreign assets in order to preserve some independence from the government. One governor, for example, confided that the position of his bank would be impossible if he had to go to the finance minister to ask for a budget to meet the bank's payroll. Capital-importing countries, which considered that their reserves existed by virtue of the nation's foreign borrowing, felt that the reserves should earn interest as a partial offset to the interest payments on their foreign debt. And a few countries, very few in fact, held their reserves largely in dollars simply because they felt it was just not rational economic behavior to hold non-interest-bearing gold.

The countries that maintained a substantial portion of their reserves in gold looked upon the matter quite differently. They were high-income countries, relatively few in number, where the earning of interest on reserves was not considered a basic function of the central bank. The monetary authorities in these countries had several reasons for preferring gold that were not dependent on tradition or the "mystique" of the metal.

First, gold was the only asset that was not matched by a liability, whereas dollar assets had to have their counterpart in liabilities of either a borrower in the money market or a bank. Hence, gold could be physically held in and freely disposed of by the country that owned it. While it may have seemed highly unlikely for the time being, the possibility existed that dollar balances could be blocked by the United States in times of trouble, such as war. And, in fact, there had been incidents of that kind. Hence, holding gold was considered to be an essential aspect of the maintenance of sovereignty. This political consideration was known as the "war-chest" motive. The governor of a smaller industrial country put it in the following terms: "We have to have gold; otherwise we would be completely in the hands of the United States." One of the factors that contributed to the emergence of the Eurodollar market was the desire of Eastern-bloc countries to hold dollars outside the immediate jurisdiction of the United States. The motive was similar to the war-chest motive in the case of gold. For considerations of sovereignty also, many countries were unwilling to denominate the par value of their currencies in terms of dollars.

Also, some central banks preferred gold to dollars because they considered that there was a risk of the dollar being devalued. For quite some years, this risk seemed negligible. But those monetary authorities were conscious that if the risk materialized, it would be difficult to get out of dollars in time. They therefore preferred to forego interest earnings on dollars in favor of the greater safety of gold. In such countries, a governor could be highly criticized for the devaluation losses on exchange reserves, but he was never criticized because gold reserves did not earn interest. After sterling depreciated in 1931, the governor of the Netherlands bank was obliged to resign because of the exchange loss the Bank suffered on its sterling reserves—and other governors were fully aware of his unhappy experience.

Another motive for holding gold that influenced some central banks was the belief, quite early in the game, that the international price of gold was one day bound to rise. They feared that they would be open to criticism if that should come to pass and their country was not in a position to profit by it.

For some years, the Bank of England believed that its reserves should be held in gold because sterling was a reserve currency. In effect, the Bank centralized the reserves of the sterling-area, while the sterling-area countries held their reserves in sterling. If the Bank of England had held a large share of its reserves in dollars, the whole point of centralized reserves for the sterling area would have been weakened—as it was from the late 1960s onward.

In addition, some central banks felt it appropriate to convert at least part of their countries' surpluses into gold in order that the United States should be subjected to balance-of-payments discipline. Discipline was imposed on other countries by the loss of any reserves, foreign exchange or gold, and even by increases of official foreign liabilities. But for the United States, loss of gold was the only effective discipline.

Finally, central-bank attachment to gold was reinforced by the interest in gold of the private sector—individuals and enterprises. In quite a few countries, it was illegal for residents to buy or hold gold, except for numismatic purposes. In a country like the United States, the vast majority of the population had no interest in acquiring non-interest-bearing gold as a form of saving, and most economists and bankers thought the very idea was ridiculous; they were not at all worried about the decline of the dollar in terms of gold, which seemed a remote possibility. But in many other countries, depreciation of the currency against gold had occurred frequently, and was still going on. Usually blocked from holding stable foreign currencies, such as the dollar or the Swiss franc, by restrictions or by the impracticality of investing small sums abroad, people protected their savings by keeping them partly in gold. This happened on a large scale even in countries where it was illegal to import and hold gold. In India, for example, the black-market import of gold was estimated at between $150 million and $200 million a year in the mid-1960s. In France, trading in existing gold hoards was freely allowed, and while importation of gold was illegal, it was well known that a significant volume of the metal was smuggled into the country. The difference in attitudes to gold saving between Frenchmen and Americans reflected the different experiences they or their families had undergone.

The private belief in gold showed itself in exceptional buying pressure on the gold market from time to time when political or monetary difficulties threatened. It also extended to the idea that currencies required the support of gold reserves, even though the old gold standard had gone completely into disuse. This applied particularly to the dollar because U.S. reserves were almost entirely in gold. Very many persons, who had only nebulous ideas about the international monetary system, believed in the idea of the gold backing of the dollar, and they invested in dollar securities because they thought the safety of the dollar was thus amply assured. Their confidence in the dollar would be bound to weaken should the dollar become inconvertible because they thought the dollar would necessarily be less safe if it lost its gold backing. Hence, inconvertibility was sure to lead to a flight from the dollar.

While the U.S. authorities could not cater to primitive monetary views, the belief in gold was so widespread and deep in the world that an abandonment of gold involved great risks for the dollar. Before World War II, Keynes frequently inveighed against the gold standard, calling it a barbarous relic. In his proposals for an international clearing union, however, he said: "Gold still possesses great psychological value which is not being diminished by current events; and the desire to possess a gold reserve against unforeseen contingencies is likely to remain. Gold also has the merit of providing in point of form (whatever the underlying realities may be) an uncontroversial standard of value for international purposes, for which it would not yet be easy to find a serviceable substitute. Moreover, by supplying an automatic means for settling some part of the favorable balances of the creditor countries, the current gold production of the world and the remnant of gold reserves held outside the United States may still have a useful part to play."[16] When its problem arose, the United States ignored these insights into the functions of gold and the psychology of many savers and investors.

The Dynamics of the System

With gold no longer used as domestic money and central banks having no rigid economic calculus for the composition of reserves, it was not feasible for economists to formulate a pure theory of the gold-exchange standard— analogous to, and derived from, the pure theory of the gold standard. The best that could be done was to analyze the behavior of the countries involved in the system and to note the conditions required for keeping the system operational. As the world economy was growing and as economic conditions changed rapidly in the two decades after the war, there was ample scope for divergent ideas. For example, a few observers concluded that the stable-par-value rule would always lead to trade and payments restrictions and should, therefore, be replaced by floating exchange rates. But there was quite wide agreement among the experts on two aspects of the system.

1. *The growth of reserves.* First, it could readily be seen that in an expanding world economy, with growing international trade and payments, total reserves would also have to grow to keep pace with the essential need for them (see the section on Surplus Payments Positions, earlier in this chapter). The essential need was to enable countries that maintained reasonable monetary discipline to handle the usual seasonal and cyclical fluctuations in external payments without jeopardy to par values or recourse to restrictions on trade and current payments. Indeed, reserves could hardly be considered adequate unless minor lapses from strict discipline could be financed in the exchange market without significantly weakening confidence in the currency. Of course, exceptional demands on a country's reserves could be met in part by credit facilities, available from the IMF or other official arrangements and from commercial banks, but easy access to credit itself depended in some measure on adequate reserves. And as the amount of exchange transactions grew, the fluctuations in external balances would also grow and their

financing would require larger reserves. If total reserves were to remain static, any country that fell into deficit would have to try to extricate itself by pressing on the reserves of other countries—a condition that would greatly hamper the working of the adjustment process.

When the IMF was designed at Bretton Woods without the power of creating reserve assets, it was not intended to deny the need for the growth of total reserves. But the problem was left to future ad hoc arrangements as the need might become manifest. The only means specified in the agreement was a uniform increase in the price of gold in terms of currencies, which could be effected by a large majority of the total voting power, but with the United States having a veto. In practice, a general increase in the price of gold depended on the United States alone. If the United States decided, say, to double the price of gold, other countries would be forced to follow suit because otherwise their trade and payments positions would be drastically worsened by the relative rise of their currencies against the dollar. When the United States raised the price of gold by 60 percent in 1934, a few gold bloc countries tried to hold out for a while—with disastrous results.

The Bretton Woods Agreement envisaged that the need for reserves would be met partly through wider use of official credit. As far as the resources of the IMF itself were concerned, the agreement specifically provided that "[T]he Fund shall at intervals of five years review, and if it deems it appropriate, propose an adjustment of the quotas of the members." This provision meant all quotas, and thus the total size of the Fund's resources, since the next sentence states, "[The Fund] may also, if it thinks fit, consider at any other time the adjustment of any particular quota at the request of the member concerned." In fact, after the postwar transition the growth of liquidity, reserves, and reserve credits never became an acute problem. Not only were the Fund's resources raised regularly, but, more particularly, there was continuous growth of dollar reserves. It was the dollar that gave an essential flexibility to the system. Dollars could be borrowed quite readily for capital import needs by foreign enterprises and borrowed also by foreign monetary authorities for reserve purposes. They could be held, ready for intervention purposes, in the New York money market. The actual use of the dollar for these purposes was on the initiative of the foreign countries themselves, and it is difficult to imagine how the prosperity of the world over the past thirty years could have been organized without it. Certainly, the international monetary system could not have been run on gold alone.

As the necessity for growth of reserves was recognized, the question of the desirable rate of growth was much investigated by economists and official bodies.[17] Relating reserve growth to the rise of imports was a common approach, but other criteria, such as the relation of reserves to the money supply and to the size of balance-of-payments fluctuations, were also developed. In a practical sense, such measures could readily be applied to the growth of total reserves but were much more difficult to assess for individual countries because it was the very purpose of reserves to fluctuate in use. Of course, only surplus countries accounted for the growth of reserves, but beyond the vague idea of "extreme surplus," precise criteria of appropriate reserve growth for individual countries were not worked out. The only central bank that did so was the Netherlands Bank; for several years, it published a formula in its annual report in which the Netherlands reserve growth target was a function of the domestic money supply. At the time, in the early 1960s, the target figure came out to about $50 million, and as the actual increase was running at about $100 million, the excess was attributed to imported inflation. Annoyed with this self-serving analysis, I had one of my staff calculate the amount of additional reserves that would be needed annually to allow all countries to apply the Dutch criterion. The figure turned out to be $8 billion a year, which shocked the Netherlands Bank into dropping the whole algebraic formula; the actual total reserve growth at the time was $2-3 billion a year.

2. *Harmony between gold and dollar reserves.* The second requirement for the stability of the system was an adequate harmony in the composition of total reserves between dollar balances and gold. If dollar reserves alone were to grow or to outpace substantially the growth rate of gold reserves, the volume of dollar holdings would sooner or later threaten the ability of the United States to maintain the convertibility of the dollar at its declared par value. This outcome would be certain even if, for a time, all other countries took their accumulations of reserves in dollars—although, in fact, some of them preferred substantial accumulations in gold. In this respect, the gold-dollar system was similar to the former bimetallic system of free coinage of gold and silver at a fixed price ratio. That double standard required that new output of the two metals remain in harmony to assure stability of their fixed price relationship. When the output of silver soared through improved mining and refining techniques, the free coinage of silver at the ratio of 16 to 1 to gold was abandoned, and it was not considered feasible to fix a new price of silver that had assured stability with gold.

This was an example of the famous Gresham's law: bad money drives out good. Bad money simply meant plentiful money, while good money meant scarce money. Throughout history there have been many cases of too much paper money driving gold coins into hoarding and the value of the paper money depreciating against the value of the gold coins. The same thing would happen in the gold-dollar system if the growth of dollar reserves outpaced the growth of gold reserves.

At the time of Bretton Woods, the United States held more than $20 billion of gold reserves, and as the dollar reserves of other countries were quite small, the possibility of official dollar liabilities endangering the convertibility of the dollar was remote. Nevertheless, the skilled economists among the negotiators clearly saw the possibility of a general shortage of gold, and they provided a way out of the difficulty in the Articles.

Keynes once said that the IMF Articles of Agreement were written in Cherokee, by which he meant that the legal language used was unnecessarily abstruse in a number of areas. Instead of borrowing from the Fund against the collateral of a deposit in domestic currency, a member was "entitled to purchase the currency of another member from the Fund in exchange for its own currency"; repayment of the loan by the member was to be effected by a "repurchase from the Fund for gold of the Fund's holdings of its currency in excess of its quota." While technical refinements may account partly for this legalistic phraseology, the obscurantism on the price of gold was due to political considerations. Ever since Roosevelt had raised the U.S. gold price, the very idea of changing the dollar price of gold was anathema to some conservative members of the Congress. To avoid controversy, therefore, the Fund rules provided that "the Fund by a majority of the total voting power may make uniform proportionate changes in the par values of the currencies of all members." A uniform change in par values of all members' currencies was simply Cherokee for a general rise in the price of gold. There was no practical possibility of a general reduction in the gold price.

It will be recalled that in providing for changes in par values of currencies, the Fund rules merely stated that "a member shall not propose a change in the par value of its currency except to correct a fundamental disequilibrium." It was not said that in case of fundamental disequilibrium, a member *should,* or *ought to,* change its par value. Similarly, as regards a general rise of the price of gold, the rules did not *direct* the Fund to raise the price in the event of a gold shortage. But the eventuality was allowed for, and neither for individual par values nor for uniform par values was it anticipated by the rational drafters of the agreement that fanatical obstinacy against obviously needed changes would be a major difficulty in the future.

It was entirely possible, of course, for a disequilibrium between the totals of dollar reserves and U.S. gold reserves to arise for which a uniform reduction of par values would not be the appropriate adjustment mechanism. Dollar reserves could rise because the U.S. current external balance developed a persistent deficit due to relative internal price-cost inflation or to a slower increase of productivity and export potential than in foreign countries; they also could rise because U.S. net investment abroad was being pushed substantially in excess of a comfortable current-account surplus. A persistently large deficit in the U.S. balance of payments caused by such developments would indicate a fundamental disequilibrium of the dollar. And the appropriate adjustment instrument, just as with any other currency, would be devaluation of the dollar's gold parity vis-à-vis the gold par value of other currencies.

But another peculiarity of the dollar was that its devaluation against all other currencies was a most unlikely event. Most other currencies were pegged on the dollar, and a great many of them were generally under strain to maintain their fixed rates with the dollar. In the event of a dollar devaluation, they would be obliged to follow the dollar to maintain their precarious balance-of-payments positions. Hence, a devaluation of the dollar to correct a fundamental disequilibrium in the U.S. balance of payments would necessarily have to be selective, relating solely to countries in large surplus. It would necessarily have to be an exercise in monetary diplomacy, with the United States, supported by the IMF, using the weight of its prestige to assure an adequate adjustment.

It was possible also that a U.S. external deficit could arise because a few of its trading partners had developed a very strong competitive position and extreme surpluses; in that case, the appropriate correction would be re-valuation of the currencies of the extreme creditor countries. But this was less likely because extreme surpluses would almost certainly impose correspond-ing deficits on a large number of other countries, rather than being concentrated on the United States. In any event, the remedy of a uniform change in par values or a rise in the general price of gold would fit the case only when new gold itself was in such short supply that the balance between dollar and gold reserves tended to become upset.

The Impact of a Shortage of Gold

The bulk of the new gold, which came into the market from current mining operations and from sales by the Soviet Union, went to supply the gold demand for industrial uses and for private gold savings. Only the residual supply was available for increasing total gold reserves. Assuming that reserves in dollars were on a reasonable upward trend, the flow of new gold into the monetary system would not be fully adequate unless it covered the incremental demands of other countries and still left a sufficient margin of new gold for the reserves of the United States to maintain confidence in the convertibility of the dollar. If the flow of new gold were less than adequate when the increase in dollar reserves was not excessive, the imbalance would not be a disequilibrium of the dollar but a disequilibrium of the gold-dollar system. This situation would lead to a crisis of the system, necessarily involving the dollar.

The arrival of the crisis could take a considerable time if the shortage of gold was moderate or, as was the case, if the U.S. gold reserves at the outset were very large relative to its official dollar liabilities. The time would be shorter if the new gold available for reserves at the existing price was small because then the demand for gold reserves by other countries would be met largely by their presenting dollars for conversion to gold at the U.S. Treasury. The United States was the only gold seller of last resort in the system; the IMF and the United States were buyers of last resort, but the IMF sold gold only to accommodate its own needs, as did other countries. The crisis would be virtually upon the system if the new gold available for reserves became negative because gold from reserves would then be used to make up a deficiency of market supply relative to private demand.

In all these potential situations where gold was in short supply, the system would be in fundamental disequilibrium. The only way of imposing an effective adjustment process would be by a general rise in the price of gold. No other remedy would produce an appropriate adjustment within the limits of the existing system. On the contrary, any other corrective would mean a change in the system, either by allowing exchange rates to float or by limiting the free choice of monetary authorities between gold and dollar reserves. It was evident, therefore, that the price of gold was an important macro-economic variable for the world economy, with a key influence on the structure and equilibrium of the international monetary system.

When the shortage of gold became apparent in the 1960s, and the demand for gold reserves of other countries was leading to a rapid decline in U.S. reserves, there was confusion on this point. The idea was put forward that equilibrium for $n-1$ exchange rates (with n being the number of countries in the system) would determine equilibrium for the system. The implication was that the general level of the gold price was not relevant and that equilibrium could be achieved as readily by revaluation of surplus countries' currencies as by devaluation of the dollar. However, this conception neglected the fact that every country with a fixed exchange rate had a gold parity so that the number of parities was n. Even if all exchange rates could be so accurately adjusted as to wipe out all payments surpluses, the United States could still lose gold if the gold shortage prompted other countries to shift the composition of their reserves in favor of gold. But of course, such fine tuning of exchange rates was not conceivable in the face of the ineluctable tendency for the balance of payments of nondollar countries to fluctuate and for some of them to be in surplus at any given time. The surplus countries would be bound to include some that would present dollars to the U.S. Treasury for conversion into gold. Moreover, revaluations would tend to aggravate the monetary gold shortage by lowering the price of gold in the revalued currencies and thus encouraging larger private purchases.

Suppose, it may be asked, monetary authorities just did not want gold? Then, of course, the system would not have been a gold-dollar system. And if monetary authorities did not want dollars, it would likewise not have been a gold-dollar system.

It must be emphasized that a shortage of new monetary gold was not a matter simply of the physical quantity of gold but of the number of ounces times the price. It was the *value* of the growth in gold reserves that had to be kept in harmony with the growth in the value of dollar reserves. If a shortage in the value of new monetary gold developed, how would a general rise of the gold price restore the balance between gold and dollars? The higher price would make it profitable to exploit marginal gold deposits and, thereby, increase physical gold production. At the same time, the higher price would reduce private industrial demand, as gold would become too costly in its borderline uses where substitutes could be found. Likewise, it would reduce the quantity going into new hoarding and speculation. Hence, the physical flow of new gold into reserves would be further increased. But the main factor would be that the value of the new monetary gold would rise substantially because of the higher price, and all that was needed was to make the price boost large enough to restore the harmony between dollars and gold in reserves.

This simple adjustment process has been denied by some writers on the ground that a rise in the gold price would have been ineffective because it would have increased the demand for gold by central banks and induced greater private hoarding of gold. Such a perverse effect, however, is against both past experience and logic. After the 1934 gold price increase, production went up, hoarding declined in physical terms, and U.S. reserves increased by leaps and bounds. If something like this did not happen again, it would only mean that the price increase had been too small and had left expectations of a further increase after a relatively short time. The increase in the price had to be large enough to be convincing so that any repetition would be well in the future.

At times of weakness of the dollar in the exchange market, U.S. officials often tried to bolster confidence by stressing the inherent strength of the U.S. economy and its potential for expansion. Such pronouncements had no impact because they had nothing to do with the matter; what was needed was an adjustment process for the deteriorating position of U.S. official reserves. Where the great economic strength of the United States could have been telling, on the other hand, was in its unquestionable power to outbid the rest of the world for an appropriate share of gold output to add to its reserves. If the authorities did not have the ingenuity to figure out what price of gold would assure this result, they could have used the experimental method of Franklin Roosevelt and his secretary of the Treasury, Henry Morgenthau. After they found out the ruling price in the gold market each morning, they would have a bid put in above the market price to assure that the United States got the gold. Of course, their main interest was to raise the price, but the same strongarm technique could have been used to strengthen the U.S. international liquidity position in the 1960s. The reason the United States did not use its economic power for this purpose was that it did not want to raise the price of gold, and the argument that the adjustment process would backfire was a rationalization.

The Growth of Dollar Reserves

The growth of total gold reserves reflected a surplus of gold supply in the market over private demand. Why was there a growth of reserves in dollars? Given the fact that the dollar was a valued reserve asset, the growth of dollar reserves could have been due to the United States conducting its affairs so as to produce an external deficit and pushing dollars into the reserves of other countries. But in fact, the rise of total dollar reserves became evident quite soon after the war, when there was still a general shortage of dollars and defensive restrictions against dollar payments; the United States was giving large amounts abroad for economic aid, and its competitive position was extremely strong. The total dollar holdings of central banks continued to go up year after year in a way that was clearly not accidental but was rather a behavioral characteristic of the system. While there had to be a supply of dollars to make their accumulation possible, the causation for quite some years came actually from the desired net payments surpluses of nondollar countries.

The essential factor behind these net surpluses was that many countries took seriously the objective proclaimed in the IMF Articles of maintaining exchange stability. If they fell into a deficit on the balance of payments, which would soon become a threat to exchange stability, they took corrective measures rather promptly. Moreover, in a case of persistent deficit, a country would be obliged to adjust by devaluation sooner or later, and the new parity was aimed to provide for at least some surplus as a margin of safety and as a means of recouping net reserves previously lost. As explained earlier, however, countries were quite tolerant of a surplus position as it removed all threat to the par value and, indeed, was the source of a desirable growth of reserves for a dynamic economy. In the rare cases of revaluation, the change of parity was never fixed so as to shift the external surplus to deficit or even to stop reserve growth. Hence, while there were always some countries in deficit, the algebraic sum of balance-of-payments positions, apart from the United States, was a net surplus.

The United States, on the other hand, accepted the accumulation of official foreign dollar liabilities and the reserve function of the dollar as a matter of course; the parity of the dollar was protected by its huge reserves in gold. The U.S. monetary authorities did not become concerned about U.S. deficits until the shortage of gold began to endanger the dollar. In fact, the United States encouraged the buildup of foreign official reserves in the interests of a strong free-world economy. What the authorities tried to do when they became concerned is described in Chapter 6.

Conditions of Equilibrium for the System

Thus, it is apparent that equilibrium, always a crucial objective in economic affairs (as well as in an analysis of them), was attainable for the dollar and for the system—just as it was for nondollar currencies. For any nondollar country, assuming an adequate level of external reserves to start with, equilibrium required a rising trend of gold and dollar reserves appropriately related to the growth of its foreign transactions. There was no impediment to the accumulation of dollars, and even with an overall shortage of new monetary gold, the U.S. gold reserves could be tapped as a substitute for the missing gold mines. A persistent deficit or persistent extreme surplus was a fundamental disequilibrium that required a change in the par value of the currency as a necessary condition for adjustment to equilibrium.

For the United States, the accumulation of dollars by other countries meant a rising trend of dollar liabilities against its gold reserves. Without a superabundance of new monetary gold, external equilibrium would still involve a deficit on its balance of payments; this situation would be stable, provided that U.S. gold reserves had a rising trend adequate to maintain the gold convertibility of the dollar. The dollar differed from other currencies also in that gold was the only freely usable reserve that the United States could hold. Under the condition that the flow of new monetary gold was adequate to cover new incremental reserve demands for gold at existing par values, the dollar would be in fundamental disequilibrium when the United States allowed a persistently large deficit in its balance of payments. The only remedy in accordance with the par-value rules would be a selective devaluation of the par value of the dollar against currencies in more than adequate surplus.

Equilibrium for *the system* required that the flow of new monetary gold be adequate to meet the incremental demand for gold reserves by countries other than the United States, plus an amount freely flowing to U.S. reserves to maintain harmony between dollar reserves and gold reserves. Without an adequate flow of new monetary gold, the system would be in fundamental disequilibrium, even though the rise in dollar reserves was reasonable. A uniform reduction of par values—a general rise in the price of gold—would be required to effect an adjustment. Of course, the dollar would be having difficulties under the condition of gold shortage, but the basic cause of its difficulty would be the disequilibrium of the system.

It is apparent, therefore, that in the double reserve system of gold and dollars there could arise a need for an increase in the price of gold; indeed, in an expanding world economy with even a minimal tendency toward inflation, there was a likelihood that it would arise. To take an adamant stand against any rise of the gold price in such circumstances would deny the system an essential adjustment mechanism and make it unworkable. Nonetheless, that is what the U.S. monetary authorities proceeded to do.

Part II

2
The Pound Sterling

From the end of World War II, Britain repeatedly suffered a precarious or adverse balance-of-payments position. Time and again, the external payments problem imposed itself on policy, and restraining measures tempered domestic economic expansion to a greater degree than for most other industrial nations. Britain's experience was not simply a reflection of the hard domestic and international realities that the country faced. Political leadership was often confused in its choice of objectives and the policies for attaining them.

Two sequences stand out prior to the breakdown of the gold-dollar system in August 1971: the postwar adjustment period, culminating in the devaluation of sterling in 1949; and the exchange crises from 1964 onwards, with devaluation in 1967. Both were long-drawn-out affairs involving a span of years.

PEACETIME RECONVERSION AND THE DEVALUATION OF 1949

Just after the war ended in Europe, the Conservative party headed by Winston Churchill was defeated in a general election. Churchill stood at the pinnacle of his triumphant leadership and was adored as a heroic figure in many countries, including Britain. It seemed unimaginable that a victorious leader could have been rejected by the voters—yet the election gave the Labour party a majority in Parliament of almost two to one, the worst Conservative defeat since 1906. After this defeat, the Conservative party never again dared to be really conservative.

In rejecting the Conservatives, the voters were not, of course, rejecting Churchill's wartime leadership. The immediate reaction of *The Economist* was that the country wanted a socialist program.[1] But since the British electorate was not prone to follow ideological doctrine, this explanation was clearly an oversimplification. More to the point was the observation of a

Labour candidate from an industrial district: "Abstract questions such as controls versus freedom . . . seem terribly far away in the streets and factories here. What people want to talk about is 'redundancy,' housing, pensions and what will happen to the ex-servicemen after the war."[2] Thus, a large majority of voters were deeply concerned with future job opportunities and the assurance of better living standards. They abandoned the Conservative party for its failures in the 1930s and felt that Labour would be more responsive to their needs. After the privations of the war, the notion of further sacrifices to reestablish and maintain sterling as a strong international currency was not among the major objectives of either Labour or its supporters. The Labour party believed in economic and social reform rather than in a progressive rebuilding of the economy.

Dollar Shortage

When peace came, the Labour government faced the tasks of demobilization (about one quarter of the British work force was in the armed forces) and of reconversion of output to peacetime uses. Wartime destruction and the rundown condition of Britain's productive equipment needed making good. There was also pressure to ease restraints on consumption. These formidable tasks strained the resources available.

Two particular problems weighed heavily during the transition. One was the large balance-of-payments deficit. With the economy geared to war needs, exports had been curtailed to about 40 percent of the prewar volume and were much exceeded by imports—even though imports were restricted to essential war supplies and minimal civilian requirements. The current payments deficit in 1945 amounted to £875 million and was covered largely by U.S. lend-lease, together with some borrowing from the United States, Canada, and the sterling area.

Moreover, it was evident that the external deficit would not be eliminated solely by regaining prewar levels of production and exports. Britain's basic position on external account had worsened over the war years. Foreign assets had been liquidated to the extent of £1.1 billion to help finance the war so that income from foreign investment was lower. Then, too, substantial spending abroad had been financed by credit, which meant that external sterling liabilities had risen from about £500 million before the war to £3.7 billion at the end of 1945, more than six times the size of the official reserves. Interest would have to be paid on these debts, and it also seemed likely that reserves would be drawn down to some extent over the next few years by some members of the sterling area. In addition, the terms of trade were less favorable than before the war so that the prewar volume of exports could not cover the same volume of imports. Also, the operation of the economy at full-employment levels would inevitably raise the demand for imports and require correspondingly higher exports.

All these factors meant that the volume of exports would have to be lifted much above its prewar level to create a sustainable balance-of-payments position. The additional export volume requirement was estimated officially to be of the order of 75 percent, and the adjustment was expected to take about three years.[3] The difficulty of achieving such an increase in exports was compounded by the weakening of Britain's competitive position relative to the United States. Prices had risen much less in the United States, and more important, U.S. industry had been vastly enlarged and improved over the war years and was in a position to convert rapidly to peacetime goods; it could easily overcome British competitors in both traditional and new lines of output. U.S. exports were about double the prewar level, without any increase of imports, and there seemed no challenge ahead to the maintenance of this dominance over other industrial countries, particularly Britain, for some time to come.

The other particular problem of the transition period was the inflationary overhang from the war. It had not been feasible to implement fully Keynes's scheme for financing the war with minimum inflation.[4] The money supply had increased by 370 percent, from £1.64 to £4.42 billion, over the war years. But the increase in the cost of living and in wages had been held down to about 50 percent by direct controls and subsidies on key consumer goods. Besides, with consumer spending limited by strict rationing, personal savings had gone up from 5 percent of personal income before the war to 11 percent in 1945—just for lack of goods to buy. Britain faced, therefore, the threat of an explosion in consumer purchasing power.

The Labour government expected that help to cope with reconversion difficulties would be available from continued U.S. aid, at least for a time. This expectation was reasonable in view of the Anglo-American wartime partnership and the notion of a fair sharing of the war burden. From an economic standpoint, peace would not be a reality until after demobilization. Moreover, the allied war-production planners had geared the British economy more highly to the war effort than that of the United States because it was closer to the battlefront. But postwar planning on this matter was fumbled in both Britain and the United States, partly because it was expected that the war with Japan would continue for at least another year, during which time Britain could make a good start on reconversion. In fact, the bombings of Hiroshima and Nagasaki brought the Japanese war to an end much more quickly, in mid-August 1945. President Truman accepted a narrow interpretation of U.S. aid legislation, primarily from Leo Crowley, the lend-lease administrator, and abruptly cut off the flow of U.S. aid to all its allies, including Britain, just after the end of the war with Japan. This was done in spite of contrary advice by the Departments of State, Treasury, and Commerce, which felt that such an action imposed an immense burden on our allies. Truman acknowledged in his memoirs that his action was ill-timed. But in 1945 he lacked the vision he subsequently demonstrated in sponsoring the Marshall Plan.

The reaction in Britain over Truman's decision ranged from dismay to angry resentment, although it met with overwhelming approval in the U.S. Congress. Suddenly, the British were confronted with magnified difficulties. Keynes believed he could convince the Truman administration of the justice of reestablishing aid, but when he was sent to Washington to explore this prospect, he found official opinion was closed to any such suggestion.[5] So Britain was left with the alternative of borrowing abroad, mainly from the United States. Even with such help, the disbursement of foreign exchange would have to be kept within bounds by continued strict import and exchange controls.

The Labour government was in any case control-minded. There was widespread apprehension in Britain about a postwar depression, and the government believed that planning, which it did not define precisely, was the key to full employment. Controls were looked upon as an essential adjunct of planning. In addition, controls and rationing were the weapons that the government expected would check the overhang of purchasing power. Unlike Belgium, the Netherlands, or Germany, Britain was not only a victorious nation but one that had not suffered enemy occupation. Hence, a currency reform or temporary freezing of excess bank balances was not even considered. Taxes could not be increased above the very high wartime levels without setting off a political reaction, and a once-and-for-all increase in prices to absorb the inflation hangover, the technique used in the United States, was thought to be inequitable.

Given this situation, the question naturally arises whether postwar adjustment would not have been made easier by an early devaluation of sterling. At the time, the British authorities were determined to maintain the pound at the rate of $4.03, which had been fixed on the outbreak of war in 1939, and declared that rate as its initial par value when the International Monetary Fund began to operate at the end of 1946. The general case for such an initial par value was best made by Camille Gutt, the managing director of the Fund, in a well-known address on "The Practical Problem of Exchange Rates," which he delivered at Harvard early in 1948 as a response to criticism of prevailing exchange-rate policy.

The normal functions of an exchange rate for any country, according to Gutt, were to allow exports to flow and to limit imports to the capacity of the country to pay for them. In the light of the great import needs for reconstruction and reconversion, however, it was not possible for the exchange rate to perform the second function—imports could not be sufficiently compressed by depreciation of the currency. Hence, for initial parities, the one practical test of the suitability of an exchange rate was whether it enabled the country to export. Gutt's exposition stressed that initial par values might have to be changed, that temporary floating was useful in certain circumstances, and that inflation had to be brought under control. But his main thesis was particularly unsatisfactory as a justification for the initial sterling parity of $4.03. In the first place, it did not allow adequately for the function of the exchange rate with respect to imports. The exchange rate should have been fixed so as to allow for the gradual relaxation of import controls as the volume of exports expanded. Moreover, the British had to have an eye out for the sterling-area countries, where the exchange rate could and should have played an immediate role in limiting import demand and thus preventing the British reserves from being used to supply these countries with cheap imports. Second, sterling's initial par value was, even from the standpoint of export performance, too high, since it was not until 1951, after sterling had been devalued, that Britain reached its target of a 75 percent increase in export volume over its prewar level.

This judgment about the initial par value was borne out by the events of 1947. After the United States refused to mount a new aid program, the government called on Keynes to negotiate a loan to cover the inevitable payments deficit of the transition period. Britain's needs were manifest, and the United States soon agreed to extend a credit of $3,750 million (apart from credit for $650 million in the lend-lease pipeline), and Canada a credit of $1,250 million, both on very favorable terms. The U.S. loan was to run for 50 years at 2 percent interest, with the first payment of interest and amortization delayed until 1951.

But there was a stinger attached. Washington insisted that the current earnings in sterling of foreigners be made convertible within a year after the loan agreement became effective. This provision was included in the bargain without the suitability of the exchange rate having been brought into the negotiations. The U.S. negotiators wanted to commit the United Kingdom to move toward a multilateral regime of trade and payments, and they bargained with the zeal for commercial advantage that is characteristic of tariff negotiators. While the British were loath to accept this commitment, they had no alternative. Once they agreed, Congress approved the loan in July 1946.[6]

The British authorities tried in the first half of 1947 to anticipate and hence temper some of the strains of convertibility by easing bilateral restrictions on transfers of sterling among non-sterling-area countries for use in current-account transactions. But when convertibility came into force in July of that year, it proved a disaster that showed the authorities to be shockingly out of touch with sentiment about sterling, both in the market and among foreign governments and central banks. The rush to convert at $4.03 was enormous.

Almost one third of the U.S. loan was used up in the mere five weeks that the experiment lasted.

It is evident that convertibility should not have been attempted until a more realistic rate for sterling had been established by an appropriate devaluation. Immediate postwar devaluation may not have been appropriate because it would have added to inflation at an inconvenient time, but it was surely the case that the external account could not be brought into true balance, free of the distortion of quantitative import restrictions and extensive exchange controls, without devaluation sooner or later. In his otherwise excellent study of sterling-dollar diplomacy, Richard Gardner expressed the rather comical view that the convertibility experiment failed because it was just not carried out right in not blocking the sterling balances sufficiently. As he took his analysis only though 1947, Gardner was not obliged to explain the 1949 devaluation of sterling.[7]

Even without the convertibility losses, the amount of the U.S. and Canadian loans would have been inadequate—as Bernstein had predicted in a memorandum to the U.S. secretary of the treasury. With the convertibility losses, the entire borrowings were used up by the end of 1947, having lasted 18 months instead of the three years originally intended. But then help with the dollar shortage came from the Marshall Plan Aid.

The convertibility fiasco, although magnified by conversions of sterling on capital account, was clear evidence of fundamental disequilibrium. The inadequacy of Britain's postwar adjustment, however, was also partly a result of the way in which the domestic economy was managed. After the failure of convertibility, the proper role of financial policies in curbing excess demand was seen more clearly, and both tax increases and reductions in public capital spending were introduced in the fall of 1947. In 1948, the financial position of the public sector showed a £459 million surplus, as compared with a deficit of £2 billion in 1945. Even so, total demand remained very strong throughout these years. Instead of the expected postwar recession, unemployment after 1947 was at about the frictional minimum of 1.5 percent of the labor force. Labor unions pressed for increased wages, and the tightness of the labor market, with vacancies exceeding unemployment, lent strength to their bargaining position. Wages rose by 20 percent over 1945 to 1948, exceeding the increase in productivity by more than 2 percent a year. This pressure added to the inflationary hangover and required adjustments in controlled prices, with the result that the cost of living had risen 16 percent by 1948, despite a large increase in subsidies on consumer goods.

But Britain's price-wage inflation was no worse than elsewhere, and actually was better contained than in most countries. In particular, prices in the United States rose 35 percent from 1945 to 1948 and wages rose 30 percent. Therefore, Britain did not have exceptional wage-price inflation to account for the persistence of its external deficit. However, whereas price controls and rationing had been abandoned by the United States in 1946, the British government was still resorting to these measures to hold back excessive demand pressures.

The spillover of this demand into imports could not be completely prevented. Their volume was allowed to rise by 28 percent from 1945 to 1948 despite the sharp reduction in military needs. Nevertheless, at their 1948 volume, imports were still only about four fifths of their prewar level.

In addition to the trade deficit, there was a continual leakage on capital account because exchange controls were evaded in one way or another or because the sterling liabilities were not tightly blocked. The trade and capital deficits of 1946-48 not only used the outside aid made available, but also reduced official reserves from $2.5 billion at the end of 1945 to $1.8 billion at the close of 1948.

It was sometimes argued that the failure of balance-of-payments adjustment was attributable mainly to unrequited exports to the sterling area paid for out of accumulated assets in London. But, in fact, sterling balances were drawn down only from £3.6 billion at the end of 1945 to £3.2 at the end of 1948. A few countries, such as India and Egypt, drew fairly heavily on their sterling assets, but others added to theirs out of payments surpluses. As Thomas Balogh, a pro-Labour economist, noted: "The repayment of balances actually accumulated during the war . . . can hardly be awarded a decisive role in British embarrassments, as so many have suggested it should."[8]

Fundamental to the continued difficulties was Labour's overreliance on the wide network of direct controls on imports, foreign exchange, and prices without any effective plan for their progressive relaxation to regularize the situation. Observers as different as Lionel Robbins and Oliver Franks argued at the time against excessive resort to controls, contending that controls were an obstacle to recovery. When high standards are set for the performance of the economy, controls can be a useful adjunct to other policy instruments, and it is quixotic to forswear their use entirely as a matter of principle. But experience, as in France, Italy, Spain, and quite a few developing countries, has shown again and again that substantial excess demand combined with an overvalued exchange rate introduces strains and distortions that controls cannot counteract. And controls lose their impact the longer they are kept in place.

The Devaluation of 1949

The IMF Annual Report of 1948 openly discussed the desirability of adjustments of some European exchange rates, although without specific mention of sterling. A devaluation of the pound had been expected by the

French authorities from the beginning of 1948, and when it did not take place, they proceeded with a further devaluation of the franc in October.[9] But it was in the United States that official opinion on the matter really crystallized. Andrew Overby, the U.S. executive director to the IMF, began to raise the exchange-rate question in 1948, and Frank Southard, his successor, continued the attack.[10] Southard saw clearly that the need for Marshall Plan Aid to Britain would never come to an end without a substantial sterling devaluation.

In the spring of 1949, the foreign-exchange market became aware of this official behind-the-scenes talk of devaluation. The result was an outflow of funds from London and losses of reserves. At the same time, the first postwar recession in the United States led to a decline in U.S. imports from the sterling area. Although dollar imports into Britain were further restricted in June and July, confidence in sterling did not strengthen. In fact, the loss of reserves mounted. By mid-September, reserves had fallen to $1.3 billion from $1.9 billion at the end of March. Devaluation had become the only practical way to stop the crisis. Dow has said that, "had sterling been devalued in April, it would have been a considered move, instead of a crisis measure."[11] True enough, but it is more to the point to say that a much earlier devaluation would have been still better.

Once the need for devaluation was accepted, the first problem for the government was what the new parity should be. Rough calculations were made by the Treasury, using scattered data and assumptions about price elasticities, but the existing conditions of price and import controls made it difficult to work out reasonable estimates. The exercise indicated that a rate of $2.80 or $3.00 would be about right. Returning to London from Washington, the chancellor, Sir Stafford Cripps, stopped in New York, where he met Ernest Bevin, the foreign secretary, and asked his opinion. Bevin thought it better to take $2.80 in order to have a bigger margin, and Cripps recommended $2.80 to the Cabinet, which adopted it.

Since the government seemed truly to believe, as late as the beginning of the summer, that no adjustment was called for, the devaluation by 30.5 percent announced on September 18 appeared to be a high figure. Cripps explained in the House of Commons that at least $3.00 was needed to make British exports competitive in the North American market. He went to $2.80 because "it was necessary to make it absolutely plain that this was not a tentative first step but . . . that we had without doubt gone far enough."

Much more important than the choice of the new parity, however, was that Labour failed to make use of the adjustment as a unique opportunity for seeking a real equilibrium—one that would allow a rapid removal of controls on imports, foreign exchange, and prices and put sterling on the road to being a strong currency. These objectives could have been accomplished by the temporary use of a floating rate, which had some supporters. As *The Economist* commented just after the event: "The government would have been far wiser to have fixed no new parity at all for the time being, but to have allowed the pound first to find its own level. This may, in fact, turn out to be Sir Stafford's greatest mistake. Nobody can confidently assert that any rate is 'correct' in the present confused and distorted state of the world economy— let alone one that will still be appropriate when it has had time to settle down. If, as Sir Stafford says, the present exchange control would be unworkable with fluctuating rates, then so much the worse for the present exchange control."[12]

Cripps believed that floating would have a destabilizing effect because of the existing speculative pressure on sterling. He missed the point that the existing speculative pressures had built up in anticipation of devaluation and would have progressively declined as the pound floated down. Sterling was, in fact, oversold at the time of devaluation, and it might not have reached $2.80 under floating. In any case, the government's *dirigiste* ideology precluded giving priority to decontrol. As Cripps explained: "If by a floating rate its sponsors mean to imply that all our exchange and import controls should be taken off and the pound allowed to find its own level, we could not possibly think of such a course. . . . The only question we considered was whether the pound should be left to find its own level within the limited range of transactions which are at present permitted over the exchanges."[13]

Besides an appropriate exchange-rate policy, disinflationary measures were needed to ease excess demand and facilitate the removal of controls. While the government recognized that demand was excessive, it was not prepared to put full employment in jeopardy, particularly with a general election in prospect. Following the September devaluation, it announced in October that cuts were to be made in capital outlays and in government expenditures, but these measures only amounted to about £250 million. Moreover, they were cuts against a rising trend rather than actual reductions, and they were only to become effective in the second half of 1950—if ever. All through 1950, demand remained pressing and unemployment stayed at the low figure of 1.5 percent of the labor force. Roy Harrod observed at the time: "The poor figure cut by the British authorities was not mainly due to lack of executive capacity, but to something deeper, the lack of a theory in regard to how the economic system works. It is not so much a question of hesitation before imposing some drastic measure but lack of any conception as to what kind of drastic measure would be a remedy."[14]

Also, the devaluation was not well managed in that no attempt was made to consult with the other principal countries, apart from the United States, with the purpose of negotiating a new exchange-rate structure based on the actual and prospective positions of each currency. The French in the devaluation of

1936 had given some precedent for such consultation, and it would have been in the spirit of the Bretton Woods Agreement. To be sure, such a negotiation might have been difficult to carry out in the wide forum of the Fund. But the OEEC was available, established precisely for European economic coopera-tion, or the Bank for International Settlements in Basel. As some countries protested at having been confronted with a *fait accompli,* lack of experience does not entirely excuse the failure to consult and negotiate. From Britain's standpoint, the action that other countries might take was pertinent to its own decision on the new parity. But it seems that the government conceived the operation simply as a devaluation against the dollar area.

As it turned out, the unilateral British action triggered a wave of devaluations that was wider and deeper than necessary, substantially reducing the effective devaluation of sterling. Weighted by British export shares, the new exchange rates yielded an average devaluation for the pound of about 10 percent, although in the distorted trade conditions of the time too much importance cannot be attached to that precise figure. The question of competitive depreciation was raised in the IMF by several Latin American directors, but only with respect to devaluations by dependent territories of the United Kingdom. The European devaluations were not questioned. Of the industrial countries, only Japan and Switzerland left their parities un-changed. Belgium devalued by only 12.3 percent despite the 30.2 percent devaluation by Holland and 20.6 percent by Germany.

The market accepted the devaluation as establishing a favorable rate for sterling so that the previous outflow of funds reversed itself. British reserves had risen to $1.7 billion by the end of 1949, an increase of $400 million from the devaluation level, and to $3.3 billion by the end of 1950. Exports increased substantially in 1950, both in volume and in value, accompanied by a rise in invisible earnings. The sterling value of imports increased because of their higher sterling cost, but their volume, under tighter controls, was unchanged. These rapid adjustments, helped by an upturn in the U.S. economy, indicated that the devaluation was producing the right kind of results. The political impact of devaluation in Britain was not marked. Labour won in the general election of February 1950, but its parliamentary majority was reduced to 18 seats. With the country enjoying full employment, however, devaluation was not an important influence on the voters.

THE ROAD TO 1967

The new par value of the pound was held stable for 18 years, until it was again devalued in November 1967. In the intervening years, sterling did not have smooth sailing. On the contrary, it was subjected to a series of crises that

TABLE 1 United Kingdom Balance of Payments, 1946-78

annual averages (millions of £ sterling)

Items (net)	1946-49	1950-51	1952-57	1958-62	1963-68	1969-71	1972	1973-76	1977-78
1. Trade deficit	-188	-370	-169	-145	-360	+16	-722	-3,614	-1,460
2. Government invisibles[a]	-176	-147	-119	-284	-607	-762	-703	-1,427	-2,692
3. Private invisibles	+217	+486	+407	+512	+851	+1,558	+1,633	+3,380	+4,815
4. Current account (1 to 3)	-147	-31	+119	+83	-116	+812	+208	-1,661	+663
5. Sterling balances[b] (gross)									
Official[c]	-49	+218	-72	-11	-75	+407	+287	-113	-69
Private	-14	+68	+18	+94	-15	+307	-91	+237	+891
6. Special grants, capital transfers, investment and other capital transactions including balancing item[d]	+167	-134	-86	-69	-416	+181	-1,669	-341	+1,633
7. Balance for official financing (4 to 6)	-43	+121	-21	+97	-622	+1,707	-1,265	-1,878	+3,118
8. Gold subscriptions to IMF (-)	-14	—	—	-18	-7	-13	—	—	—
9. Allocations of SDRs (+)	—	—	—	—	—	+99	+124	—	—
10. Official financing (increase in reserves -)	+57	-121	+21	-79	+629	-1,793	+1,141	+1,878	-3,118

[a] Interest, profits, and dividends are included under private invisibles up to and including 1962. Public corporations are included under private invisibles.
[b] Up to and including 1962, the figures are calculated from statistics relating to outstanding stocks.
[c] Excluding IMF.
[d] Including EEA loss on forward commitments.

required the adoption of restrictive policy measures to safeguard the parity. Outside events had a significant influence in some instances, but the gradual deterioration of sterling's position over the years reflected the relative failure of the domestic economy. The critical analytical question was posed in the Bank for International Settlements (BIS) Report for 1968: "While the immediate causes of devaluation were to some extent accidental, its origin lay in the history of weakness for some years before. The question, therefore, is why the currency had been subject to repeated crises and why earlier periodic efforts with restrictive policies failed to establish a firm external base for untroubled economic growth."

The Korean War and Its Aftermath

The first shock to sterling came from the Korean war, which reversed the favorable balance-of-payments situation of 1950 and resulted in a fresh sterling crisis in the second half of 1951. Even before hostilities broke out, the world economy was in a phase of very rapid expansion, with international demand for raw materials already rising. The prospect of wartime shortages triggered a heavy wave of panic purchases that sent prices of industrial materials soaring. British export prices also rose rapidly, by about 20 percent over these 12 months, but prices of imports increased much faster—by 40 percent. This deterioration in the terms of trade was quickly reflected in an adverse shift of the trade balance. Import controls on dollar goods were held very tight in 1950, having been strengthened the year before, in the belief that the commodity price outburst would be temporary—which proved to be the case. But because inventories of materials were drawn down, they had to be renewed at higher prices the following year. In addition, the government added to imports by the stockpiling of strategic materials. In all, imports increased from £2.6 billion in 1950 to £3.9 billlion in 1951—about two thirds of the rise attributable to price increases and one third to volume; and the visible trade deficit went up between the two years from £50 million to nearly £700 million.

The war in Korea led Washington to emphasize to Britain and its other allies in Western Europe the danger of Communist aggression. Urged by the United States to join in raising defense capabilities, and spurred by an American pledge to aid in this effort, Britain responded with a new three-year defense program of £3.6 billion, subsequently raised to £4.7 billion in January 1951. The program was a considerable burden on the economy. Hugh Gaitskell, the new chancellor, sought to restrict government spending, but made only a half-hearted attempt to cover the added costs of defense. Both income and purchase taxes were increased, initial depreciation allowances on new investment were suspended, and small charges were imposed for the first time in the health services (which provoked a bitter dispute within the Labour party). In all, the increase in revenues was estimated at only £150 million, and the budget position shifted from a surplus of £339 million in 1950 to a deficit of £133 million in the following year. Thus, the net effect of the defense program was to increase pressures on demand; unemployment in 1951 fell to the very low level of 1.2 percent, and was far exceeded by registered job vacancies. Defense output also added to import requirements and usurped part of the limited capacity of the engineering industries, limiting their exports.[15]

Another factor initially adverse to sterling was the OEEC Code of Liberalization of Trade. This committed member countries to liberalize 60 percent of intra-European trade 15 days after the establishment of the European Payments Union (EPU), which was approved on September 19, 1950. The immediate effect for Britain was to worsen the trade balance. British imports from European countries increased without being matched by a higher volume of exports. Moreover, the sterling area's payments balance with the OEEC area entered into Britain's net position in the EPU.

Finally, wage restraint started to break down in October 1950. Restraint had been initiated by Cripps in February 1948, and was effective with labor mainly because he was able to communicate his own high sense of purpose. While it lasted, restraint held the increase in wage rates to 5 percent over a period of two and a half years. But once its bind was loosened, there was a wave of large wage increases, resulting in an 8 percent overall increase from 1950 to 1951. From that point on, wage pressures were a persistent problem for the British authorities.

The collective impact of all these factors was to turn the payments balance on current account from a surplus of £300 million in 1950 to a deficit of more than £400 million in 1951. In the second half of 1951, the rest of the sterling area also went into deficit and drew on its balances in London as its export materials prices began to decline while its previous high income still prompted strong demand for imports. Britain's official reserves began to decline in July and, with speculative outflows added to the basic payments deficit, fell by $1.5 billion in the second half of the year. By the time the severity of the deterioration was recognized, the government had scheduled a general election and was hardly free to take new measures.

The election was a victory for the Conservatives. Churchill again became prime minister and R. A. Butler the chancellor of the exchequer. Although the sterling crisis was a factor in the election, the disillusion with the Labour government's domestic economic management was even more of an influence.

To deal with the crisis, the new government imposed sharp cuts in imports by tightening direct controls on dollar goods and retreated from the commitment to liberalize trade within the OEEC area. Further restrictions took place during the first months of 1952, reducing Britain's liberalization in intra-European trade from 90 to 60 percent by the end of 1951 and to 46 percent in 1952. Reductions in imports were made by other sterling area countries after discussions at the January 1952 conference of Commonwealth finance ministers. As world raw-material prices were falling rather rapidly also, the crisis melted away quickly, and as early as March 1952, the loss of reserves was down to $65 million per month. By the fourth quarter of 1952, official reserves began to rise again, limiting the loss for the year to $490 million. Nonetheless, the Korean crisis had drained the reserves from $3.3 billion at the end of 1950 to less than $2 billion two years later.

From the start of 1952, the pressure of demand began to recede. The large price rises of the previous year limited the real purchasing power of consumers, and restrictions on consumers' credit introduced in January further curtailed spending. In addition, enterprises began to trim inventories after their buildup in 1951. Industrial output actually declined in 1952, and unemployment rose to 2 percent. The balance of payments showed a large turnaround in 1952, with the current account in substantial surplus. Despite the recession, however, wage rates rose by 8.3 percent, and partly because price controls began to be relaxed, retail prices showed a similar advance—even though import prices were falling. In the face of weakened demand, Butler's budget in March was fairly neutral. At the same time, however, monetary policy emerged from the freeze that had been imposed since the beginning of the war, with the bank rate being raised from 2 to 2.5 percent in November 1951 and to 4 percent at the time of the budget.[16]

All in all, the effects of the Korean war crisis, accompanied by increased defense spending, the initial effects of the liberalization of European trade, and the breakdown of wage restraint, had by the early 1950s significantly eroded the benefits derived from the 1949 devaluation of sterling. In future years, the market quickly showed a distrust of sterling whenever signs of trouble appeared. While Britain's reserves subsequently rose somewhat, they never became adequate to support the sterling system. Frequent statements were made of the intention to increase reserves, but somehow the strength of will to attain this objective against the various pressures on the balance of payments never materialized.

The Floating Rate Plan

Although the Conservative government had felt obliged to resort to drastic import controls to check the crisis of sterling in 1951, its basic philosophy was against controls. Whenever conditions allowed, it sought to restore an increasing measure of freedom to the market economy. In particular, the Conservatives (as well as the Bank of England) looked upon the reestablishment of London as an international financial center to be a necessary source of earnings for the nation and a means of holding the sterling area intact. They believed that this objective could not be realized unless sterling was made convertible.

But the sorry experience of 1947, and the weakened confidence after the Korean crisis, meant that there was no simple road to convertibility. To press deflationary measures in the face of the emerging recession was not an attractive or feasible political alternative. Given this situation, a secret plan for convertibility was developed, with the code name of Operation Robot. It was the brain child of Leslie Rowan and Richard "Otto" Clarke of the Treasury and George Bolton of the Bank of England, who together won over Butler early in 1952.[17]

The key elements of the plan were to extend convertibility for the current earnings of nonresidents, while allowing sterling to float for a transitional period, with the safeguards of a freeze on sterling balances and maintenance of import controls. While floating might be used to absorb some of the strain on the exchange rate rather than having it fall on the reserves, the idea was not the usual one of letting the currency depreciate so as to allow a free path for domestic expansion. On the contrary, the plan's proponents did not consider British goods to be uncompetitive or the balance-of-payments deficit to be anything but transitory. Their idea rather was that, with sterling floating, any weakness on the exchange market would oblige the authorities to take measures to support the rate and thus to effect some shift in policy priorities from very full employment to the balance of payments and the suppression of inflation. There were known to be leakages in the exchange controls (in part through the EPU mechanism), and while decontrol of imports could come more gradually, it was thought that convertibility had to come by a sharp break.

Armed with these ideas, Butler went to Washington to solicit support from the United States. In view of the low level of Britain's reserves, he believed that help should be available in case temporary pressures threatened the exchange rate too strongly. But John Snyder, the secretary of the treasury, was not interested. It was an election year in the United States, and it would have taken some imagination—and courage—to find a way of giving support to Britain. In addition, the United States was not ready to ease its bind on IMF resources, maintained over the transition and Marshall Plan years. But it is ironic that, having insisted on convertibility in 1947 with the pound at $4.03, the United States did not encourage it in 1952 with the pound at $2.80.

Butler was prepared to go ahead in any case, but ran into strong opposition in the Cabinet. Lord Cherwell, the paymaster general and an intimate friend of Churchill's, was a powerful opponent.[18] Cherwell argued that the world dollar shortage was still too great to make convertibility feasible and that there was the danger of a drastic decline in the sterling exchange rate. It was necessary to concentrate on building up British production and export potentials before convertibility could be attempted. Christopher Dow, writing more than 10 years later, also argued that Operation Robot was premature, and his view cannot be lightly dismissed.

Yet there was considerable merit in the proposal of a managed float as a temporary adjustment technique. Sterling at $2.80 was not an unrealistic rate in the absence of excess demand, and speculative pressure was likely to be calmed by a relatively small easing of the exchange rate. Moreover, the wider changes in policy priorities envisaged by the authors of the scheme, including greater emphasis on export potential and the international position of sterling and a less ambitious target for full employment, might well have improved Britain's long-run economic performance.

Recalling the situation later, Butler observed that he wanted expansion but believed it was capable of achievement "only if the fresh winds of freedom and opportunity were allowed to blow vigorously through the economy."[19] Still, lacking American encouragement or cooperation, the plan was finally abandoned in June 1952. Butler has said that the senior members of the government were responsible for its defeat and that he received consistent support only from Oliver Lyttelton, secretary of state at the Colonial Office.[20]

The Specter of Overvaluation

To return to the march of events during the 1950s, the sterling parity seemed adequate to the needs of external balance. With the current account in reasonable shape, the solid accomplishments of 1953-54 included trade liberalization and the ending of food rationing and price controls. But recurring crises in 1955-1957 made it evident that the position of sterling was fragile.

The 1955 crisis broke out in July, when the market became suspicious about the maintenance of the exchange rate. Negotiations were then in process on a scheme for replacing the EPU with a looser European Monetary Agreement. This proposal had been made by the British authorities primarily to prepare the way for sterling convertibility, but also because they thought that the EPU clearing system contained leakages that were unfavorable for sterling. At a meeting of the OEEC, the United Kingdom proposed that the exchange margins in the new agreement be widened to 5 percent (which contrasted to the 3/4 of 1 percent rule in the EPU) to give more maneuverability in dealing with day-to-day market forces. The leak of this proposal, which was not favored by Britain's partners in the EPU, was a bombshell to the market. Traders were convinced that sterling would be the prime candidate for a decline, and strong selling pressure broke out.

More fundamental to the crisis, however, was the fresh development in

Britain of excess demand, accelerated inflation, and an adverse trade balance. Unemployment fell to barely 1 percent in 1955; wages and prices jumped by 7 and 6 percent, respectively; imports increased by almost £500 million; and the current balance shifted to a £155 million deficit from its £120 million surplus of the previous year. Of course, the exchange crisis had to be met by new restrictive measures, which included restraint on investment by nationalized industries and local authorities. Moreover, an exceptional budget, which partly reversed a number of tax cuts made in April, was introduced in October after the Conservatives had won the 1955 election.

The flare-ups of the exchange market in 1956 and 1957 were quite different from that of 1955 in that the current external account was in surplus on both of these occasions. The selling pressure on sterling in the second half of 1956 arose from the seizure of the Suez Canal by Egypt and the crisis that followed. The United Kingdom drew $560 million on the IMF and arranged further credit lines also with the IMF and with the United States.

The exchange-market crisis in the second half of 1957 was also an affair of confidence, though the threat to exchange rates in this case had more substance. Germany had been running a strong external surplus, particularly in the EPU, and several countries in the OEEC were urging a revaluation of the deutsche mark as an act of good creditor policy. A leak of this discussion in the press set off the crisis. In fact, while the German authorities were not willing to take unilateral action, Ludwig Erhard, the minister of economics, suggested informally that several countries might act together to adjust the exchange-rate structure. But the speculative furor, far from having the effect of goading the authorities into a useful exchange-rate adjustment, scared off the authorities in Britain and Germany, leading them to drop the whole idea. In the United Kingdom the bank rate was raised to no less than 7 percent, bank advances and new capital issues were restricted, and public spending on investment was limited. In addition, a Council on Prices, Productivity, and Incomes was established in the hope that it would contribute to better performance of the economy by pointing the way to a reduction of inflation.

Despite the speculative outbursts of selling in the market, the basic position of sterling did not seem compromised. While a policy of restraint was necessary in view of the exchange crisis and output remained on a plateau, it was not an obvious "dilemma" situation because it was clear that excessive demand existed. Whereas the Treasury's confidential target for full employment was an unemployment rate of 1.8 percent, the actual rate during 1956-57 averaged 1.3 percent. Thus, it appeared that the failure of reserves to grow was due to an overly high level of domestic demand.

At the same time, the competitive position of the United Kingdom was being weakened, partly because of continual inflation and partly because the growth rate of the economy was trailing behind the dynamic increases in other countries, such as Germany, Italy, and Japan. Neither industry nor the trade unions made increased productivity a prime objective, and the budget demands of the welfare state required high taxes, which were a damper to incentive; the government for its part had no lever with which to attack the growth problem. With respect to inflation, there was some support for the view that fiscal and monetary policy should give more priority to its suppression. Peter Thorneycroft, the new chancellor, resigned in January 1958, skeptical of the government's firmness in this matter. The prevailing view, however, was that wage push was the basic inflationary force, and it could be seen that the round of wage increases year after year exceeded the increase in productivity. Sir Robert Hall, the Treasury's economic advisor, suggested that the OEEC charge a group of experts to study the causes of inflation; its report *The Problem of Rising Prices* was issued in 1961 and emphasized the importance of cost-push inflation.

The Critical Test, 1959-60

The sterling crisis of 1964 is often taken as the precursor of the devaluation of 1967. But the critical test for the pound really came in the 1959-60 expansion effort. The cumulative impact of restraint over the previous three years and the easing of international economic activity and trade brought a recession in 1958. British industrial production declined and unemployment rose to a postwar high of 2.9 percent in February 1959. Excess demand was clearly eliminated for the first time since the war, and with the help of a drop in raw-material prices, the balance of payments improved substantially. External convertibility was established generally in Europe at the end of 1958, when the EPU was liquidated and replaced by the European Monetary Agreement. Sterling participated in this move, and the United Kingdom's liberalization of inter-OEEC trade stood at 95 percent.

Cautious relaxation of restraints on credit and public investment was begun after the summer of 1958, and some further budgetary stimulus in the spring of 1959 was appropriate. However, the strong stimulus actually given—which included substantial reductions in both direct and indirect taxation—once again had an election-year flavor and clearly involved the risk of a renewal of excess demand. Moreover, these measures were taken at a time of general economic upswing in Europe.

The response of the economy was rapid throughout 1959 and the first quarter of 1960, with the lead taken by consumer demand and, subsequently, private capital outlays. It seemed as though the previous three years of stagnation had stored up a large expansion potential. Industrial production rose by 12 percent, and the increase in total output was 8 percent. Yet, after only five quarters of growth, strains on resources became apparent. These showed in a rapid decline in unemployment—from 2.3 percent at the end of 1958 to 1.6 percent by April 1960—and a rise in the rate of wage increases to almost 5 percent in 1959 and 5.5 percent in 1960.

Equally significant was the rapid deterioration in the balance of payments, mostly on the trade account. From a surplus of £344 million in 1958, the current balance shifted to a deficit of £245 million in 1960. Imports had risen rather rapidly in the second half of 1959, partly because controls on dollar imports had been eased and partly because inventories were being rebuilt after the previous recession. More striking, however, was the modest performance of exports, especially in relation to the gains of other countries. After a rise during the second half of 1959, the growth of exports tapered off until the fourth quarter of the following year. From 1959 to 1960, British exports increased by 7 percent, which compared with an increase of almost 20 percent for the countries in the Common Market. This weakness of exports was of some years' standing. From 1953 to 1960, for example, when the volume of world exports had risen by 50 percent, British exports had risen only 26 percent in volume. In contrast, German exports had gained 150 percent, Italy's 180 percent, and those of the Netherlands and Switzerland 88 and 67 percent respectively.

One explanation offered for the sluggishness of British exports was that British enterprises were not sufficiently aggressive in seeking foreign markets and that they found it easier to serve the home markets under the conditions of active domestic demand that had prevailed over most of the postwar period. While this factor may have played some part, the argument neglected the fact that British firms had a long tradition and experience in exporting and that the range of British export goods was wider than that of many other industrial countries. Moreover, there was a network of importing distributors and agents of British goods throughout the world with every desire to do business.

Given these favorable circumstances, it was clear that British goods were less competitive than were those of most other industrial countries. In Germany, Italy, and the Netherlands, for example, the sweep of expansion in the 1950s had been led by exports that were outcompeting the products of other countries. These countries had a favorable position in the exchange-rate structure after the 1949 adjustments, and they held this position over the next decade, a period when the British competitive position was deteriorating. The most important reason for this relative deterioration was the continual tendency toward excessive wage increases through organized wage bargaining that exerted an upward push on costs and prices. Although British wages did not rise more rapidly than did wages in most other industrial countries, they had a larger cost-push effect because productivity gains and profit margins in Britain were less substantial.

The Phillips curve[21] attempted to explain wage movements by reference to the level of unemployment, with the implication that wage inflation stemmed from demand pressure on the labor market. But while excess demand played a role in the United Kingdom, particularly in the period from the second half of 1954 to mid-1956, the fact was that the rate of wage increases was persistently too high. Wage increases were larger when demand was high and lower when demand slackened, but in both instances, they exceeded the gain in productivity, with inevitable price effects. From 1954 to 1960, wage rates increased more than 30 percent while productivity rose less than 20 percent. By the late 1950s, the problem of cost-push inflation through the pressure of organized labor was widely recognized.

Owing to this cost-push inflation, British export prices showed a distinct upward tendency, rising by about 10 percent from 1953 to 1960. In contrast, export prices in Germany and the Netherlands were almost stable, while they showed moderate declines in Italy, Switzerland, and Japan. Thus, during the years following the Korean war episode, Britain not only lacked an exchange rate conducive to export-led expansion at the outset, but also lost further ground in international competitiveness. The conflict between pursuing the objective of economic growth and maintaining the external balance had already forced the government to change its policy from stimulus to restraint and back again a few times, a phenomenon characterized in the press as a stop-go policy.

The issue in 1960 was whether the current-account deficit could again be corrected simply by following a cautious demand policy or whether the disequilibrium was fundamental and required a devaluation. The former course of action was unlikely to succeed, not only because it would be difficult to keep wages down enough to gain a competitive advantage, but also because of the size of the turnaround required in the balance of payments. It would not be enough just to wipe out the 1960 current deficit; there had to be a surplus large enough to cover investment abroad of at least £200 million, plus a reasonable margin for building up the reserves.

For the moment, however, the authorities marked time. They were helped in doing so by the fact that during the second half of 1960 the current balance-of-payments deficit was more than covered by capital inflows. The revaluation of the deutsche mark in March 1961 triggered heavy sales of sterling in the exchange markets, but with the government reluctant to dampen the economic expansion at what seemed like an early stage, the loss of reserves was handled by $900 million of short-term borrowing from central banks—the first major inter-central-bank support operation. Nor was any significant corrective action taken in the April 1961 budget.

The market was not convinced by this wait-and-see attitude. The strain on resources and wage inflation continued, with the balance of payments showing a persistent deficit and sterling remaining weak into the summer. By July, policy action had become imperative and comprehensive restrictive measures were initiated to stop the boom. Besides a broad package of monetary and fiscal restraint, Chancellor Selwyn Lloyd put a freeze on public-sector wages and salaries for the coming six months and appealed to the private sector for similar wage restraint. To provide further help to the balance of payments, capital exports were to be restricted more severely, and business was to repatriate the profits from foreign operations more fully. With the support of these measures, a drawing of $1 billion was made on the IMF to repay the short-term central-bank credits and a further standby credit from the IMF was arranged to strengthen confidence in the sterling parity.

This strong dose of restraint reversed the upswing, as business fixed investment and inventory buying dropped off; over the next 18 months unemployment rose steadily. Import growth slowed down, and with some rise of exports, the current account of the balance of payments showed a surplus in both 1962 and 1963, though not a sufficient one to cover fully the export of long-term capital. Wage increases moderated, particularly during the pay pause, but rose to the 4 percent level afterwards in spite of the recession, again outpacing productivity gains. Evidently, wage increases could not be moderated enough to allow a significant gain in the competitive position nor could the restraint be held indefinitely.

To limit the upward drift of unemployment in 1962, the authorities began to loosen their restrictive posture. The bank rate was lowered from its crisis level of 7 percent during the second half of 1961. From mid-1962 onward credit restraints were further eased, and purchase taxes on consumer durable goods were cut from 45 to 25 percent. Also, plans to raise public investment and to increase the tax allowance on new private investment in the coming year were announced while social security benefits were increased early in 1963. These measures probably would have started an immediate recovery had it not been for the very severe winter weather.

The months before budget time in 1963 were marked by dissatisfaction with unemployment and stagnation. The slow growth of the British economy since 1955 compared to other industrial countries was frequently noted. Above all, a general election was due not later than 1964, and the prospect of facing it with the economy held in check to promote the strength of sterling was politically unattractive. So the decision was made that the budget in April would be expansionary. The chancellor, now Reginald Maudling, put a bold front on this change of policy by stating in his budget speech: "I absolutely reject the proposition that a vigorous economy and a strong position for sterling are incompatible." He added that the reserves and IMF credit would be used if they were needed, a view later seconded by the leader of the opposition. A fanciful theory of the adjustment process was relied on to justify this strategy. By stimulative demand policy, the economy would be lifted to a higher growth trend, with an annual rate target of more than 4 percent, and higher productivity in turn would overtake wage-cost inflation and improve the competitive position of British industry. Coupled with wage restraint, this process would correct the fundamental disequilibrium. On this reasoning, the 1959-60 experiment in expansion was to be repeated.

A large rise in public expenditure was projected for the coming fiscal year together with a reduction in taxes, concentrated on the personal income tax so as to stimulate consumer spending. The budget deficit, held to £66 million in the fiscal year 1962-63 under the restraint phase of policy, was estimated to increase to £687 million under the new order of the day in the fiscal year 1963-64. Although the actual deficit was not quite so large, the economy bounded ahead. Naturally, however, imports also bounded ahead, and the current external account moved into deficit. In 1959-60, a current payments deficit had appeared after five quarters of expansion. This time it came after only four.

THE CRISIS OF 1964 AND THE DEVALUATION OF 1967

The external deficit on current account in 1964 amounted to £360 million; capital outflows raised the overall deficit for the year to nearly £700 million. Until late in the year, the true situation was again hidden from the market by an inflow of money, particularly from higher sterling-area earnings. In any case, firm corrective action was inhibited as in the past by the prospect of the general election in the fall. In the summer, the deficit began to take its toll of the reserves, and there was some outflow of funds as the election approached. The Bank of England mobilized a credit package of $500 million from central banks to help in the financing.

Meanwhile, the IMF standby credit of $1 billion, dating from 1962, had to be extended without arousing suspicions in the market. After informal discussion at the July BIS meeting, the standby was renewed by the IMF Board on July 28 without embarrassing questions being raised. In the October election, the Conservatives were defeated, and the Labour party returned to power with a narrow parliamentary margin. Harold Wilson became prime minister, James Callaghan, the chancellor, and George Brown, minister of a newly created Department of Economic Affairs.

Even before taking office, the new Labour government knew it would be faced with a balance-of-payments problem, but it was stunned by the size of the deficit with which it was confronted. A white paper on the economic situation revealed that the total payments deficit for 1964 would be between £700 million and £800 million. A major change in policy was evidently required, with an unhappy choice between the Scylla of a devaluation and the

Charybdis of a deflation severe enough to preserve the existing exchange rate. The three economic advisors appointed by the government, Thomas Balogh, Robert Neild, and Nicholas Kaldor, counseled immediate devaluation.

The government, however, rejected both options. As the Labour party had been in office when sterling had foundered in both 1931 and 1949, the policy-making triumvirate of Wilson, Brown, and Callaghan decided against accepting the political onus of yet another devaluation. Wilson is cited by Richard Crossman as saying: "You're talking nonsense. Devaluation would sweep us away. We would have to go to the country defeated. We can't have it."[22] At the same time, the white paper declared that "the Government reject any policy based on a return to stop-go economics," asserting that there was no undue pressure on resources calling for action. This view was absurd when registered unemployment was at 1.5 percent, despite a large spillover of demand into imports.

With effective restriction of the domestic economy and outright devaluation of sterling both ruled out, compromise measures were the only tactic left. On the external side, a half-step to devaluation was taken. All imports, except those of food and raw materials, were subjected to a 15 percent surcharge (later reduced to 10 percent), which effectively about doubled the level of tariffs, while exports benefited from small (1-3 percent) rebates of indirect taxes that entered into their cost. On the domestic side, as a partial offset to the effects of the surcharge on demand for home-produced goods, an autumn budget included tax increases designed to reduce the 1964-65 budget deficit from £550 to between £400 and £500 million. In the event, the deficit proved to be £576 million.

The foreign-exchange market did not panic when the large payments deficit was made known and the surcharge imposed. It waited somewhat anxiously to see whether supporting restrictive action would be taken. It was only when the market realized that no effective check on the boom was intended that the flight from sterling grew to crisis proportions. The official reaction was to attribute the whole affair to anti-Labour speculation, with George Brown deriding the speculators as the "gnomes of Zurich," which gave small comfort to corporate treasurers and bank directors who had a duty to protect the assets of their institutions. To stem the tide, the bank rate was raised from 5 to 7 percent on November 23, but the chancellor took the edge off his measures by declaring that "it is not the Government's desire or policy that there should be a downward revision of investment plans." Then, on the 25th, the Bank of England announced that new credits of $3 billion for the support of sterling had been arranged with the central banks of other countries in the Group of Ten, Switzerland, Austria, and the BIS. A week later, the $1 billion IMF standby facility and a medium-term loan from the Swiss National Bank were drawn to repay the previous short-term borrowing from central banks.

The underlying facts of the 1964 crisis foreshadowed the devaluation of sterling. The real surprise was that devaluation was fended off for three years. This delay was not secured by severe restrictions on demand and wages, although restraining measures were taken to suppress the exchange crises that erupted in 1965 and, more especially, 1966. Rather, by quite fantastic maneuvering, the government found the means to finance and disguise the basic deficit and the flights from sterling.

Essential to this effort was the active support of the United States in mobilizing rescue credits. American officials were concerned to defend sterling because they foresaw that a devaluation would lead to enormous pressure on the $35 official gold price, which they were publicly committed to maintain. So, on one occasion after another, the British authorities borrowed from the central banks and the IMF, they used official reserves, and they also mobilized the government portfolio of $1.5 billion in American securities, which had been taken over from private holders during World War II, to throw into the breach. These defensive measures, although of questionable wisdom, were at least orthodox.

What was more than questionable, and completely unorthodox, was the hiding of actual reserve losses from the market by means of overnight end-of-the-month borrowings from foreign monetary authorities—a device that enabled the British authorities to issue quite arbitrary figures of monthly changes in reserves. Equally dubious was the giving of instructions to the Bank of England to avoid a collapse of the spot exchange rate by undertaking support operations for sterling in the forward exchange market that in the end ran into billions of pounds.

While the reserve losses in the 1964 exchange crisis were followed by some recovery, they raised the threat that the reserves would not be adequate to handle fluctuations in the external sterling balances. A group of experts was appointed by the BIS governors in November 1965 to study this problem, and after much negotiation, another special credit facility of $1 billion was set up in June 1966. It came to be known as the First Group Arrangement. It could be drawn upon only to offset reserve losses corresponding to changes in the sterling balances, and the credits extended were mutually guaranteed by the participating central banks. The BIS was to supply the funds in the first instance either from its available resources or by recourse to the money market.

The announcement of this facility did not bring an end to the weakness of the pound in the exchange market. For the facts remained that the basic balance of payments was in deficit, aggregate demand excessive, and wages rising by some 8 percent per year, much faster than the productivity rate. After a new exchange crisis in July 1966, the government was forced to adopt a fresh series of monetary and fiscal restrictions, as well as a freeze on prices and incomes until the end of the year, to be followed by continued restraint.

These measures were hailed as "perhaps the most drastic stabilization program ever to be put forward by a democratic Government in peace time,"[23] praise that failed to take account of the size and character of the disequilibrium that needed correcting. While the overall budget deficit for fiscal 1966-67 was estimated at £287 million, the result turned out to be a deficit of £740 million, partly because the program dampened economic activity and had the usual "automatic stabilizer" effect of holding back tax receipts and boosting social security outlays. Unemployment began to rise and reached 2.3 percent by mid-1967. As the halting of the boom reduced inventory buying and imports, the balance of payments improved during the fourth quarter of 1966 and the first quarter of 1967, despite the ending of the import surcharge in November 1966, but the situation remained fragile and confidence in sterling weak.

The adverse factors over the next six months preceding the devaluation were, in part, accidental, but what made the currency vulnerable was its basically unsound position. The Labour government was in a political bind. It simply could not accept a policy of severe restriction of the economy and high unemployment, which was the only real alternative to devaluation.

As unemployment mounted, some steps were taken to ease credit restraints. Wages accelerated considerably after the first half of the year, and hourly rates for the year as a whole rose by 6.2 percent, partly because of commitments made before the 1966 freeze. The basic external balance was back in deficit in the second and third quarters of 1967. Confidence had already been weakened in June by the impact of the war in the Middle East, which blocked the Suez Canal, and received another blow from the strike by British dockworkers, which started at the end of September. Sometime in early November, Labour's leaders accepted the need to devalue. In contrast to 1949, when Britain acted unilaterally, this time Leslie O'Brien, the governor of the Bank of England, discussed the devaluation with the other governors in the Group of Ten at the BIS monthly meeting in November. He told them that the only alternative to devaluation was a large long-term credit. Such a credit would have required legislation in most countries, and was hardly a practical possibility at this stage. The governor obtained agreement from his colleagues that other currencies (notably the French franc) would not follow the pound if the devaluation did not exceed 15 percent. A devaluation of this magnitude was within the range indicated as appropriate by the calculations of the Treasury's economic section, mainly Wynne Godley, based on the foreign trade matrix of the IMF.

The Cabinet's formal decision to devalue was taken on Thursday, November 16, 1967. On the same day, Chancellor Callaghan was asked pointedly in the House of Commons whether the government was seeking a long-term foreign loan. He could not bring himself to utter a direct lie, and the market had no difficulty in drawing its own conclusion. On Friday, there was a flood of sterling sales, and Bank of England reserve losses for the day exceeded $1 billion. Because of the red tape involved, the Bank of England could not withdraw its support and close the market in the course of the day. The devaluation from $2.80 to $2.40 was announced on Saturday, November 18.

The immediate problem for the government was the measures to be taken to reinforce the new exchange rate. The accepted view among experts was that a strong program of demand restraint was essential to establish the new parity firmly. But the full-employment fetish was still so strong that the government did not impose an adequate program. It believed that the existing unemployment rate of more than 2 percent would be an adequate damper on potential postdevaluation forces. The immediate steps taken were to raise the bank rate from 6.5 percent to a new crisis high of 8 percent, to strengthen somewhat existing directives to limit credit, and to affirm a stricter wage restraint. It was also announced that the planned increase in government expenditures would be reduced and that the corporation tax would be raised in the next budget. To bolster the reserves and strengthen confidence, a fresh standby credit of $1.4 billion was requested from the IMF, and central-bank credits were arranged to bring the potential new resources up to $3 billion.

The inadequacy of this program was soon felt. After a short-lived return flow of funds, sterling weakened again in the last weeks of December and required heavy support in both the first and second quarters of 1968. Besides, the reserves had to be drawn down to meet the loss of about £350 million involved in the liquidation of the forward-exchange contracts entered into before the devaluation to help hold the market. The large wave of gold buying, which had been anticipated by the United States, was also an adverse factor in the sterling exchange market, both for psychological reasons and because foreign-held sterling, converted to dollars, was used to buy gold. There was also a speculative rush into Australian mining shares in the early months of 1968.

But the reaction of the domestic economy was itself a severe cause of strain. Consumer expenditures had already begun to expand owing to the stimulus given in 1967. After the devaluation, a large buying wave developed, partly in anticipation of higher prices for imported goods, partly because the government had indicated that indirect taxes were to be increased in the April 1968 budget. Durable goods purchases increased exceptionally in the first quarter of 1968 and bank lending exceeded the high level of the previous quarter. In these circumstances, the date of the budget was advanced to March 19, and Roy Jenkins, Labour's new chancellor, proposed tax increases to yield more than £900 million. In May, the Bank of England took steps to intensify the credit squeeze, and in November, import deposits were imposed, which further tightened credit conditions. Thus, after considerable delay, a program adequate to support the devaluation was put together. In the following year's budget, taxes were further increased by £450 million so that the projected budget surplus for 1969-70 came to more than £800 million, as against the deficit of £1.5 billion recorded in 1967-68.

The other postdevaluation problem that emerged concerned the sterling balances. Official holders of sterling, having suffered a second postwar devaluation, were not disposed to maintain such large reserves in London. While a sudden flight out of sterling balances was perhaps unlikely, it seemed probable that the sterling-area countries would tend to draw on their sterling reserves when they were in deficit, but to accumulate dollars and other currencies when they had a surplus. Hence, a constant drain on the British reserves could be foreseen. The prospect was such that a temporary floating rate seemed essential until arrangements with the sterling-area countries could be made.

During the Basel meeting of November 1967, O'Brien asked me if I agreed that devaluation was necessary, and I told him that I had agreed with the view of the economic advisors in London in 1964. But now, I added, it was essential to let sterling float awhile or else there would be constant trouble from diversification of sterling-area reserves. O'Brien may have considered this prospect, but the government decided on the orthodoxy of a new fixed par value, partly on the advice of U.S. officials. After a few months, however, it became abundantly clear that the problem of the sterling balances could not be handled for long by the available reserves and credit lines. Britain made a fresh approach to its partners in the Group of Ten, and they indicated a willingness to provide new support for the sterling balances. But they insisted that the British authorities make arrangements to ensure that the sterling-area countries maintained their sterling reserves at a reasonable level. The British accomplished this by providing a guarantee on the exchange value of the bulk of the sterling funds involved. The financial negotiation resulted in the Second Group Arrangement to support the sterling balances by a credit line of $2 billion provided by 12 central banks and the BIS.

Playing politics with the adjustment process had been a costly game. The basic deficit on current and long-term capital accounts for the years 1964-67 amounted to £1,571 million, of which £578 million was on current account. With the flight of money added in, the official financing over this period totaled £2.3 billion, plus more than £2 billion of forward exchange contracts outstanding at the time of devaluation. Besides using up the government's dollar portfolio of £520 million, £522 million had been drawn from the IMF and £1.3 billion from other monetary authorities. In 1968, further net official financing of £1.4 billion was required.

The aim of the devaluation had been to obtain a £1 billion swing from deficit to surplus on current payments. Owing to the delay in taking support measures, the deficit remained large in the first half of 1968. Thereafter, however, the gains were rapid and sizable, and by 1970 the turnaround exceeded the £1 billion target. In the exceptional year 1971, the current-account surplus was about £1 billion (2 percent of GDP), partly reflecting the weakness of the domestic economy. Thus devaluation was clearly successful in the medium term.

The long history of sterling's weakness reflected several factors. These included bouts of demand inflation and the high priority assigned to full employment, as well as weak management in substantial sections of industry. But the most important and persistent factor was wage-push inflation, which successive governments, Conservative as well as Labour, could not effectively resist. The frequency of wildcat strikes and other labor troubles, which I had called "a tinge of anarchy" in a BIS annual report, left no doubt about the hard bargaining attitude of unionized labor. Unions wanted large wage increases, as in other countries, but in Britain they were less willing to cooperate with management by assuring the productivity increase and the expansion of output that were needed to validate the higher wages. As a result, wage gains were eroded by increasing prices, and British workers fell behind workers in other countries in their rise in real income.

FLOATING THE POUND, JUNE 1972

Although industrial production rose by 7 percent in 1968, it flattened out in 1969 under the government's restrictive policy designed to consolidate the new parity of sterling. While the balance of payments improved and there was a huge reflow of money to London, unemployment edged upward, and the strong emphasis put on incomes policy limited the wage increase in the 12 months to November 1969 to 5.5 percent. In the course of the year, the government attempted to obtain a legal basis for incomes policy and to put some restrictions on the rights of trade unions, but it was forced to abandon these efforts because of strong union opposition.

The breakdown of wage restraint started at the end of 1969, when several wage settlements were made much in excess of the guidelines. As unemployment at 2.5 percent was comparatively high and registered vacancies low, there was no pressure on the labor market. The jump in wage rates was caused by the pure force of bargaining power. One labor leader said at the time that if the government would not stimulate the economy then the trade unions would. Thus began a wave of two-digit wage increases, beginning with 12.7 percent in 1970 and continuing with more than 11 percent in 1971, 14 percent in 1972, and 12 percent in 1973. At the same time, by early 1972 registered unemployment had risen to the high figure of 4 percent, and industrial output had shown no growth for three years. All credit restraints had been removed in the course of 1971, and in March 1972, the government took the risk of giving a £2 billion budgetary stimulus to the economy. In addition, sterling was attached to the Common Market snake, or fixed-exchange-rate arrangement (see Chapter 9), in anticipation of Britain's membership in the EEC. In the April budget speech, however, the chancellor, Anthony Barber, had said that "It is neither necessary nor desirable to distort domestic economies to an unacceptable extent in order to retain unrealistic exchange rates, whether they are too high, or too low." At the time, many felt that this new attitude to the exchange rate promised an end to stop-go management of the economy. In the event, the government's overall economic strategy, based on strong monetary and fiscal stimulus, only provided another instance, similar to that of 1963-64, of domestic expansion being put in front of monetary and external payments stability.

As these measures were being taken, the trade balance began to deteriorate, although the current account was still in surplus. Since wages and prices were continuing their upward course and the economy was headed toward an expansion likely to worsen the balance of payments further, the market began to revise its views on the outlook for the pound. Revision was hastened when a new dock strike threatened to accelerate the rate of inflation. All at once, massive selling of sterling erupted once again. During the third week of June, sterling had to be supported to the extent of $2.7 billion. Rather than risk a struggle with a new fixed exchange rate, the Conservative government decided to let the pound float.

Sterling rapidly fell by about 7 percent against the dollar, and with some ups and downs, the decline amounted to more than 10 percent by the end of October. At this point, the government introduced a statutory wage-price control program similar to the measure that had been taken by the United States in August 1971. In the first phase of the program, wages and certain other incomes were frozen for the period November 1972 to March 1973, with the price freeze to continue for an additional month. This freeze resulted in a lull in the wage spiral. But the main price indices continued to advance at a rather high rate because prices of foods and imported raw materials, which were exempt from the freeze, were rising rapidly in international markets. When the second phase of the control program was initiated in April 1973, the ceiling on wage increases was set at 8 percent, though even this high margin could not be held tightly.

The general tendency of sterling in 1973 against other leading nondollar currencies was downward, reflecting continued monetary expansion and a worsening balance of payments on current account. As the crisis of the dollar came to a head in February with its second devaluation, the dollar itself declined sharply, and the sterling-dollar rate improved, reaching a high point of $2.59 in the early days of June. The rate fluctuated in the following months according to how the market was affected by interest-rate differentials, anticipated public-sector borrowing, and uncertainties about the future of the guarantees on official sterling-area balances. In the late months of the year, sterling fell sharply against the dollar, which also was rising against the joint float of European currencies; between the beginning of November and the middle of January 1974, sterling declined to $2.15, a drop of almost 30 cents.

The third phase of the wage-price control program was instituted in November 1973. Allowing for greater flexibility in wage settlements, it was still aimed at maintaining some restraint over wage demands. Its great weakness was that it effectively guaranteed a pretax real wage increase of 3 percent. The average basic pay increase allowed under the scheme was 10 percent. On top of this, there were "threshold arrangements," which indexed earnings during the year beginning in October 1973. Under these arrangements, earnings might increase further by some 1 percent if and when the increase in the retail price index since October 1973 reached 7 percent and by a further 1 percent for every subsequent percentage point increase in prices. This would have been a recipe for trouble in any event. The increase in commodity prices, and above all the quadrupling of the price of oil, made it a recipe for disaster.

Shortly after the OPEC price of oil was boosted at the end of 1973, the coal miners demanded a 30 percent wage increase. Prime Minister Edward Heath recognized that meeting this demand would not only mean an end to all wage-price restraint but would probably also set the scale of wage increases in other sectors of the economy. Heath resisted, which prompted a strike by the miners, who refused to compromise. He called an election on the issue of whether the miners had to abide by a reasonable degree of wage restraint, but during the course of the election campaign, his position was damaged by the findings of an independent commission that a large settlement was warranted.

The stalemate election result was effectively a defeat for Heath and the Conservative party. Labour was returned to power still headed by Harold Wilson, despite his disastrous economic and monetary leadership after the 1964 sterling crisis. It was, in effect, a vote for inflation, in which Heath's unconvincing handling of the situation and sympathy for the miners played a part. Wilson quickly settled the strike on the miners' terms, and the British economy went into the most serious phase yet of wage-price anarchy. The inflationary spiral was greatly aggravated by the indexation provisions of phase three of the Heath government's incomes policy. The rise of more than 17 percent in the retail price index in the year from October 1973 meant that the threshold arrangements were triggered 11 times. Altogether, wage rates increased by 24.3 percent in 1974 and by a further 29.3 percent in 1975. By May 1976 sterling was at $1.70, even though the dollar itself was depressed against the joint float of European currencies.

On the occasion of Wilson's retirement in March 1976, Anthony Lewis summarized Wilson's two terms as prime minister in the title of his *International Herald Tribune* column: "Wilson: the Rudderless Years."

3

The French Franc

Like Britain, France frequently suffered balance-of-payments deficits in its postwar history. Unlike Britain, France did not try to maintain an unrealistic par value of its currency but accepted more readily the adjustment process through devaluation. In France, the problem of governing effectively was complicated by the multiplicity of political parties, all jockeying for position, and by the existence of a large communist minority, both in parliament and in the labor unions. Nonetheless, through the functioning of the Commissariat du Plan, successive governments placed a high priority on rebuilding and expanding the economy, even though it was hard going at times because of the monetary situation and the wars in Indochina and Algeria.

Between the liberation of France in July 1944 and the return of General de Gaulle to power in 1958, the Ministry of Finance and the prime minister's office changed hands 24 times. Over these years of revolving door politics, inflation became the way of life. It may be argued whether weak coalition governments were the cause of inflation or inflation the cause of the parliamentary game under the Fourth Republic; certainly they reacted on each other. De Gaulle once asked how a country that had 360 varieties of cheese could be governed.

Between the liberation and the stabilization of the franc under de Gaulle, the currency was, in one way or another, devalued seven times. The subsequent phase of relative monetary stability lasted ten years, until the outbreak of the social disturbances in May-June 1968. This eruption ushered in a new inflationary wave and led to another devaluation of the franc in August 1969.

THE POSTWAR TRANSITION

France did not have the advantage of a postwar military occupation that could impose monetary reform. Nor did it have a bold economic statesman, like Ludwig Erhard, to sweep away wartime controls and give the economy the benefit of adjustment through a free market process. In consequence, the postwar transition was a long drawn out affair marked by very substantial inflation and currency depreciation. France suffered more from these evils than did other industrial countries, not because its basic economic situation was inherently more difficult, but because of political weakness. In the first instance, the failure resulted from a decision made by General de Gaulle.

During the war, the Bank of France had been obliged to finance the heavy expenses of the German occupation forces. The Vichy government also had had recourse to inflationary financing because prevailing conditions made it difficult to levy adequate taxes. As a result, the money supply had increased about 3.4 times from the end of 1939 to the liberation. At the same time, total output fell drastically to less than half its 1939 volume, and a significant share was drained off in net exports to Germany.

Even so, with the occupation authority maintaining fairly firm price controls, consumer prices increased only 2.7 times—although effective prices were higher when the black market is taken into account. Moreover, because the occupation authorities wanted cheap labor and an inducement for workers to move to Germany, controls had held the rise in wages to only 1.6 times. It was evident, therefore, that the money supply was vastly excessive and that after the liberation it would threaten to break the bind of price controls by an inflationary outburst. A great clamor for increases in wages was also foreseen.

The Attempt to Undertake Monetary Reform

In Britain, which had not been occupied by the German army, monetary reform had not even been considered. In countries that had been occupied, however, it was natural to think of this way of eliminating excess liquidity. The Free-French government in Algeria considered the problem and, in July 1944, decided that a rigorous monetary reform was the only way to wipe out the excess purchasing power. This reform was to be effected by restricting depositors' access to their swollen bank balances and by issuing limited amounts of new bank notes in exchange for a multiple of outstanding paper money. The program was intended to prevent a postwar inflationary surge and to provide a firm monetary base for the reconstruction of the economy. It was also intended to deprive of their tainted profits those who had traded with the enemy and dealt in the black market.

General de Gaulle had fully supported the decision on monetary reform agreed to in Algeria. But after the interim Provisional Government was installed in Paris, and the time for action began to slip by, a fierce dispute on the matter arose among his ministers. There was little popular support for reform. Both the business and financial communities were united in their opposition to it because the losses it might entail were more obvious than the benefits it promised. Farmers had no inclination to give up any of their hoarded currency. Even the labor union leaders, including the communists, were lukewarm toward the reform, although it could have ended the black market quickly, to the immense benefit of their members; instead, the unions, occupied with the struggle between communist and noncommunist leadership, concentrated on obtaining wage increases, which were then frittered away in the subsequent inflation.

Pierre Mendès-France, the minister of economic affairs, was the chief advocate of the reform plan, which he had helped design. Addressing a passionate letter to de Gaulle in January 1945, he pleaded for its implementation. With clear insight, he stated that the inflationary process had been unfolding transparently in the previous six months and that prompt action on the reform plan was the only practical way of avoiding cumulative disorder. The options were clear: either a sharp stop to the inflationary process in its tracks or an indefinite devaluation of the franc. He accused the opposition of finding one pretext after another for delaying action, but stated that General de Gaulle had the prestige to overcome it. The opposition, he said, was hoping for a miracle, but past experience gave no precedent for anticipating one.

Leading the opposition was Minister of Finance René Pleven, who had been appointed by de Gaulle only in mid-November 1944, after Aimé Lepercq, the original minister and a leading architect of the reform plan, had been killed in an automobile accident. Although Pleven was an acute politician, he was somewhat demagogic, and had little taste for unpopular causes. He replied to the arguments of Mendès-France in a report to de Gaulle in February 1945[1] and in his presentation of the government's program to the Assemblée Consultative in March. Pleven invented a variety of arguments against the reform, the key one of which was simply an assertion that public confidence demanded that the issue of new currency be made franc for franc and without any restriction of bank deposits. The excessive money supply was not the cause of the existing internal monetary disequilibrium, he said, but merely a symptom of it. The government would aim to cure the problem at its source by promoting a vigorous expansion of production—a hoary fallacy. Meantime, it would contain inflation by maintaining price controls and rationing and by siphoning off redundant purchasing power into a large government loan. This argument neglected the fact that controls could not be held against the pressure of the vastly excessive money supply and that the restoration of output itself would create an additional new money demand for the goods and services produced.

General de Gaulle had to resolve the dispute, as he recounts in his Mémoires.[2] The monetary reform in Belgium had been held up as an example to him. In October 1944, the Belgian Finance Minister Camille Gutt had acted to stabilize the Belgian franc by severely restricting the use of existing currency and bank deposits and by freezing prices, wages, and salaries. But de Gaulle said he considered that the material and moral conditions in Belgium and France were profoundly different. Belgium had suffered much less during the war, and it had had help from the American and Canadian supplies for the allied armies entering Europe through the port of Antwerp. France did not have these advantages. Hence, after long consideration, he supported the minister of finance, choosing what he called the "voie progressive" and rejecting monetary blockage. Although published as late as 1959, the *Mémoires* did not mention the subsequent inflation in France. Nor did they refer to the later monetary reform in Germany. Mendès-France resigned from the government, as de Gaulle put it, "naturally and with dignity," and France lost the chance to enact its own economic miracle.

In a fascinating review, "Le Général de Gaulle et la Monnaie,"[3] Olivier Wormser gave two possible reasons, not mutually exclusive, for de Gaulle's decision. First, he might have been seduced by Pleven's arguments. Second, he might have thought the country too worn out to bear the rigorous program of reform sought by Mendès-France. Whatever de Gaulle may have thought his reasons were at the time, the general did not have the background to appreciate the dire consequences of the feeble program proposed by Pleven or the rapid benefits that would follow monetary reform. Since he did not lack courage to fight for an unpopular course he considered essential, one must believe that had he clearly seen the advantages of monetary reform he would not have kept a minister opposed to it. It is significant that upon his return to power in 1958 he gave a high priority to monetary stabilization and chose a finance minister, Pinay, who shared that view.[4] Evidently, he had learned that political power was related to economic strength and monetary stability. On the other hand, he never developed any real expertise in monetary affairs, as could be seen by his advocacy of a return to the gold standard in 1965.

The Pleven policy let loose a violent price-wage inflationary spiral. Controlled prices had to be continuously revised upward and the prices charged by public enterprises continuously raised. From the end of 1945 to 1949, the consumer price index rose over four times. Wages, first increased by 50 percent in August 1944, were raised substantially on six further occasions. The money supply increased by more than three times, almost as fast as during the war. This inflationary atmosphere seriously slowed economic recovery, and was clearly an obstacle to sound organization of the public finances.

As with other war-torn countries, a deficit in the balance of payments was inevitable during the transition period, but in France, it was aggravated by the severe inflation. The current-account deficit amounted to $5.6 billion for the years 1945-48 and was financed by almost exhausting official reserves of $2 billion, by borrowing abroad to the extent of over $3 billion, and by running deficits in bilateral payments agreements. Toward the end of this period, Marshall Plan aid came to the rescue. From the liberation to the general realignment of exchange rates in 1949, the franc was devalued five times, declining from 43.8 to 350 to the dollar.

The Situation Post-de Gaulle

After de Gaulle withdrew from power in 1946 because his proposal for a strong presidential system of government was not accepted, and the Blum socialist coalition that followed failed to cure inflation by preaching self-restraint, the first serious stabilization effort was initiated in 1948 by René Mayer, the new minister of finance. Subsidies on consumption goods were reduced and new taxes imposed, which could be avoided partly by subscribing to a government loan. What was more important, many price controls were abolished and the charges of public enterprises raised to allow prices to adjust to costs and inflation to catch up with the excess money supply. The price of coal was doubled, electricity rates more than doubled, and rail fares raised by 32 percent.[5]

On the external side, the principal measure was the substantial devaluation of the franc in January 1948, followed by a further devaluation in October.[6] The rates were not unified, however, as Mayer allowed the franc to float against the dollar and the Swiss franc, while applying the new fixed exchange rate to other currencies, where France had bilateral payments agreements.

This arrangement was not accepted by the IMF's Executive Board on the grounds that broken cross-rates contravened the Fund's Articles and that they would have adverse effects on other countries. The French were very annoyed with the IMF and went their own way. Peace was not made until a few years afterward. In the meantime, France was not in any event eligible to draw on the Fund's resources because she was receiving aid from the United States under the Marshall Plan. France's exchange-rate arrangements were modified later in the year when all trade transactions were made subject to fixed rates.[7]

Prices in 1949 were up about 10 percent over the previous year, partly because of the tax increases. But wage increases were more moderate in 1948 and 1949, and rationing was brought to an end. The situation was improved considerably by U.S. assistance to France under the Marshall Plan totaling $830 million in 1948 and $1,070 million in 1949. This aid not only relieved the balance-of-payments deficit, but also gave support to the first Plan of Modernization that concentrated on the expansion of basic industries, making no concessions to demands for housing or consumer durable goods.

With the devaluation of the franc in September 1949, a uniform exchange rate of 350 francs to the dollar was adopted for trade transactions and soon afterward the free-market rate came into line. Stabilization efforts were pushed further in 1950. The overall budgetary position was considerably improved by increases in indirect taxes, and liquidity was absorbed by a fresh government loan. The currency reserves increased moderately in 1949 and more substantially in 1950. Thus, it appeared that France's belated struggle for monetary stability was succeeding.

However, the objective of stability was not firmly rooted, and the basic weakness in the political sphere caused by the multiple party system and the possible resurgence of excessive wage demands hung over it. When Maurice Petsche became minister of finance in late 1949, he was determined to strengthen the collection of taxes. But when vigorous measures were suggested to him by a young expert in the Département des Impôts, his reaction was: "*Delouvrier, pas de terrorisme fiscal!*" Clearly, the French difficulties with the adjustment process and stabilization were in no way caused by the international monetary system.

TOWARD THE DEVALUATION OF 1957

The exchange parity of the franc was held constant from 1949 until 1957. Long before that, however, the position of the franc had been undermined by renewed inflation, which was touched off by the steep rise of international commodity prices that came with the outbreak of the Korean war. By the end of 1950, wage demands were strongly on the increase. These developments meant that a deterioration of the balance of payments in 1951 could hardly be avoided. But the political reactions to domestic pressures were what turned it into a major crisis.

After six changes of government in three years, parliamentary elections were held in June 1951. They brought some major shifts of strength among the parties, the most important being the initial upsurge of the Gaullists. A new coalition was finally installed in August, which proceeded to settle the prevailing unrest by a series of inflationary measures, raising the minimum wage, social security payments, and civil service salaries by 15 percent or more. Most outrageous was a 40 percent rise in the price of wheat to appease farmers. Other wage and price increases spread throughout the economy. Average wage rates in 1951 rose more than 20 percent above the level of the previous year, while the consumer price index was 18 percent higher. During 1951, rates of increase were even steeper.

In the face of this inflationary outburst, and with the trade balance adversely affected by higher prices of raw-material imports, confidence in the franc began weakening. The external surplus turned to deficit, and the loss of reserves accelerated because of the threat of a new devaluation. By the end of the year, a crisis situation had developed, and a newly reshuffled government was installed in January 1952.

While it withdrew from the liberalization of trade under the OEEC Code and allowed some remission of taxes and social charges on exports to help the trade balance, the government was unable to obtain support for a program to deal with the crisis—a program that might well have included a devaluation. Less than two months later it fell, leaving the sharp battle over the exchange rate still unresolved. On March 8, Antoine Pinay became prime minister, serving also as his own minister of finance.

Pinay was conservative in his approach, and saw the primary problem as one of slowing down the inflationary spiral, by holding the major elements in the situation as they were, rather than by bold restrictive measures. He was aided in this objective by the decline of raw-material prices in 1952, by the recessionary tendencies in the international economy, and by the restrictive effect of the previous year's inflation on real domestic demand. When he met with the parliamentary Commission des Finances and was confronted by the deputies' demands for a variety of increased budget expenditures, he told them, "I am not going to give anybody an increase. The only thing I will give you is a stable franc."

In line with his policy conception, Pinay did not try to increase taxes. But he made a substantial cut in the public investment program, which helped to take the edge off the boom. In addition, a large loan was floated to mop up excess liquidity. The loan had the unusual provision of being indexed to the gold Napoléon; that is, the redeemable value of the bonds would rise when the price of the Napoléon rose in the Paris free market. At the same time, an amnesty was declared to allow the repatriation of funds from abroad without penalty, but it met with only mild success.

In order to reduce the frequent demands for wage increases, the mechanism of indexing the minimum wage, which was a bellwether for other wage increases, to the cost-of-living index was introduced. But while the rise of prices was slower than in 1951, it still continued, and in September, a price freeze was imposed in order to provide a breathing space.

Besides inflation, the pressing problem for the government was the balance of payments. Senior officials recommended that the franc be devalued so as to eliminate the external deficit and enable France to conform again to the OEEC Code of Liberalization. The evidence, both in the movement of the trade balance and in the studies made of comparative prices at home and abroad, clearly indicated that the franc had become overvalued. But Pinay refused any such suggestion. Instead, he maintained tight quantitative controls on imports.[8]

It was not clear what Pinay's expectations were at the time. Probably he believed that the balance-of-payments position would recover by itself if given the chance in a noninflationary and temporarily recessive economy. Or he might have thought that to devalue promptly would lessen the chances of restoring internal stability and that a continued deficit was worth the cost. In fact, the trade balance recovered very little in the next few years, despite fairly tight control of imports, since exports did not increase until very strong foreign demand developed during 1955-56. As both French and foreign opinion recognized that the franc was overvalued, how was a devaluation of the currency forestalled until 1957?

The critical factor was U.S. aid. After the Korean war began and Marshall Plan aid was brought to an end, the United States began military assistance on a substantial scale to help build up the defense capabilities of its NATO allies. To support France's war effort in Indochina, aid to France was not only large, but was mainly in the form of dollars rather than military supplies. The location of NATO headquarters in France and the spending of dollars by U.S. forces also brought in a sizable amount of foreign exchange. These various receipts more than covered the deficit on other items, allowing the reserves to increase from $616 million at the end of 1951 to almost $2 billion at the end of 1955. With rising reserves, import controls on intra-OEEC trade were substantially relaxed.

An additional factor that forestalled devaluation was that the economy was held on a recessionary plateau through most of this period, with both industrial output and employment remaining flat. The second Modernization Plan, due to start in 1953, was not approved by the government until April 1954. Although Pinay resigned at the end of 1952, the series of governments that followed were cautious about stimulating the economy for fear of inciting inflation. Consumer prices remained fairly stable, and the upward trend of wages was moderate.

"L'Opération 20%"

This interval of stability in France was brought to an end ostensibly by the war in Algeria. But the failure to conduct this struggle without a renewed inflationary upsurge must be laid to the ineffectiveness of government. The case was similar to the Vietnam war inflation later in the United States.

The war in Algeria began in November 1954. Its effect on the government budget, however, remained fairly slight throughout the following year. But in 1956, a sharp increase in war spending took place. The consolidated budget deficit, officially termed *"l'impasse budgétaire,"* rose from the previous noninflationary level of about 600 billion francs to just over 1,000 billion francs in 1956 and somewhat more in 1957. At the same time, a general election was held at the beginning of 1956 in which the middle-of-the-road parties lost seats to the communists and to the right-wing Poujadists. A new government took office at the end of January, with Guy Mollet as prime minister and Paul Ramadier as minister of finance. It was a definite shift to the left intended as a counterattack against the communist electoral strength.

Output had started expanding in 1955, stimulated by an increase in public investment outlays. Although the increase in activity initially had only a small impact on employment, production accelerated rapidly in 1956 as the outlays for the war increased and total demand became excessive. As a consequence, inflationary pressures became evident, the balance of payments deteriorated, and there was a sharp loss of reserves. In contrast to 1951, when wage push was the primary inflationary factor, the instability of 1956-57 was initiated by the increased budget deficit; the Suez Canal blockage in the fall of 1956 was an added complication.

Confronted with the growing disequilibrium, the government was unable to put together an effective stabilization program because it could not obtain the approval of the National Assembly for strong measures.[9] An increase in taxes in July 1956 and a loan floated in September were both inadequate. In addition, controls on consumer credit were tightened. For the rest, the government resorted to new tricks with the cost-of-living index to hold down increases in index-linked wages and hence in the general level of pay. The game was to control the prices of the specific goods and services included in the cost-of-living index and to allow the prices of alternative or supplementary goods and services not included in the index to rise.

Policy measures continued to be weak and indecisive in 1957. Economies of 250 billion francs in government expenditures were projected in the budget, but in fact, the budget deficit increased. The Bank of France raised its discount rate from 3 to 4 percent in April and to 5 percent in August, but the discount rate played a minor role in the management of bank credit because large credits were under direct administrative control by the National Credit Council, an official interagency committee. More significant, perhaps, was the 20 percent reduction in the ceiling on the banks' rediscount facilities at the Bank of France.

In June, the liberalization of trade was suspended, and the prices of most industrial goods were frozen. But with the budget deficit continuing to exert its pressure, and with private investment, consumer expenditures, and wage increases adding to the boom conditions, the government's mild policy restraints did not check the sharp rise of output. Imports increased by 300 billion francs in both 1956 and 1957, while the trade balance swung into deficit because exports could not make much headway against the unfavorable position of the currency. From almost $2 billion at the end of 1955, the official reserves declined to $645 million at the end of 1957, despite a drawing of $260 million on the IMF. Over the same two years, wages rose by 12 percent while the rise of the consumer price index was held to 5 percent.

As the summer progressed, the loss of reserves continued, and the authorities were obliged to consider some kind of remedial action. Instead of an outright devaluation, the barely camouflaged alternative of "l'opération 20%" was imposed. This involved a 20 percent levy and premium on visible trade transactions, with the exception of fuel and raw-material imports and certain exports. It was a political dodge intended to avoid the stigma of devaluation. The second stage of this *de facto* devaluation was instituted in October when *all* imports and exports were brought under the scheme. It lasted until June 1958, at which time a new parity of the franc was formally recognized, reducing the exchange rate on the dollar from 350 to 420 francs— a devaluation of 16.7 percent.

THE DEVALUATION OF 1958

The government of Guy Mollet had fallen in late May 1957 so that "l'opération 20%" had been instituted by Félix Gaillard as minister of finance for the first stage and as prime minister for the second. Apart from the price freeze in August, the authorities took no domestic restraint measures to support the de facto devaluation for the rest of the year. Hence, the pressure on resources and the inflationary atmosphere continued, with import prices and wages both rising sharply. In these circumstances, there was no improvement in the payments position or in the hectic state of the exchange market. It was amazing to see that "l'opération 20%" had passed by as if nothing had happened, largely absorbed in the accelerated inflation. By the end of 1957, the war in Algeria was at its height with no end in sight, and the need for more thoroughgoing stabilization measures became evident.

In February 1958, firmer policy actions were taken in both the fiscal and the monetary domains. The budget deficit was to be reduced from the level of more than 1,000 billion francs in the previous two years to 600 billion, as it had been in 1955—an objective that was substantially achieved. Not only did Gaillard have stronger qualities of leadership than Mollet, but the two years of dilly-dallying with inflation had shown parliament that real action was required.

The April budget law also stated that net advances by the Bank of France to the government should not be increased during the year. In addition, a ceiling was put on short- and medium-term bank credits, penal rates were imposed on banks that exceeded their rediscount ceilings and the added penalty of a cut in rediscount facilities was imposed on banks that overshot the credit limitations. The effect of these measures was immediate. Industrial production fell off despite involuntary accumulation of business inventories, and unemployment began a sharp rate of increase that went on into the following year. When the statistics became available after their usual lag of a month or two, it was evident that the excessive pressure on resources had been eliminated before the end of the second quarter.

On the basis of the restrictive program they were about to launch, the authorities sought additional credit through a $200 million extension ("rallonge") of the French quota in the European Payments Union (EPU)* and a further drawing of $160 million from the IMF. The EPU Managing Board agreed informally to the French request, even though the shaky government was not proposing to change the parity of the franc. Knowing that the deal had already been made, I nevertheless intervened at the formal meeting of the board, as economic advisor of the OEEC, to put on record the view that a full adjustment of the balance-of-payments deficit was not possible without a devaluation of the currency. Of course, nothing immediate could come of such an intervention, but it did guarantee that the political authorities would hear an outside opinion that devaluation was essential. Surprisingly, the French member of the board, Pierre Calvet of the Bank of France, responded very mildly; it seemed evident that he and other senior French officials had reached the same conclusion.

Around that time, the continuing war in Algeria was leading to a political crisis, for public opinion had become divided over the justice of trying to maintain Algeria as a Department of France. The Gaillard government fell on April 15, and after an interim government under Pierre Pflimlin lasting only two weeks, General de Gaulle was returned to power provisionally on June 1. He was pledged to maintain "Algérie Française" and to submit to popular referendum a new constitution that would establish a Fifth Republic with a strong presidential system. The new constitution was duly accepted, and came into force in October. De Gaulle was elected the first president of the Fifth Republic, and the Gaullist party won an absolute majority in the Assemblée Nationale. It was the first elected government with such a strong position in the postwar period.

The change in de Gaulle's attitude toward monetary stability was immediately apparent when he named the conservative Antoine Pinay as minister of finance. A few adjustments were made in the budget in July while maintaining the target figure of 600 billion francs for the "impasse." An amnesty was

*Quotas set limits to the cumulative surplus or deficit that an EPU-member country could accumulate in intra-European payments for settlements through the EPU mechanism. For further details see BIS Annual Reports, especially 21st Annual Report, Basel, Switzerland, 1951, Chapter VIII.

declared on funds repatriated from abroad, without much success because of the overvaluation of the franc, and as in 1952, a government loan indexed on the gold Napoléon was floated and drew in some foreign exchange.

Something else was obviously needed, and a group of experts, under the chairmanship of Jacques Rueff, the prominent conservative economist, was set up to work out a stabilization plan. Its report, largely written by Rueff himself, reflected his orthodox conception of public finance. It proposed sharp restrictions in public expenditure and barely recognized that the economy was in full recession. A number of senior officials felt that the report was too severe.[10] The director of the Commissariat du Plan, Étienne Hirsch, protested to Pinay, with Rueff present, that restricting investment under the Modernization Plan was no longer necessary and would only deepen the recession. This reasoning prevailed in the main, although the existing restraints were firmly continued in 1959 and various fiscal reforms were introduced.

On the external side, the Rueff report recommended the liberalization of trade and the relaxation of exchange controls. Although it was not mentioned in the published report for obvious reasons, a return to liberal trade and payments implied a devaluation of the franc, and both Pinay and de Gaulle accepted the necessity for it.

Size of the Devaluation

The question was what should be the size of the devaluation. Given the fact that the franc had been devalued in 1957, some officials favored a moderate devaluation of 6-8 percent, a figure they could support by international price comparisons. Other officials, believing that such a moderate devaluation would merely overcome the existing disadvantage of the French competitive position, argued that the intended liberalization of trade would be an additional burden for the balance of payments. They argued also that an increase of prices in France would be inevitable, particularly as charges of public enterprises had to be raised significantly. They also pointed out that it was necessary to aim at an external surplus so that the foreign debts incurred in the past few years could be repaid. Foreign monetary liabilities at that time were actually larger than gross reserve assets. Another factor that weighed heavily in this view was the prospective reduction of tariffs among the Common Market countries. As French import duties were much higher than those of Germany and the Low Countries, it was expected that the same percentage reductions in tariffs would increase French imports more than exports.

All in all, therefore, the size of the devaluation had to depend on a comprehensive judgment rather than on a limited comparison of prices and purchasing power parities. A study of the question prepared in October by Henri Koch, director of research at the Bank of France, evaluated the price disparity that had to be corrected at 7-10 percent and suggested a devaluation of 12 percent to take care of other factors as well. When the time for action arrived, however, it could be seen that the further rise in prices had been rapid and that more was in prospect. The devaluation, finally made on December 27, 1958, reduced the par value by 15 percent to 1.8 milligrams of fine gold. Although the franc was pegged to the dollar in practice, most French people thought of the matter in terms of the gold content. Against the dollar, the new rate of exchange was 493.7 francs, compared with the previous figure of 420 francs. At the same time, liberalization of trade was restored, and France participated in the general move to external convertibility that was agreed upon as the EPU was liquidated. These measures were welcomed by France's trading partners, and the new par value was promptly accepted by the IMF.

Because of the firm policy actions and restrictive measures taken earlier that year, the devaluation quickly proved successful. Exports advanced strongly, outpacing imports, and by March 1959, the balance of payments had regained a surplus position, which increased in subsequent months. The reserves rose significantly for the year as a whole and allowed a start to be made on repayment of foreign liabilities before their due date. At the beginning of 1960, the new franc was introduced, substituting 1 new franc for 100 old. This measure aimed to enhance prestige and to signal the regained stability of the currency.

During the years 1960-67, French reserves rose by $5 billion. In addition, the foreign debt liabilities of $1.6 billion were completely liquidated. So favorable a development had been quite unexpected. In addition to the stabilization program of 1958-59, three factors help account for it. First, the convertibility of the currency, supported by the political stability under de Gaulle, gave foreign investors a new confidence in France. The inflow of foreign capital averaged more than $400 million a year, and was particularly large from the United States. Second, for several years, rising prosperity in Europe swelled the earnings of France from tourism. Third, starting with the stimulus to exports, French private industry vigorously pursued expansion and improvement of its output, helped by the favorable financing provided under the Second Modernization Plan. Foreign-owned enterprises also contributed their share to the advance of the French economy.[11]

LES ÉVÈNEMENTS DE MAI 1968

The years 1959-67 were not without serious problems—above all, the war in Algeria, the revolt of a diehard group of generals, and the attempted assassinations of de Gaulle. His qualities as a statesman were never more evident than in the handling of these problems. The independence of Algeria was finally achieved on July 1, 1962, and the French African colonies were given their independence later by de Gaulle without prior turmoil.

Nor was the French economy without problems. It was disturbed by excess demand and the wage-price spiral, as well as by the structural difficulties involved in the repatriation of about 1 million people from Algeria. In the fall of 1963, a stabilization program for the domestic economy was instituted, including a price freeze and attempts to temper the increase of wages. From 1959 to 1967, consumer prices increased more than 30 percent and hourly wage earnings by almost 80 percent. But the external value of the franc was not threatened, although the trade balance gradually lost its earlier strong position despite inflation in other countries.

The exchange value of the franc was, however, abruptly challenged by the sociopolitical uprising of May 1968. The trouble was started by left-wing university groups, on the model of student protests in other countries, and became universitywide after violent attempts at suppression by the police. The disturbances then spread to the factories and culminated in a general strike against the public authorities. Raymond Aron called it "one of those queer crises of which France possesses the secret"[12] and cited de Tocqueville on the revolt of 1848. For several weeks, there was extreme violence and a near paralysis of government, except for the activity of the police.

Finally, in mid-June, after de Gaulle had appeared on television, calling for a return to reason, an agreement was reached with the trade unions on the basis of a 17 percent increase in wage rates, and the temper of the public gradually calmed down. A rapid inflation, however, was set in motion that, in 1968-69, raised average earnings by 12 percent and consumer prices by over 10 percent. The outbreak provoked an immediate exodus of money from France, and by the end of 1968, the loss of reserves amounted to $2.8 billion, with the external balance in deficit month after month. Despite de Gaulle's hostility to the United States over leadership in NATO and over the reserve currency status of the dollar, the Bank of France drew on its swap line with the Federal Reserve (see Chapter 6), which was increased twice before the end of 1968. France also made use of its automatic drawing rights in the IMF.

THE DEVALUATION OF 1969

During the next few months, the question of devaluation was explored secretly in Paris. At one extreme, there was a proposal for a large devaluation that would put sterling and the dollar on the spot and perhaps lead to a rise in the price of gold, which the French had thought necessary for some years.[13] This tactic was not accepted, however, and instead, a decision was made to try for a joint realignment of the par value of the franc and deutsche mark. This proposal was discussed with the German authorities in early November.

At the monthly BIS meeting of central bank governors in Basel on November 17, Jacques Brunet, governor of the Bank of France, obviously under instructions, set out the French position in precise terms. The government had decided to devalue the franc, Brunet explained, because of the disequilibrium that had arisen and the continuing loss of reserves. But the government considered the disequilibrium to stem not simply from the problems of the franc, but to reflect undervaluation of the D-Mark as well. Hence, the French authorities believed that a joint and simultaneous devaluation of the franc and revaluation of the D-Mark was essential to a sound adjustment. The French proposed that the parities of both currencies be changed by 7.5 percent. If the German authorities were unwilling to participate in this move, the franc would be devalued by 15 percent.

This presentation appeared to be a bargaining position rather than a firm decision, and events showed that it was. In any case, the link between the change in the par values of the two currencies was not inextricable. A revaluation of the D-Mark by 7.5 percent was warranted on its own merits; it could not have had a decisive influence on the French trade and payments positions. It was clear, though, that the French authorities recognized the franc to be in fundamental disequilibrium and that a devaluation was necessary. The link with D-Mark revaluation was no doubt designed to soften the political onus in France.

No conclusion could be reached at the BIS session, and the problem was passed on to the meeting of ministers and governors of the Group of Ten in Bonn a few days later. Just before the meeting, Germany had announced the imposition of a 4 percent tax on exports and a 4 percent tax rebate on imports—a quasi-revaluation applicable to visible trade. When the meeting opened on November 20, the German authorities refused to revalue outright or to increase their tax measures from 4 to 7.5 percent, as was suggested to them by several other countries, including the United States.

François-Xavier Ortoli, the French minister, was under instructions only to explore the matter, and he was frequently on the telephone to Paris as the discussion proceeded. Strong opposition to a devaluation as large as 15 percent was raised by other ministers, and threats were made that the measure would be opposed if it came to the IMF for approval and that swap credits between central banks would not be made available. The French delegates finally suggested that a devaluation of 11 percent might be acceptable in Paris. This figure implied a reduction in the par value of the franc from 1.8 to 1.6 milligrams of gold. The meeting was adjourned with the expectation of such a devaluation, and the international press carried headline stories to that effect. The German ministers, Schiller and Strauss, had been briefing the press quite openly. Happily, the foreign-exchange market had been closed.

The pros and cons of devaluation were being debated excitedly in French official circles, where opinion developed against the move. Raymond Barre and Jean-Marcel Jeanneney, two prominent advisors, opposed it. One view was that the restraint of domestic demand and the restoration of internal stability would themselves be adequate to restore confidence in the franc and to correct the basic balance of payments. Another view was that a devaluation of 11 percent was too small to cure the disequilibrium, particularly as the rate of inflation would be accelerated by the devaluation itself. On this view, the devaluation should be postponed until internal stability could be regained.

The result of discussion in the cabinet was a position against a change of parity, which had de Gaulle's support. In a press conference shortly afterward, he confirmed that the franc would not be devalued and that other measures would be taken to correct the situation. Holding the parity had all the appearances of a decision based on considerations of political prestige and pique over the press headlines and the uncooperative attitude of the German authorities. But the antics by both sides were unlikely to enhance anyone's prestige.

In the oversold position of the franc, the exchange market was rather quiet in January and February 1969. For the first half of the year, however, the reserves continued to fall, and the trade balance worsened sharply. The market still expected the parity to be adjusted sooner or later, as did most experts. But it was not to be accomplished by de Gaulle, who resigned from the presidency on April 28 after having been defeated in a referendum on regionalism and reform of the Senate that he had made a condition of his continuation in office.

The New Government Devalues

Georges Pompidou, who had been prime minister, was elected the next president, and Valéry Giscard d'Estaing was named minister of finance. After a little more than two months in office, the government devalued the franc. It was a surprise move made in the middle of the summer holidays, well executed, and with no prior leaks to the press or to the market. The parity was reduced by 11.1 percent, and the rate on the dollar moved from 4.937 francs to approximately 5.55.

The principal opponent of devaluation in France was Jeanneney, who argued that the previous, more rapid rise of imports than of exports was not caused by a price disparity but by excess demand and that this could be corrected without involving a period of high unemployment.[14] But in fact, the government did impose monetary and fiscal restraints along with the devaluation, and there is no reason to believe that an adequate adjustment of the trade balance would have occurred without devaluation. Apart from the necessity of regaining confidence in the franc, some surplus had to be achieved on the external account so that the various debts incurred could be repaid. Even with the successful change in parity, the reserves at the end of 1969 were lower than a year earlier and the gain in net reserves (that is,including repayment of official monetary debts) in 1970 of $1.9 billion owed much to a substantial repatriation of money from abroad. The $3.4 billion gain in net reserves in 1971 was bound up with the flight from the dollar.

Difficulties encountered by the franc in the 1970s will be considered after discussion of the breakdown of the fixed-exchange-rate system. Summarizing the story up to this point, it may be said that, while France suffered much inflation over the years, once a situation of fundamental disequilibrium had been recognized, governments did not tarry long before devaluing the currency. The high-level civil servants of the Inspectorate of Finance had much influence on these decisions, and prominent ministers had risen from that corps of experts. The French economy, while not experiencing an economic miracle, made impressive progress and gained an assured place in the industrial world.

4

The Deutsche Mark

Once its monetary situation had been normalized after the war, Germany emerged as the largest and most persistent surplus country among the industrial nations. With almost continuous accumulation, official reserves increased from virtually zero to $7 billion during the years 1951-60 and by a further $7 billion to the end of 1970. This impressive performance was bound up with the high growth rate of the economy, which owed much to progressive industrial leadership, a disciplined labor force, and government policies that gave scope and incentive to initiative. But the undervalued position of the D-Mark at the beginning of the 1950s was itself a factor facilitating the growth of exports and serving as a spur to industrial expansion. The vigor of the German economy was evident from the facility with which it absorbed the refugees from East Germany and attracted many foreign workers to handle its industrial machine. Of course, this additional manpower also constituted a productive human resource, which made its own contribution to the German economic "miracle."

From 1955 on, analyses of statistical returns clearly revealed that the German external payments position was in "extreme" surplus and that, at the prevailing parity of the currency, there was frequently a conflict between the objectives of domestic monetary stability and balance-of-payments equilibrium. The D-Mark was a "dilemma case" because restrictive measures to curb internal inflationary forces would accentuate the external surplus. Yet the government continually resisted an adjustment process adequate to resolve the dilemma, although the remedy of revaluation of the currency was well known and was in fact advocated by private economic research institutes. The government took refuge in characterizing the problem as imported inflation. The German surplus contributed at times to the payments difficulties of some other countries, notably Britain and France. The effect on the operation of the gold-dollar system of any one surplus, even a large one, was marginal. Nevertheless, exchange-market disturbances over expected revaluations of the D-Mark did weaken general confidence—just as the crises over devaluation of sterling after 1964 weakened confidence not only in Britain but in the monetary system at large.

Otmar Emminger has provided many interesting details of the official policy struggle.[1] And while he writes from a German viewpoint, he is frank enough to say that recourse to revaluation of the exchange rate in the pre-1973 period was insufficient. The principal milestones in the D-Mark's external history were the currency reform of 1948, the devaluation of 1949, the revaluations of 1961 and 1969, and the temporary adoption of a floating exchange rate in 1971.

THE CURRENCY REFORM

The real start of postwar reconstruction in Germany was delayed several years by the circumstances of defeat and subsequent military occupation. In fact, the occupation authorities added to the money supply already swollen by the financing of the war, while price controls and rationing were kept intact. Output had sunk to a low level, a huge excess of purchasing power had been accumulated, and money had lost much of its function as an effective medium of exchange and store of value. It was often said that cigarettes were a more valuable money than the currency.

This chaotic monetary situation was cleared up almost overnight by a currency reform based on the plan of a young American expert, Edward Tenenbaum. The plan was put into effect by the Allied authorities on June 20, 1948. It is often said that Germany accepted monetary reform the easy way: by having it imposed. But Belgium and Holland adopted reforms themselves, and in Germany, the currency would probably have broken down anyway and have required a self-imposed reform—as happened during 1923-24.

The main provisions of the reform were as follows. The reichsmark currency and bank balances were declared to be no longer legal tender and a new currency, the deutsche mark, was created. Individuals, business firms, financial institutions, and public bodies were given small initial allocations of D-Mark in exchange for their reichsmark balances; demand and savings deposits in reichsmarks were made convertible into D-Marks at a rate of 10 to 1, except for interbank and public-authority balances, which were canceled; and outstanding debts, apart from liabilities of financial institutions, were scaled down in the ratio of 1 to 10. The measures reduced the money supply to somewhere between 7 and 9 percent of its former total and brought it into a reasonable relationship with the availability of goods.

The favorable impact of the reform was immediately apparent as goods appeared in the stores, the black market disappeared, production spurted ahead, and money became a thing of value, worth working for, and worth saving. While there were some complaints about the inequities of the operation, it was universally recognized as successful and a great improvement over the inequities and inefficiencies of the black-market economy. In any case, political opposition to reform was not possible in occupied Germany. The currency reform was followed by the program on the "equalization of burdens" resulting from war damage and property losses incurred by the refugees from Eastern Germany. This program evened out the starting position for most of the population, and it was important in securing social peace during the difficult phase of reconstruction.

The liberating impact of monetary reform was reinforced by the simultaneous removal of price controls on manufactured goods and even on some foods. Although controls were maintained for the time being on raw materials, rents, and most foods, market conditions were rather chaotic for about six months, during which prices of decontrolled items rose appreciably from their previously unrealistic levels. There were price excesses in this adjustment period, but as prices came to reflect basic market conditions and the price mechanism functioned in allocating resources, the economy bounded ahead on its reconstruction and expansion miracle.

Ludwig Erhard, minister of economics in the Christian Democratic government then in office, spearheaded the decontrol policy, which he announced in a famous radio speech.[2] But the policy was progressively supported by the political opposition. A dictum of a rising star among the Social Democrats, Karl Schiller, was widely approved: "As much freedom as possible, as little control as necessary." Decontrol came as a surprise to the Allied authorities. E. F. Schumacher, an economist with the British mission, complained sarcastically that the Germans wanted to go back to Adam Smith. In fact, the Germans were enthusiastic about decontrol because they had had their fill of queuing up and rationing during the Hitler years. Moreover, the reconstruction period was facilitated by the fact that wage demands did not force prices to increase. The German people were in a sober mood after their defeat, and it was widely recognized that only by getting the economy going could jobs and real gains in living standards be provided. As a result, business profits were high, and their reinvestment gave a firm base of new capital for the growth of output.

The Dread of Inflation

Another factor played a major role in Germany's subsequent monetary history. Past experience had given Germany a dread of inflation. Having had the national currency wiped out after both World Wars made a lasting impression. There was always the fear that allowing significant wage and price increases would risk a flare-up into runaway inflation, and the great mass of the people, as well as the three political parties, shared this view. Even after new generations, which had not witnessed monetary collapse, came along, they grew up in an atmosphere in which the word "inflation" carried a more menacing connotation than it did in most other countries. Full employment was more of a priority in Britain, France, and the United States.

In the law written by the occupation authorities, the central bank was charged with the responsibility for strengthening the currency, and while this phrase was not defined, it was taken to embrace stability of prices. After power was handed back to a national government, this provision in the law was made firmer. The record shows that wholesale industrial goods prices increased in Germany by 14 percent between 1953 and 1970, while in Britain the rise was 54 percent, and in France 64 percent. Even in the United States, which had a relatively good record during this period, the increase was 30 percent. Until the end of this period, wage-push inflation was not the significant force in Germany that it was in other countries. The archetypal German was against inflation; the same could not be said about the archetypal Briton, Frenchman, or American.

Clearly, there were striking differences between German and British policies and attitudes in the transition period. In Britain, the emphasis was on reducing inequality in the distribution of income by welfare programs,[3] highly progressive taxes, and the socialization of a few industries, with heavy reliance on controls to allocate resources and to keep inflation in check. In Germany, the emphasis was on rehabilitation of the currency, rapid removal of controls to let the price mechanism work freely, reliance on the business system for reconstruction and expansion, without begrudging a high rate of profits both as an incentive and as a major source of finance for investment outlays. German labor did not stand in the way of technological and managerial improvements in production methods, and the high rate of productivity increase was a noninflationary source of rapid gains in real wages. It is no mystery why Germany rather than Britain had an economic miracle.

At the same time, in contrast to France, Germany had a stable government and a head of government, the chancellor, who had greater power in law to form policy than is usually given to a prime minister. The constitution of the Federal Republic was prepared with the disasters of the Weimar Republic in mind. In the last election before Hitler came to power, 32 political parties had contended for seats in the parliament, and the prime minister had only equal standing in the cabinet with the other ministers. The new constitution aimed to avoid the instability that came from splinter parties, which could maintain a foothold because of the system of proportional representation. While it provided a degree of proportional representation, the main principle was the majority of votes in the election districts. The new constitution also provided that only political parties that gained a minimum of 5 percent of the total votes could be represented in parliament. Hence, the evils of splinter parties were wiped out. The Communist party was represented for a short time, but soon lost its seats under the 5 percent rule. Three parties remained: the Christian Democrats, the Social Democrats, and the much smaller Liberal or Free Democrat party. Since the first national government was formed, there have been only five chancellors: Konrad Adenauer, Ludwig Erhard, and Kurt Kiesinger (all Christian Democrats) followed by Social Democrats Willy Brandt and Helmut Schmidt.

THE DEVALUATION OF 1949

As foreign trade resumed in the early days of economic recovery, it was conducted without a fixed or unified rate of exchange. Goods were sold abroad for what they could bring in foreign currency, and German producers were paid at the internal reichsmark price. On May 1, 1948, in anticipation of the currency reform, the Allied authorities fixed a unified exchange rate of 3.33 marks to the dollar, confident that this rate would assure the competitiveness of German industry. Exports rose rapidly in the months that followed, limited more by their availability than by their price.

The whole structure of exchange rates was put in question when sterling was devalued on September 19, 1949. The government of the newly formed Federal Republic asked the Allied authorities, who had retained power over the exchange rate, what should be done about the D-Mark. They told the Germans to do whatever they thought was best. There was considerable discussion among the German monetary authorities of the pros and cons of devaluation, weighing the danger of greater competition from the industrial countries that devalued, against the disadvantage of higher import prices. Finally, on September 29, a new rate of 4.20 D-Marks to the dollar was announced, a devaluation of 20.6 percent.

This decision was arbitrary, reflecting the uncertainty of the future payments position. The actual rate chosen was influenced by the irrelevant fact that it restored the pre-1933 relationship to the dollar. In light of the subsequent undervaluation of the currency, the most reasonable course, at least for a trial period, would have been to hold the existing rate, as was done by MacArthur's experts in Japan. This course would have been in accord with Camille Gutt's concept, mentioned earlier, of a proper "transition period" exchange rate.

Wages in Germany, having risen only by 40 percent from their prewar level, stood at about 1 DM per hour—which was low enough for all the exports that could be produced to be sold. The fact was that the adjustment by devaluation necessary for sterling had already been accomplished for the D-Mark by the currency reform. But there were no objections to the devaluation from outside Germany. Even U.S. officials, who had been urging the need for adjustment of exchange rates, had no plan for a reasoned realignment of currencies or much awareness that the United States had an interest in having the exchange-rate instrument used properly. They were preoccupied with bringing Marshall Plan aid to an end.

The Korean War Crisis

The fear of shortages that arose with the outbreak of the Korean war in 1950 induced an international buying wave in which German firms participated. Imports increased fairly sharply, and a payments deficit of $200 million developed in the EPU in the third quarter of the year. This figure was small for a country the size of Germany, but it nonetheless threatened to exhaust Germany's modest quota in the EPU and its very small cushion of official reserves. To explore the appropriateness of a special credit, the EPU Managing Board sent the economic advisors of the OEEC and the BIS, Alec Cairncross and Per Jacobsson, to Germany. They found that the real trouble was the low level of official reserves, which left no margin for accidents. The difficulty was cleared up after the EPU extended a credit of $120 million and certain restrictive measures were taken. By the second quarter of 1951, the payments position was back in surplus, as the experts had predicted.[4]

What is of interest in this episode from the standpoint of the functioning of the system is that there was some loose talk in the OEEC about a possible need for further devaluation of the D-Mark, indicative of the confusion that still prevailed about exchange-rate policy in the transition period. The economic advisors took it seriously enough to devote a section of their report to the question, rejecting further devaluation out of hand. At the same time, they recommended that, despite the great needs of domestic reconstruction, "the replenishment of the monetary reserves should be one of the main objectives of policy." This result was readily achieved because of the favorable position of the D-Mark relative to other currencies, which the German authorities maintained by insistence on price stability.

THE 1957 CRISIS

Once established in the second quarter of 1951, the external surplus grew steadily. From under $200 million at the end of 1950, the reserves rose to over $4 billion by the end of 1956, with an increase of $1.2 billion in that year. A revolution in the balance of payments had taken place. A deficit on goods and services account of DM 2.5 billion in 1950 had become a surplus of DM 5.7 billion in 1956 as exports soared from DM 8.4 to DM 30.9 billion. Expenditures of the Allied forces stationed in Germany amounted in 1956 to DM 1.8 billion, but half this sum was offset by indemnification payments made to Israel and elsewhere.

The German surplus in the mid-1950s tended to be concentrated within the EPU, with the United Kingdom and France usually having most of the counterpart deficits. Germany was soon considered to be in extreme surplus and was constantly urged to follow a good creditor policy by taking measures to share the burden of the adjustment process. As the rate of expansion of output, helped by the influx of labor from Eastern Germany and the stimulus of exports and reconstruction outlays, was already spectacular, the adjustment could not be induced by more active fiscal policy unless this simply meant an adjustment by inflation. The German authorities rejected this course; some of Germany's trading partners on the other hand considered that a certain amount of inflation to offset their own would be quite reasonable. In fact, the sizable budget surpluses from 1952 to 1956 were sterilized by deposits at the central bank to avoid inflation and leave room for private-sector expansion.

The German authorities used a variety of measures to adjust the balance of payments. Trade was liberalized rapidly, including trade with the dollar area; tariff rates were reduced unilaterally in 1955 and 1956, and in the later years, all restrictions on capital exports were removed. In addition, some foreign debts were repaid before maturity. While the German contribution to the cost of maintaining Allied forces in the country had been stopped by this time, the German authorities purchased part of their defense supplies abroad to help with the balance-of-payments problem. The beginning of foreign indemnification payments was not strictly a balance-of-payments measure, but its start was facilitated by the large external surplus, as was the aid to poorer countries that began later. These measures certainly made the external surplus less than it would have been otherwise, but the significant fact was that the surplus and reserves continued to grow nonetheless.

For a few years, monetary policy was very easy. From the 6 percent level imposed at the time of the 1950 crisis, the discount rate was brought down in several steps to 3 percent, and reserve requirements were also lowered. In 1955-56, however, the production boom began to press against resources and prices began to rise. The central bank promptly reversed its policy of ease and moved to monetary restraint, increasing the discount rate in several steps to 5.5 percent by May 1956.

Continued monetary ease, however, would have been appropriate to deal with the external surplus. Furthermore, it became evident that the disequilibrium was "fundamental" since the current balance-of-payments surplus had actually increased during a period of easy monetary policy and rapid expansion of output. Clearly, then, Germany was in a "dilemma" situation. The trouble went back to the devaluation of 1949, which by this time could be seen to have been much overdone.

No Compulsion to Revalue

By late 1956 and early 1957, it became known among high officials of a few other countries that revaluation of the D-Mark was being considered by the German authorities. Informal discussion at the technical level had in fact taken place earlier. Revaluation was advocated strongly by Ludwig Erhard, but he was unable to convince Konrad Adenauer, the chancellor. Wilhelm Vocke, president of the central bank, was also against revaluation, and he carried most of the Central Bank Council with him. As an alternative to unilateral action, Erhard proposed a wider realignment of parities involving revaluation of the D-Mark and devaluation of the French franc and sterling. At OEEC meetings, great pressure was put on German officials to take effective action, but the authorities decided that revaluation was too venturesome a step to be risked.[5]

I urged U.S. officials to use their influence with the Germans in support of the move, but they dismissed the idea, calling the disequilibrium a European affair. They did not accept my argument that it was in the interest of the United States to establish the principle that surplus as well as deficit countries had a duty to contribute to the adjustment process by a change of par value in the case of fundamental disequilibrium. None of us could know that the beginning of large U.S. deficits was only a year and a half away.

Why did the German authorities refuse to revalue? It was not just the influence of domestic politics. Nor were they lacking in cooperative spirit, which was at the heart of the OEEC. Adenauer, in particular, repeatedly demonstrated his devotion to Western cooperation and unity. Germany was very aware of the iron curtain. As there was no good argument against a change of parity in a dilemma situation, the opponents of revaluation simply contended that the surplus was temporary, caused by inflation abroad, by a lag in German imports and capital exports, and by particularly favorable terms of trade, which they claimed would not last. They were certainly influenced also by the idea that the large foreign-exchange receipts from the Allied forces in Germany might disappear in the future—although they wanted the foreign forces to remain and although there seemed little likelihood of a major improvement of relations between the NATO countries and the communist countries of Eastern Europe. Another argument was that revaluation in terms of the dollar was not appropriate because Germany was not in surplus with the dollar area.

It was easy for Germany to procrastinate in the face of a surplus. Making forecasts of a lower surplus next year or thinking up arguments against revaluation came naturally when there was no monetary compulsion to adjust. Otmar Emminger[6] has reported that a phrase that carried much conviction in German discussions of the matter was that revaluation would be equivalent to "curing the healthy man instead of the sick one," meaning that the responsibility for adjustment ought to be on the "sick" deficit countries. Only the United States had the influence with the German authorities to counterbalance this kind of reaction, and its officials did not see fit to intervene.

When discussions in the OEEC in June 1957 on the problems of exchange rates leaked to the market, the exchange crisis, already noted in the chapter on sterling, was set off. The flight of funds into the D-Mark during the summer was very large, both through transfers of money and through the change in the terms of payments; German firms temporarily withheld payments to nonresidents, while foreigners rushed to cover outstanding D-Mark obligations. To discourage the inflow, the German authorities banned the payment of interest on nonresident bank accounts and lowered the discount rate.

While any intention to change the parity of the D-Mark was officially denied, the devaluation of the French franc in August was evidence that other exchange rates were not firmly entrenched. Finally, however, at the IMF meeting in September, both Germany and the United Kingdom made strong statements reaffirming the maintenance of existing parities. Calm then returned to the exchange market, and for a few months, the hot money flow reversed itself and Germany's reserves declined somewhat.

THE REVALUATION OF 1961

The international recession of economic activity in 1958 and the first few months of 1959 had little effect on the German surplus on trade and services account. The overall external surplus dropped to DM 3.4 billion in 1958 from DM 5.1 billion the year before, but this was due mainly to the turnaround in the movement of short-term funds. As recession in Germany took hold, the authorities moved rapidly to an easy-money policy, reducing the discount rate in January and June 1958 and again in January 1959 to a record low of 2.75 percent. This policy brought about a sharp reduction in the rate on long-term money, the yield on industrial bonds falling to about 5 percent from 6.5 percent in 1957, inducing the first large outflow of capital from Germany. With official foreign lending and transfer payments also rising sharply, the balance of payments in 1959 showed its first deficit since 1950, and the reserves declined by DM 1.7 billion.

The respite, however, was not long-lived. The German economy, stimulated by exports, began to move out of the recession early, as did that of the United States, and the upswing was exceptionally rapid—with the prospect of more to come. By the end of the summer, the Deutsche Bundesbank, as the central bank had been renamed, was convinced that inflation threatened and began to apply repeated doses of restrictive measures. Between September 1959 and June 1960, both the discount rate and the bank reserve requirements were raised on several occasions. From August 1960 onward, the banks were offered special inducements to hold dollars abroad, under swaps with the Bundesbank, rather than to convert them into D-Marks. What lent a semblance of shadowboxing to the whole affair, however, was that the previous outflow of funds turned into an inflow because of the attraction of higher interest rates in Germany and because German firms met their credit needs partly by borrowing abroad. The movement of money was magnified by the fact that interest rates in the United States were simultaneously declining because of recession there. The total credit received from abroad by the German economy in 1960 has been estimated at DM 5.5 billion. Hence, rather than slowing down the boom, the tight monetary policy brought back the external surplus—even though the payment of interest on nonresidents' bank deposits and the sale of money-market paper to foreigners were prohibited.

The situation might have been helped by the use of direct controls on borrowing abroad, but the authorities were loath to violate their free-market philosophy. By some mysterious thought process, the maintenance of an undervalued exchange rate by central-bank intervention was not considered a violation of the free-market philosophy.

The alternative of using fiscal restraint on domestic demand, which would have allowed monetary policy to be oriented more to the external account, was adopted to the extent that a budget surplus was allowed to emerge as the boom gathered strength. By itself, however, the budget surplus was just not large enough to moderate the pace of the upswing. Political reluctance to increase taxes further played its role with the government, as in Britain and France. Otmar Emminger and Eduard Wolf looked upon the monetary restraint measures of 1959-60 as an experiment to see whether the Bundesbank could discharge its domestic duty without disrupting the external accounts, assuming that the way would be clear for a revaluation if the outcome proved unsuccessful. As Emminger has stated, the attempt was "a total failure."

The failure was certainly evident to the outside world, which saw only the external surplus and not the thought processes of Bundesbank officials. In 1960, the visible trade surplus increased to DM 8.4 billion, and with the large reversal of both long- and short-term capital flows offsetting higher transfer payments abroad, the increase in reserves was no less than DM 8 billion.[8] The return of the payments position to extreme surplus again raised the question of revaluation both inside and outside Germany. The Monetary Committee of the Common Market recommended it, although, curiously enough, the step was not urged on German officials in the discussions at the annual meeting of the IMF in September. In fact, Per Jacobsson had frequently argued against revaluation with the German authorities, and was influential in maintaining the doubts of Karl Blessing, who had become president of the Bundesbank in 1958. The Washington discussions largely determined the negative outcome of the meeting of high-level German officials with Adenauer in Bonn in October 1960.

As the inflow of money into D-Marks continued, the Bundesbank began to shift the emphasis of its policy to the external situation. The discount rate was lowered from 5 to 4 percent in November and to 3.5 percent in January 1961, and small cuts were made in reserve requirements, even though domestic pressures on prices had not abated. The clear dilemma of monetary policy won further support for revaluation from the Bundesbank, including that of Karl Blessing.

The German authorities waited to see what attitude would be taken by the new administration in the United States. After President Kennedy reaffirmed the maintenance of the dollar par value, there seemed to be no prospect of a multilateral adjustment of parities. On the contrary, the United States sent a note to the German government in February, criticizing its persistent piling up of reserves and urging exports of long-term capital, especially to developing countries, as the proper solution of the problem. The final straw came in late February, when the Bundesbank again lowered reserve requirements to foster a decline in market interest rates and was greeted by complaints from the government that the action was at cross purposes with the need to prevent internal inflation.

Modest Revaluation

The German monetary authorities had been anxious to play a constructive role in the international adjustment process; they were embarrassed by the large accumulation of reserves. However, the desire to regain freedom in the use of monetary policy against domestic inflationary pressure was the decisive influence that broke the psychological barrier against a change in the par value of the currency. Once revaluation had been accepted in principle, the question for the officials then became the size of the change. On this vital matter, there were no accepted guidelines. In cases of overvaluation, such as the pound sterling and the French franc, the aim of an exchange-rate adjustment would normally be not only to wipe out the external deficit but also to allow a margin for rebuilding the official reserves that had been lost previously. Analogously, therefore, a revaluation of the currency should provide for the previous overaccumulation of reserves to be gradually drained off. But the idea of deliberately arranging for an external deficit was quite beyond accepted thinking. A few central-bank governors said at times that they would like their country to have an external deficit to strengthen the case for anti-inflationary policy, but they never made practical proposals to this effect.

In Germany, some of the experts considered that a revaluation of 15 percent was necessary to bring the balance of payments to equilibrium by equalizing price competitiveness at home and abroad, but the consensus settled around a more prudent 10 percent. At the final meeting with the chancellor, Erhard and Blessing both urged a revaluation of 10 percent. Adenauer was out of his depth in this field, and he was hesitant because export interests and other nongovernment personalities were adamantly against any parity change. A banker friend from Cologne, Robert Pferdemenges, was particularly influential with Adenauer in this regard.

After complaining about the difference between the consensus view of the officials and the outside interests who wanted the existing par value maintained, Adenauer said that he would compromise on a 5 percent revaluation. Eduard Wolf, Bundesbank director of economics, responded to this decision: "I beg you, Mr. Chancellor, not to spoil a good policy instrument by insufficient use." But Adenauer could not be budged. Significantly, it was not brought home to the chancellor that Germany had created its own problem by its 20 percent devaluation in 1949. The decision to revalue the D-Mark from 4.2 to the dollar to 4.0 was announced on March 3 —a politico-econometric solution.

Immediately, the Dutch guilder was revalued in line with the D-Mark on the initiative of Jelle Zijlstra, the minister of finance. Like Germany, the Netherlands was a "dilemma" case and had experienced a substantial accumulation of reserves from $386 million to $1,861 million in eleven years, after its ill-considered devaluation in 1949. It was generally thought desirable in Holland to maintain the exchange-rate relationship with Germany, its most important trading partner.

Commotion in the Markets

Apart from an early postwar move by Sweden, the German action in 1961 was the first revaluation in the international adjustment process. The German authorities had not consulted with other countries beforehand, so there was no opportunity for multilateral discussions about the size or the utility of the revaluation. In the event, the German-Dutch revaluations opened up the question of further exchange-rate adjustments and set off a turmoil in the exchange markets. There were fears that the revaluation might be raised to 10 percent, that the Swiss franc might follow, or that certain other currencies, notably sterling, might devalue. In addition to the demand for D-Marks in the spot market, there was considerable pressure on the forward rate, with the three-month D-Mark premium rising to 4 percent a year against the dollar. Charles Coombs of the Federal Reserve Bank of New York has described the cooperation that was organized between the Bundesbank and the Federal Reserve to offset these market pressures by strong intervention in both forward and spot transactions. Similar cooperation was soon arranged between the Federal Reserve and the Swiss National Bank.[9] (See also Chapter 6.)

At the next BIS monthly meeting, a few days after the revaluations, the governor of the Bank of England negotiated credit lines of $1 billion from the other central banks to counter the flight of funds from London and help market confidence in sterling, the first such operation since the war. Also the governors issued one of their rare public statements affirming that the central banks were cooperating in the exchange markets to maintain stability. The intervention by the central banks gradually calmed down the market.

Official foreign reaction to the D-Mark revaluation itself was mostly critical. The Swiss felt locked into the par value of their currency because a change in the gold parity of the franc could involve a lengthy process of popular referendum, and they did not like the disorder that would result in their exchange market. United States officials thought surpluses should be offset by foreign aid and capital exports. Only the Dutch strongly defended the revaluation as a means of restoring the central bank's power to control the domestic monetary situation and of contributing to the international payments balance.

The consensus of opinion among German monetary experts, as Otmar Emminger has observed, was that the revaluation was "too little and too late." Nonetheless, a certain calm descended over the external position of the D-Mark during the period 1962-67. Although during those years reserves rose by almost DM 3 billion, it was not until 1968 that an extreme surplus reemerged.

The smaller surplus has been attributed in part to the revaluation which, according to an IMF study, reduced German exports by about 10 percent from their previous growth trend and somewhat accelerated imports.[10] This conclusion is questionable, however, because it rests on the assumption that removing seasonal, cyclical, and preexisting trend influences from the time series of exports would leave only the revaluation effect. Such reasoning makes no allowance for the emergence of new forces and structures in international trade. In particular, the exports of Japan and Italy more than doubled between 1960 and 1966, while the automotive industry in the United

States was making a partially successful effort to stem the tide of imports from Germany, though it did not regain its export business. The 5 percent revaluation had little to do with such shifts in trade patterns, and it is significant that the IMF study found that much larger D-Mark revaluations later were ineffective as a means of stemming German exports. A latent undervaluation of the D-Mark remained behind the cyclical and random influences.

THE REVALUATION OF 1969

While the D-Mark did not come under pressure in the foreign-exchange market between 1962 and 1967, the possibility of a further revaluation remained an active issue. It was frequently advocated by the advisory council of the Ministry of Economics as an anti-inflation measure. The main factors that held the external position in check were net capital exports and the exceptional rise of imports during the intense boom of 1964-65. Imports advanced from DM 49.2 billion in 1963 to DM 66.6 billion in 1965, resulting in a deficit on current account in that year.

Strong measures were taken to curb the boom, bringing about a mild recession in 1966-67. The result was an upward leap of the goods and services export surplus from DM 6.8 billion in 1966 to DM 16. 4 billion in 1967. However, by that time, interest rates were at minimum levels to stimulate a revival, and there was a high outflow of short-term capital from Germany, particularly through the banks, which offset the current-account surplus and postponed the crisis until 1968.

A rapid economic revival began in the second half of 1967 and gained force in the following year, leading to a DM 10.5 billion rise in imports. Exports showed even greater buoyancy, however, basically reflecting strong demand abroad and perhaps also the gradual gain in Germany's competitive position resulting from the country's slower rate of price increase. While a large offset came from long-term capital exports totaling DM 11.2 billion in 1968, the exchange market became uneasy after the May-June political disturbances in France. There was also a suspicion that the huge capital outflow could not be long maintained once a tightening of monetary policy was needed to check the economic upswing. Hence, possible revaluation again became an issue in the market's psychology.

Strong demand for D-Marks emerged in early September 1968, and the Bundesbank had to absorb $1.4 billion from the exchange market in a 10-day period. Most of these funds were returned to the banks by means of swaps against D-Marks at favorable rates. In November, the move into D-Marks intensified; impetus was added by leakage of the discussion at the BIS meeting

TABLE 2 German Federal Republic: Balance of Payments, 1949-78

annual averages (millions of deutsche mark)

1. Items (net)	1949-50	1951-55	1956-60	1961-66	1967-69	1970-72	1973-74	1975-78
2. Foreign trade fob/fob	−2,880	+2,893	+7,276	+8,659	+21,344	+23,686	+49,008	+45,536
3. Services and transfers (1 and 2)	+2,536	+18	−2,217	−9,094	−11,557	−20,809	−30,124	−34,390
3. Balance on current account	−344	+2,911	+5,059	−435	+9,787	+2,877	+18,884	+11,146
4. Long-term capital	+268	−305	−1,180	−421	−12,390	+6,970	+3,584	−8,084
5. Short-term capital, including errors and omissions	−373	+75	+102	+1,213	+1,473	+8,138	−10,207	+6,136
6. Overall balance (equals changes in the official external position) (3 to 5)	−449	+2,681	+3,981	+357	−1,130	+17,985	+12,261	+9,198

on Sunday, November 17, concerning a possible joint franc devaluation and
D-Mark revaluation of 7.5 percent each (see also Chapter 3).

Special Measures

Although the idea had originated in the Bundesbank, the German government would not accept the proposal to revalue. An election was due in the
following year, and besides being unpopular with exporters, a revaluation
would have meant lower D-Mark prices for the agricultural products subject
to the Common Market price-fixing arrangements. With a crisis raging in the
exchange markets, the government announced on November 19 that it would
introduce a charge on exports equal to 4 percent of their value and tax relief
on imports also equal to 4 percent (farm products covered by EEC regulations
were exempted from this scheme). In effect, it amounted to a 4 percent
revaluation for trade in industrial goods. Also, foreign deposits in German
banks above the level on November 15 were required to be held at the
Bundesbank, without interest, so as to discourage the inflow of funds. A
meeting of ministers and governors of the Group of Ten was hastily arranged
for November 20 in Bonn to try to resolve the crisis, and the exchange markets
of Europe were closed to calm down the highly charged atmosphere. During
this November crisis, the German reserves increased by $2.4 billion.

At the ministerial meeting in Bonn, much pressure was put on the German
authorities to revalue, or at least to raise the amount of their tax measures on
trade up to 7.5 percent. The Germans, however, rejected any further
concession to outside pleading. As the whole affair was being aired in the
press, mainly by Schiller and Strauss, the German ministers who were
competitors in the coalition government, the political nature of their stand
was evident. The only constructive step taken was to arrange central-bank
credits of $2 billion for the Bank of France.

Despite the lack of concrete actions at the Bonn meeting, the market was
calmed down by the strong official statements that no exchange-rate changes
were projected for the near future. Hence, when the exchange markets were
reopened, the speculative atmosphere had died down, and a huge outflow of
funds from Germany was set in motion. Over the next three months, the
reserves declined by almost $3 billion. The current-account surplus, which
had been running at an artificially swollen annual rate of almost DM 18
billion, fell to a rate of DM 4.6 billion. And as long-term capital exports rose
to a new high, the basic balance of payments showed a deficit.

In these circumstances, the Bundesbank began to reverse its easy monetary
policy, partly to curb the developing strains on domestic resources, but
mainly to narrow the gap between domestic and foreign interest rates. It
announced a cut of 20 percent in rediscount facilities to the banks in March

1969 and raised the interest rate on secured advances to 4 percent. This rate was increased again in April, and the official discount rate was also raised. Long-term capital exports continued at an accelerated pace, however, and an informal rationing of foreign capital-market issues was organized to dampen the outflow.

Renewed Turmoil in the Exchange Market

It was the political uncertainty in France surrounding President de Gaulle's resignation that began to upset the exchange markets in April 1969. When rumors of exchange-rate changes circulated in the market in early May, the demand for D-Marks became high, and the Bundesbank was obliged to buy more than $4 billion in a period of little more than a week. This flight of money stopped after a firm announcement on May 9 that the D-Mark parity would not be changed, although, of course, the measures that had been taken in both Germany and France were inadequate to correct the fundamental disequilibrium.

The initial move toward a basic adjustment was the devaluation of the French franc on August 8. Having suffered a substantial loss of reserves month after month, the French authorities announced the change of parity in the calm of the summer holidays. It was a copybook operation, which at once eased the strain on the franc. Objectively, this also was a favorable moment for the German authorities to adjust the D-Mark. The Bundesbank had been urging the government to revalue the currency for almost a year. But no action was considered pending the parliamentary election scheduled for late September. As polling day approached, the exchange market became unsettled because a change in parity was thought likely after the election. The buying of D-Marks became a flood in the week before the election, particularly after Schiller, the minister of economics, repeated publicly that he was in favor of revaluation, thus making it an election issue. With the pressure on the currency intense, the authorities closed the exchange market on September 25 to avoid what would surely have been a "black Friday."

The election was won by the Social Democrats, which made it clear that the conservative forces opposed to revaluation had misjudged even the political value of their policy. At the IMF annual meeting in Washington, Emminger informed his colleagues in Working Party 3 of the OECD[11] of the state of affairs in Germany. The difficulty was that an official change in the parity could not be made until the new government took office, and the Bundesbank saw no way to control the market when it was reopened. After some fruitless discussion, a vice-governor of the Bank of France, Bernard Clappier, suggested that the only course for the Bundesbank was to refrain from intervention in the market, while allowing it to function on its own; in other words, to let the D-Mark float until a new parity could be fixed. Emminger was noncommittal about this solution. It was strongly opposed by several delegates as being against the rules of the IMF but was supported by others, including participants from the IMF and the BIS, on the grounds that it was the only way to avoid exchange-market pressure on other currencies.

In fact, the German authorities had considered temporary floating, and Emminger discussed the matter with Schweitzer and his advisors that afternoon, obtaining agreement on the written communication to the IMF to be sent when floating was declared on Monday morning. The D-Mark quickly appreciated by about 5 percent. An outflow of foreign funds and an adjustment of abnormal leads and lags in payments then began, and the Bundesbank supplied dollars to the market to meet the demand without trying to pull down the rate of exchange. After four weeks of floating, a new parity was announced on October 27, involving a revaluation of 9.3 percent.

This movement was somewhat larger than the calculated changes in purchasing power parity but was certainly not excessive, as the special 1968 tax measures on trade were eliminated. It was, however, much more than the market or other countries expected since the floating rate had been at a premium of little more than 6 percent. It thus proved convincing to the market, and there was a rapid adjustment of overbought positions in D-Marks. Indeed, as the Federal Reserve had imposed very tight conditions on the U.S. money market to dampen the American boom, the United States was attracting funds from abroad on a large scale. Consequently, there was a huge outflow from Germany in the rest of 1969 that brought the loss of reserves for the year to $3 billion.

THE FLOATING OF THE DEUTSCHE MARK, MAY 1971

Faith in the exchange rate of the D-Mark after the revaluation of October 1969 was not destined to be long lasting. Only 18 months later, the market was seized by a violent new speculative outbreak that was the prelude to the dollar crisis in the summer of 1971.

As the months passed after the revaluation, the German trade surplus continued at a high level. Although the boom in Germany went on and the volume of imports increased somewhat more than did exports, a favorable change in the terms of trade produced a small increase in the trade surplus. However, this was more than offset by a sharp rise in payments for services and transfers so that the current-account surplus was reduced from DM 7.5 billion in 1969 to DM 3.2 billion in 1970.

Under normal conditions, a current-account surplus of that size could have been easily absorbed by capital exports. Instead, as in 1960, both Germany and the United States conducted monetary policy as if they were closed economies, and with only minimum concessions to balance-of-payments considerations, and the result was a flood of money into the D-Mark.

By late 1969, the tight monetary stance of the Federal Reserve began to be relaxed; with recessionary signs developing, a policy of progressive ease was pursued throughout 1970 and into the first quarter of 1971. In Germany, on the other hand, demand pressure had remained strong, and the rate of inflation was increasing. This happened despite the anti-inflationary impact of revaluation, which reduced import prices. By this time, German labor had forgotten about self-restraint and was imposing high wage demands of the kind also seen in other countries. Average hourly earnings rose 9 percent in 1969 and 16 percent in 1970.

The government announced a stabilization program in January 1970 which involved a small shift to fiscal restraint. Federal budget expenditures were to be limited to a rise of 8.8 percent by postponing DM 2.7 billion of investment outlays, and the Länder and local authorities were to seek similar restriction. In addition, some income-tax alleviations were postponed. The degree of restraint contained in this package was mild indeed and once again left the problem of domestic stabilization to monetary policy. As monetary conditions in the United States became progressively tighter in 1969, the Bundesbank followed suit by raising rates in the German money market, particularly after the revaluation in October. Then in March 1970, it gave the signal for severe restraint in monetary policy by raising its discount rate from 6 to 7.5 percent and boosting the Lombard rate,[12] which had been increased from 7.5 to 9 percent the previous December, to 9.5 percent. These measures were taken specifically because further fiscal action was not forthcoming.

After the two previous failures, in 1960-61 and 1968, to curb a domestic boom in the presence of an external surplus by means of tight monetary policies, the same treatment was to be tried again. The result was another failure and for the same reason. The German market was swamped with an inflow of money from abroad, and German firms met their borrowing needs in the Euromarket with the help of German banks.

With the easing of Federal Reserve policy, U.S. and Eurodollar interest rates declined sharply throughout 1970 and the first quarter of 1971. The Bundesbank responded by reducing its discount rate in July, November, and December of 1970 and again on April 1, 1971, although at the same time it raised reserve requirements repeatedly. Yet the spread between international and German interest rates remained substantial, and the consequence was a huge inflow of money from abroad, much larger than had taken place previously. Official reserves increased by DM 22.7 billion in 1970 and by a further DM 8 billion in the first quarter of 1971. While the German authorities were very disturbed by this situation, they were more disturbed by the inflationary atmosphere in the country. They could not bring themselves to take nonmonetary measures to dampen it because a free-market ideology stood in the way of using direct controls. They were inclined to put responsibility for the situation on the aggressive ease of Federal Reserve policy, as they made plain in various international meetings of officials.

As market opinion had been convinced by the previous revaluation, it was more than a year before suspicions arose about the D-Mark exchange rate. Finally, the market began to be affected by speculative forces in March 1971, which grew in strength in April. On May 3, the German economic research institutes published a joint report recommending that the D-Mark be allowed to float so as to curb the dollar inflow and help suppress inflation. A wave of D-Mark purchases became a flood, and the Bundesbank was obliged to absorb almost $2.3 billion in the first few days of the month. On May 5, the authorities closed the foreign-exchange market, and on May 9, the government asked the Bundesbank to stop intervening in the market for the time being. The market was reopened the next day with a floating rate. The spot rate rose to DM 3.525 to the dollar, an appreciation of about 4 percent.

With the exchange rate now floating, the authorities took some restrictive fiscal measures, mainly in the form of reducing planned expenditures. In June, the Bundesbank raised reserve requirements so as to freeze about DM 5 billion in the banking system. But by this time, the lack of confidence in the dollar was moving toward its August climax. Whatever the German authorities did, the dollar could not go on forever at $35 an ounce of gold. Nonetheless, Germany's competitive strength and her success in curbing inflation had created the image of the D-Mark as a strong currency that was likely to be revalued—just as sterling had the image of a weak currency likely to be devalued. In these circumstances, by their reluctance to upvalue the currency promptly, to gear monetary policy more closely to balance-of-payments needs and to impose direct restraints on the inflow of funds, the authorities helped to bring upon themselves the large flights of money that troubled them—the so-called destabilizing capital flows.[14]

Part III

5

A Broad View of the Gold-Dollar System

The U.S. balance-of-payments problem, unlike that of many other countries, did not reveal itself in a series of fluctuations between deficit and surplus, because it was under the influence of the reserve-currency functions of the dollar in the monetary system. Instead, the dollar passed from strength to weakness in several phases, until the old par value was finally abandoned in August 1971. The decline in the availability of new gold to the monetary system also took place in phases. In both cases, the onset of each phase was marked by specific events. This chapter outlines in broad terms the evolving situation of the dollar and of the monetary system. The U.S. authorities' policy reactions will be reviewed in greater detail in the next chapter.

PHASE I—DOLLAR SHORTAGE (1946-49)

The first postwar phase, extending through 1949, was a period of severe dollar shortage. The U.S. economy, following its vast wartime expansion, entered peacetime as the most powerful productive machine the world had ever seen. Demobilization of the armed forces was rapid, and American industry was raring to go in the reconversion to peacetime production; rapid, too, was the dismantling of wartime controls and the restoration of a free market economy. A few years of inflation served to absorb the excess purchasing power that had been built up during the war and to fill the backlog of demand by industrial reconversion.

In contrast, other belligerent countries had suffered much destruction, and for several years after the war, their output was far below prewar levels. The demands of reconstruction and the difficulties of stabilization were severe, and they were aggravated by political obstacles and uncertainties. Even in countries that had not suffered wartime destruction, there was a great pent-up demand for goods that had been unavailable during the war.

The balance-of-payments positions that resulted from these circumstances during the transition period were, therefore, a surplus for the United States and a deficit or dollar shortage for many other countries. To overcome this imbalance, the essential adjustment processes required were physical reconstruction of homes and factories and monetary stabilization in the deficit countries. Several war-torn countries wanted to draw on the IMF, but the U.S. authorities realized fully that the situation could not be put right by the kind of credit that the Fund was designed to furnish. Instead, the United States wisely granted much greater resources in the form of long-term loans and, later, Marshall Plan aid, while largely holding the Fund's resources inactive until after monetary stability had been restored.[1] The first large use of the Fund's facilities was not made until 1956.

Despite the outpouring of economic assistance, U.S. gold reserves increased substantially in this period, rising from $20 billion at the end of the war to $24.6 billion at the end of 1949. This gain was larger than the inflow of gold to the international monetary system during those years, which amounted to about $1,750 million. In other words, the dollar shortage was drawing down the aggregate gold reserves of other countries. The fact was, as the devaluations of 1949 were to recognize, that quite apart from the problem of postwar reconstruction there was a fundamental disequilibrium between the dollar and other major currencies.

Given the conditions of 1946-49, it is hardly relevant to raise the question about a fundamental disequilibrium of the system. But in fact, a major change had occurred in the statistical position of gold from the situation before the war. After the dollar price of gold had been raised in 1934 from $20.67 to $35 an ounce, gold production showed a sharp upward trend; output reached a peak in 1940 of $1,310 million against $815 million in 1934. There was a large flow of gold to U.S. reserves and some talk of "the avalanche of gold."

The increase from $20.67 to $35 in the official gold price had not come about by economic calculations of a viable price for the metal in its monetary, investment, and industrial uses. The price was raised about as much as the previous decline in farm prices, which it was hoped would be reversed by the higher gold price (see Chapter 6). Obviously, there was nothing sacred or scientific about $35 for an ounce of fine gold.

The gold situation was changed drastically during the war, partly because of the scarcity of manpower and materials, but also because the price-wage inflation made marginal mining operations unprofitable in all gold-producing countries. The level of free world output dropped from $1,310 million in 1940 to $750 million in 1946. Under peacetime conditions, there was a small recovery to $825 million in 1949. It is significant that output in most gold-producing countries never regained its 1940 levels, despite the easier cost-price relation in many countries after the 1949 devaluations. This was the case for the Witwatersrand output in South Africa; the subsequent increase in production came from new mines in other parts of the Transvaal and in the Orange Free State. Marginal mines in South Africa and gold mining in several other countries were subsidized because the inflation since 1939 had made $35 an ounce an unprofitable price.

The gold market in London was not reopened until 1954, but in the meantime, gold was freely traded in other centers, such as Zurich, Tangiers, and Beirut, where prevailing prices were significantly above the official price. In this situation, several unanticipated questions about gold were brought before the IMF Executive Board during the early postwar years. Was it permissible for members to allow sales of newly mined gold at prices above the par value? Could countries grant subsidies to their gold producers who were caught in the inflation squeeze? A majority of the Fund's board was against such practices, although the decisions of the board allowed some flexibility.

Several executive directors also proposed that the official price of gold be increased, but the U.S. representative, Frank Southard, said that his country was opposed to any such move. He later added that he believed discussion of the question by the executive directors was appropriate but that the U.S. government was still opposed. "Although the United States was mindful of the gains that a uniform change in par values would bring to gold producers and gold holding countries, it had decided against a change in the present period of struggle against disequilibrium and inflation."[2] It is significant that this statement viewed the gains from a higher gold price solely in relation to gold producers and gold holders. There was no appreciation of gold's importance for the functioning of the world monetary system. At the same time, the statement shows also that U.S. gold policy had not yet become completely rigid.

PHASE II—MODERATE U.S. PAYMENTS DEFICITS (1950-57)

The wave of devaluations in the autumn of 1949 changed the U.S. position of large external surplus at a stroke and ushered in the second phase for the dollar. This was the phase of moderate deficits covering the years 1950-57. The dollar shortage did not cease for all countries at the same moment, but the ending of Marshall Plan aid in 1952 constituted a belated recognition that the basic situation had changed. With the scare of the Korean war and its impact on both stockpiling and prices of imported raw materials added to the effects of the devaluations, the official settlements deficit of the United States in 1950 amounted to $2.5 billion, and its gold reserves declined by $1.7 billion. Over the years 1950-57, the official settlements deficit totaled $6.8 billion, with a gold loss of $1.7 billion. The underlying trend was somewhat more adverse, but the Suez crisis gave the United States an unexpected surplus of $1 billion in 1957 and a gold-reserve gain of $1.1 billion in 1956-57. Thus, in this phase, the system's tendency to rely in large part on the dollar for the growth of total reserves became established. There was no threat to the system, however, as the U.S. loss of gold was fairly small. Moreover, problems like Suez could happen again and give the United States occasional increases in gold reserves. The one-way street for Fort Knox gold was not yet evident.

On the gold market, the devaluations of 1949 immediately produced a sharp drop in premium prices. Although the Korean war gave an impetus to the private absorption of new gold in the years 1950-52, the market price was little disturbed. When the London market reopened in March 1954, gold trading was not significantly out of line with the $35 par value of the dollar.

After 1952, the flow of gold into reserves rose sharply for some years. An essential factor was the ebbing away of private demand in 1953-55. But Soviet gold sales to the market also began in 1953, and the new South African mining areas started to produce. Production from the new mines rose rapidly; it was not until 1962, however, that world gold output regained the peak level of 1940 because the yield from other producing areas drifted downward under the disincentive of the existing price and the exhaustion of profitable gold deposits.

PHASE III—LARGER U.S. PAYMENTS DEFICITS (1958-67)

From the surprise surplus of 1957, there was an abrupt shift to a large U.S. deficit, amounting in 1958 to $3 billion, with a drain on the gold reserves of $2.3 billion. The deficit could be attributed partly to the recession in the world economy. But more fundamentally, the maintenance of U.S imports against a $3 billion drop in exports reflected the stronger expansionary trend of industrial capacity and export potential in Western Europe and Japan. This was masked briefly by the Suez crisis and the European boom of 1956-57, which boosted European imports from the United States, particularly of oil and steel—hence the large reaction of U.S. exports in 1958. In total, U.S. imports did not react to the recession because foreign industrial products had begun their invasion of the U.S. market—most conspicuously so in the case of European automobiles.

After 1958, a large deficit proved to be a persistent characteristic of the U.S. balance of payments, relieved only at times when restrictive monetary policy temporarily drew in private short-term money from abroad. While exports and the trade balance improved during the years 1960-65, an overall deficit persisted as a result of rising capital exports, the volume of which remained large even after controls began to be imposed in 1963. European currency convertibility and the creation of the Common Market helped stimulate exports of capital from the United States in the form of foreign lending and the establishment of foreign subsidiaries and branches of American business firms.

In 1968, the U.S. trade balance again deteriorated sharply; therefore, Phase III of the dollar's postwar history may be taken as covering the years 1958-67. Over this period, the cumulative U.S. official settlements deficit exceeded $20 billion. The loss of gold reserves year after year exceeded $10 billion in total, and U.S. liabilities to foreign monetary authorities increased by almost $10 billion. It was a deficit of unprecedented proportions under the pressure of which any other country would have been forced to adjust or to witness a breakdown of the par value of its currency.

Was the Dollar in Fundamental Disequilibrium?

The critical analytical question concerning Phase III was whether fundamental disequilibrium could be attributed to the dollar itself or whether a shortage of new monetary gold had brought the gold-dollar system to fundamental disequilibrium. An examination of the year-by-year increases in the reserves of other countries, to which the U.S. deficit was largely the counterpart, shows that they were quite widely dispersed.

The industrialized nations of continental Europe had a combined increase of $20 billion. Only in a few cases, however, could the reserve gain be described as large. France had the biggest increase, averaging $630 million a year, almost half of which was to be lost in 1968-69. Germany and the Netherlands also had relatively big increases—of $300 million and $160 million a year, respectively—but they were mainly acquired before their 1961 revaluations. The increase in Switzerland's reserves, at $180 million a year, was large for the size of the country but did not seem greatly excessive in view of the importance of its banking system. In the case of Belgium, about half of the $1.4 billion increase in reserves was an offset to the debtor foreign-exchange position of the banks. The United Kingdom lost reserves over this period. For the rest, Canadian reserves rose by $800 million, while Japan had an increase of $1.2 billion. For the ten other countries classified as developed, the increase of reserves over the ten years came to $2.1 billion, while for the less-developed countries in the IMF membership, 54 in all, the increase of reserves was $2.5 billion.

In short, U.S. payments deficits had assumed the function of the principal source of reserve growth for the system. This was at least partly unintentional, as the United States sought to limit its deficit. The growth of total reserve assets in the system was not overly large, being at a lower rate than the growth of world trade. Suppose, then, that the United States had wanted to adjust by devaluing the dollar moderately against other currencies. It would probably have encountered fierce resistance from all but a very few other countries. Most countries would have pegged their currencies to the dollar rather than maintain their par values in gold unchanged. Given the small number of countries that might have held their gold par value, the improvement that the United States could have anticipated in its balance of payments from this source would have been quite small. The conclusion is, therefore, that the dollar was not significantly overvalued or in fundamental disequilibrium vis-à-vis other currencies, in the usual meaning of those terms.

The Shortage of Gold

But what of the gold situation? Something was obviously wrong because U.S. gold losses averaged $1 billion a year, although from late 1960 onward foreign monetary authorities were increasingly requested not to convert dollars into gold at the U.S. Treasury. From its level of $1 billion in 1957, gold production increased steadily to $1,440 million in 1965 and then declined by $30 million in 1967. The increase was more than accounted for by new mines in South Africa, which increased output by $540 million, while output from other, older mining areas was falling. In addition, the market was fed by Soviet sales; these reached $500 million a year in 1963-65, when gold was used to pay for wheat imports. Soon after, in 1966, Soviet sales abruptly stopped.

Meantime, private demand for gold had increased considerably. The industrial use of gold as reported by the United States and some other countries rose from $200 million in 1957 to $500 million in 1966, but the total was probably above $800 million when industrial use in additional countries is considered. Buying of gold as an investment and hedge against currency depreciation was also rising.

The increase in private demand was not gradual but came in four leaps. The first, after the lessening of demand from its bulge during the Korean war, came in 1956 and was related to the Suez crisis. Private demand jumped from $350 million in 1955 to $640 million in 1956 and did not recede much thereafter.

The second leap came in 1960. By that time, the United States had been in large external deficit for almost three years, and when public opinion polls indicated that John Kennedy was the likely winner of the presidential election in November, there was a rush of demand for gold that forced the market price significantly above the official price. The U.S. gold reserves were still considerable, at $17.8 billion, but the market was influenced by a suspicion that a Democratic administration might raise the dollar price of gold deliberately as a means of solving the balance-of-payments problem. The level of private gold purchases in 1960 was $400 million higher than in the year before. And only after the United States supplied some gold to the market out of its reserves did the fever calm down.

The third leap in private demand came in 1965, and was the result of President Johnson's commitment of U.S. forces to the war in Vietnam. Private demand in that year rose to $1.6 billion, an increase of almost $500 million, and took the lion's share of the gold supply on the market. Strangely enough, General de Gaulle's press conference in early 1965 advocating a return to the gold standard and the shift in French reserve policy toward holding gold rather than dollars had little effect on private demand.

The final leap came late in 1967 with the crisis of sterling and its devaluation. Private gold purchases amounted to nearly $2.8 billion, and the gold pool established in late 1961 by the main BIS central banks had to supply almost $1.4 billion of gold to the market in a desperate effort to hold down the price to the official level. (See Chapter 6 for a fuller account of the gold pool.) The market continued to require heavy support from the gold pool in the first months of 1968. The futile effort came to an end on March 15, when the pool announced its withdrawal from the market, establishing what was called a two-tier price system—one tier official, the other private.

The upward trend of private gold demand was steeper than the growth rate of Western gold production and progressively narrowed the availability of new gold for the monetary system. When the Soviet Union stopped selling gold in 1966, the system was faced with a situation where no new gold was available to it. In the following year, the system suffered an actual loss in its stock of gold reserves through sales to the market by the central-bank pool. From the start of the period in 1958, however, the system was continuously in fundamental disequilibrium because the availability of new monetary gold fell far short of the amount demanded by monetary authorities. Free choice between gold and dollars in the composition of reserves could be exercised only by drawing heavily on the U.S. gold stock.

Two factors account for the change from an avalanche of gold in the 1930s to the gold shortage after 1958. One was the large general price inflation during the war and early postwar years, as against the constant official price of gold. The other was the recovery from the Great Depression of the 1930s and the spectacular expansion of the world economy once the postwar transition had been accomplished. The gold shortage and the need for its alleviation by a rise in the price of gold would have arrived much sooner if the new mines in South Africa and Soviet gold sales had not come onto the scene. Equally, the crisis of the system might have come later if the adjustment policies of some countries, notably the United States, had been more rigorous.

PHASE IV—FUNDAMENTAL DISEQUILIBRIUM OF THE DOLLAR (1968-71)

The next and last phase in the changing position of the dollar covers the period from 1968 to the summer of 1971, when the convertibility of the dollar into gold was suspended. The two-tier gold-price system was a time bomb, bound to self-destruct: the growth of real income and even moderate price inflation, with occasional currency crises, was bound to push up the market price of gold, and when the gap between the market and official values became significant, the $35 official price would become untenable. But the process worked rather differently in actual fact because the dollar itself got into fundamental disequilibrium. This came on top of the fundamental disequilibrium of the system so that the U.S. gold reserves were under double jeopardy.

President Johnson announced the commitment of the United States to the defense of Vietnam in July 1965. With the approval of Congress, military expenditure soon rose rapidly and led to a growing budget deficit, an excessive demand on resources, and an accelerating price-wage spiral. The president was urged strongly by William McChesney Martin, chairman of the Federal Reserve Board, to seek a sound war finance policy by increased taxes. But Johnson refused the advice. He wanted to pretend that there was no war and thus no need for war taxes; he also did not want to risk congressional cuts in the social spending program to which he gave a high priority. Taxes were not increased until July 1968.

The shift to Phase IV, or to fundamental disequilibrium for the dollar, became clear in the statistics for 1968. In that year, there occurred a sharp deterioration of the U.S. trade surplus as imports spurted ahead more than $6 billion, while exports rose less than half that amount. From an average of $4.2 billion in 1965-67, the trade surplus dropped to $600 million in 1968. To some extent, this change reflected the pressure of demand at home, but at the same time, the U.S. competitive position had been weakened both by domestic inflation and by the continuing gains made in the export potential of several other countries. Japan in particular had become a large producer of industrial exports, and its trade account shifted from deficit in 1967 to balance in 1968, and to surplus in 1969. Between 1957 and 1968, Japan's exports increased four-and-a-half times in value, and they almost doubled again by 1971. Another clear sign that the dollar had become overvalued against a selected group of other currencies in this period was the several revaluations that occurred—the deutsche mark in 1969 and the Swiss franc and Austrian schilling in May 1971. In that same month, the deutsche mark and the guilder were allowed to float up against the dollar.

In 1970, the U.S. official settlements deficit soared to almost $10 billion. Flight from the dollar accelerated sharply in the first half of 1971 and reached such proportions in the summer that decisive action could no longer be postponed. On August 15, gold convertibility of the dollar was' formally suspended and the curtain finally brought down on the gold-dollar system.

TABLE 3   United States Balance of Payments, 1946-78

annual averages (billions of U.S. dollars)

Items (net)	1946-49	1950-56	1957	1958-59	1960-64	1965-67	1968-69	1970-72	1973	1974-76	1977-78
1. Merchandise trade	+7.0	+2.6	+6.3	+2.3	+5.4	+4.2	+0.6	-2.0	+0.9	-1.9	-32.3
2. Military transactions	-0.6	-2.0	-2.8	-3.0	-2.4	-2.8	-3.2	-3.2	-2.1	-0.6	+1.1
3. Services	+1.8	+2.5	+3.6	+2.8	+3.9	+5.3	+6.1	+7.2	+12.2	+16.5	+22.3
4. Balance on goods and services (1 to 3)	+8.2	+3.1	+7.1	+2.1	+6.9	+6.7	+3.5	+2.0	+11.0	+14.0	-8.9
5. Remittances, pensions and other unilateral transfers	-3.9	-2.8	-2.3	-2.4	-2.6	-3.0	-3.0	-3.6	-3.9	-5.6	-4.9
6. Balance on current account (4 + 5)	+4.3	+0.3	+4.8	-0.3	+4.3	+3.7	+0.5	-1.6	+7.1	+8.4	-13.8
7. U.S. assets abroad, excluding U.S. official reserve assets [increase, or capital outflow, (−)], of which:	-3.2	-2.5	-5.9	-4.3	-7.1	-8.2	-10.3	-13.7	-23.0	-40.3	-48.6
7.1 Other U.S. government assets	-2.2	-0.3	-1.0	-0.6	-1.3	-1.9	-2.2	-1.7	-2.6	-2.4	-4.2
7.2 U.S. private assets, of which:	-1.0	-2.2	-4.9	-3.7	-5.8	-6.3	-8.1	-12.0	-20.4	-37.9	-44.4
7.21 Nonbanks	-0.9	-2.0	-4.3	-3.3	-4.4	-6.2	-7.9	-9.5	-14.4	-19.8	-22.2
7.22 Banks, n.i.e.	-0.1	-0.2	-0.6	-0.4	-1.4	-0.1	-0.2	-2.5	-6.0	-18.1	-22.2
8. Foreign assets in the U.S. other than assets of foreign official reserve agencies [increase, or capital inflow, (+)]	-0.3	+1.6	+1.3	+2.6	+1.5	+3.0	+12.5	+1.9	+13.3	+19.2	+24.1
9. Assets of foreign official reserve agencies [increase, or capital inflow, (+)]					+1.2	+0.9	-1.2	+15.0	+5.1	+9.5	+33.2
10. Allocations of SDRs	–	–					–	+0.8	–		–
11. Statistical discrepancy	+0.7	+0.3	+1.0	+0.3	-0.9	0	-0.5	-4.0	-2.7	+4.8	+4.9
12. Change in U.S. official reserve assets [6 to 11; increase, or capital outflow, (+)]	+1.5	-0.3	+1.2	-1.7	-1.0	-0.6	+1.0	-1.6	-0.2	+1.6	-0.2
Memorandum item: official settlements balance [9 + 10, with sign reversed, +12; net increase, or net capital outflow, (+)]	.	.	.	.	-2.2	-1.5	+2.2	-17.4	-5.3	-7.9	-33.4

6

The Defense of the Dollar, 1958-71

During the years of severe dollar shortage after World War II, policy measures adopted by the United States on the international monetary front were generally excellent. It simply disposed of the bulk of the unprecedented surplus in its balance of payments by means of official foreign loans and generous economic aid. In the following years up to 1957, the cumulative external deficit it registered was relatively modest and, in view of the large gold reserves at Fort Knox, presented no real problem. Practically speaking, the United States had the advantages of a floating exchange rate without its disadvantages. It could concentrate policy measures on the domestic situation without fear of flights from its currency. Responsibility for intervention in the exchange market was up to other countries. But then trouble came, and the United States lost its way.

Between 1958, which marked the beginning of the period of large U.S. payments deficits, and 1971, when gold convertibility was abandoned, the loss of U.S. gold reserves totaled $12.6 billion and the rise in official foreign liabilities $42 billion (Table 4). This cumulative deterioration of some $55 billion in the external monetary position of the United States took place under four administrations and five secretaries of the treasury. As these men were devoted financial generals, the question is why they permitted this huge wastage of the country's reserve position, and the contortions of the international monetary system that went with it. Each of them waged what came to be called "the defense of the dollar." But in reality it was, first to last, a defense of the U.S. legal gold parity at $35 an ounce; $35 an ounce was their sacred cow.

GENERAL OBSTACLES TO THE ADJUSTMENT PROCESS

To start with, several impediments to action on the adjustment process in the United States may be noted.

TABLE 4 Deterioration of the U.S. Reserve Position, 1958-71 (billions of dollars)

Date	Secretary of the Treasury	Gold Reserves (change)	Official Liabilities (increase)
1958-60	Robert Anderson	− 5.0	2.0
1961-64	Douglas Dillon	− 2.3	4.9
1965-68	Henry Fowler	− 4.6	1.8
1969-70	David Kennedy	+ 0.2	6.0
1971	John Connally	− 0.9	27.4

Shortly after his first election to the presidency, Franklin Roosevelt started to raise the dollar price of gold from $20.67 to $35 an ounce. Roosevelt had the mistaken idea that raising the gold price would help to reverse the drastic fall of domestic prices in the Great Depression and to relieve the squeeze of the debt burden on small enterprises—particularly in agriculture. This idea came from a book by two agricultural economists, Warren and Pearson,[1] which showed the historical correlation between the price of gold and the general level of prices. The Keynesian conception of demand management was not yet developed and Roosevelt was grasping at any idea that might spur a recovery of the economy. As the United States was not losing gold, the measure was not required on external grounds. At the same time, gold-clause contracts were declared null and void, and the private holding of gold was prohibited. These actions were resented by conservative interests and became a symbol for anti-Roosevelt political forces. Following the war, when memories of Roosevelt's actions were still fresh, Democratic politicians looked upon the idea of raising the dollar price of gold as a great political danger, much as Labor politicians in Britain regarded a devaluation of sterling. For the public, which could not legally hold gold, and even among bankers, who did not trade in gold, the issue had little significance.

A second impediment to action was that the chief executive officer of the government, that is, the president, did not have the power to change the gold parity of the currency, as he could in most other countries. Edward Bernstein and Ansel Luxford had inserted a clause in the Bretton Woods Act of 1944 to the effect that the president could not propose a change in the dollar's par value to the IMF or agree to a uniform change in all par values without the approval of Congress. The purpose of the clause was to gain the support of some members of Congress for establishing the IMF. What the president could do was to suspend the gold convertibility of the dollar and then ask

Congress to change the legal par value. But those in high authority who thought about this possibility believed that it would entail an interval of chaos on the foreign-exchange and gold markets. "Chaos" was a gross exaggeration, however, because market forces would soon have persuaded Congress of the need to act.

Another factor of some significance was that the official reserves of the United States were held by the Treasury Department, rather than by the central bank. This weakened the interest of the Federal Reserve in the country's reserve position. While from the early 1960s onward, the System made large resources available for operating the inter-central-bank swap network, the priority in monetary policy lay almost entirely in domestic considerations. The Open Market Committee regularly heard reports on the external developments and the exchange markets, but when a "dilemma situation" arose, it did not feel a strong responsibility to take corrective action. Governor Maisel has observed that only a small number of decisions taken by the committee were significantly influenced by the balance of payments, an attitude with which he fully agreed.[2]

Finally, an analytical and psychological obstacle lay in the fact that the adjustment process required for the dollar in the 1960s could not be brought about without a general rise in the price of gold. This remained the case even after the exchange rate of the dollar became, in addition, overvalued vis-à-vis a few selected currencies. U.S. officials often felt that the United States was somehow trapped because a 10 or 15 percent general devaluation of the dollar would not work in the same way as it would for other countries. As most currencies were pegged on the dollar in practice, and not undervalued, their exchange rates would be held constant if the dollar devalued against gold. Against the few undervalued currencies, the United States could negotiate new parity relations only under the cover of a general rise in the price of gold, rather than by pressing for unilateral revaluations with all the political onus on the revaluing countries.

First Reactions to the Deficit

The abrupt shift to balance-of-payments deficits in 1958-59 was taken to be a consequence of an earlier recovery from recession in the U.S. economy than in other countries, aggravated by a sharp increase in imports of small European automobiles and steel. Domestic steel was in short supply because of the long steel strike in the second half of 1959. Although gold losses of $3.3 billion for 1958-59 were large, no policy measures were directed specifically against the external deficit. With fiscal and monetary policies aimed at restraint for domestic reasons, economic activity declined in 1960 after the steel strike ended, unemployment rising from 5 to 6.5 percent of the labor force. The Federal Reserve began to relax its policy in June and moved to greater ease from July to September, but budgetary restraint was maintained even after the fiscal year ending June 30 showed a budget surplus.

This was the situation in the United States when the gold market broke loose in mid-October: the U.S. economy was in recession and easing of fiscal restraint was obviously appropriate; John F. Kennedy, considered the likely winner in the November election, was emphasizing the need to get the U.S. economy moving again; and it was evident that the next administration faced a policy dilemma between domestic recession and balance-of-payments deficit. An immediate devaluation of the dollar against gold, the onus for which the new president could place on his predecessor, seemed a not unreasonable game plan to many sophisticated gold buyers, including a few central banks. Hence, the sharp rise in market demand for gold. The Bank of England tried to ease the tension by allowing the market price of gold to edge upward for several days, but on October 20, increased demand pushed the price above $40. At the same time, some central banks converted dollars into gold at the U.S. Treasury, raising the U.S. gold loss for the year to $1.7 billion. Following Kennedy's forceful denial that he would raise the gold price if elected, and the United States support to market sales of gold by the Bank of England, the market price gradually returned to $35. But the gold outbreak had jolted the U.S. authorities and world opinion.

In mid-November, President Eisenhower announced a series of measures to strengthen the balance of payments by reducing expenditure abroad. These measures included a buy-American directive for military PXs and the Development Loan Fund, and a reduction in the number of dependents of military and civilian personnel abroad. In addition, Treasury Secretary Anderson visited Germany in an effort to secure a contribution from the German government toward the cost of the substantial U.S. forces stationed in that country. As he represented a lame-duck administration, little success could be expected. Moreover, Anderson's proposal that Germany make a contribution to the U.S. budget was politically impossible from the standpoint of the German government.

PRESIDENT KENNEDY'S ADMINISTRATION

Although Kennedy had talked in terms of economic activism during the election campaign, he proved cautious after taking office. His narrow victory was a handicap to his dealing vigorously with either the recession or the balance-of-payments deficit, and besides, the Congress did not warm to his youthful charm. He avoided policy problems in the inaugural address, speaking instead of sacrifices that the public would have to face. But what the sacrifices were, or to what purpose, was not spelled out. As it turned out, the only sacrifice was of Fort Knox gold.

Recognizing that the threat to the price of gold was a political hot potato, Kennedy appointed Douglas Dillon, Republican investment banker, as secretary of the treasury and Robert Roosa, of the New York Federal Reserve Bank, as under-secretary to emphasize that novel policies would be ruled out. The gold fever of 1960 alone should have underscored the importance of the problem to him. Moreover, Paul Samuelson, an economic advisor during the election campaign, later let it be known that he told Kennedy that the dollar had become overvalued and a devaluation had become necessary. It is not known exactly how Samuelson described the situation. A strong case could have been made that the United States was being harmed by the shortage of new gold for reserve purposes and that even a considerable rise in the general price of gold would have met no significant resistance from other countries in the IMF. But the case for devaluing the dollar simply against other currencies was quite another thing. Events showed that Germany and Holland would have accepted a reasonable change in the relative value of their currencies because they soon revalued on their own initiative. Perhaps one or two other countries could have been persuaded to follow suit. In general, however, the counterpart of the U.S. deficit was not persistent large surpluses, but many small and variable ones. In addition, the position of the U.S. balance of payments in 1960 did not seem so hopeless, as the trade surplus improved sharply from its 1959 low. Hence, there was no case for a devaluation of the dollar in terms of many other currencies.

Weak Defensive Measures

Theodore Sorensen has said about Kennedy at the start of his administration that "he had no intention of devaluing. Nor would he stop the outflow of dollars and gold by shutting off credit, imports, or dollar convertibility. He refused to believe that he had to choose between a weaker economy at home or a weaker dollar abroad."[3] But this refusal to believe was not based on monetary analysis. John Kenneth Galbraith, among others, had advised Kennedy against devaluation because it would be bad politics.

Whatever the president-elect thought about the basic issues, he did not want to resort to drastic measures. So, in a time-honored political tactic, he sought other advice. He told Roosa that a study should be made of ways of reconciling the steps needed to turn around the depressed economy with the steps that should be taken to close the balance-of-payments deficit.[4] An expert committee of Allan Sproul, Roy Blough, and Paul McCracken was set to work to square the circle. By inauguration day, it predictably produced a report on traditional lines.[5] Roosa has said that the report "ended any

lingering expectations that the President would embrace one or another kind
of panacea—such as a change in the price of gold, or direct controls over
capital flows." No doubt. But it also failed to nail down a solution of the
problem. And, of course, Roosa's belittling of a rise in the price of gold by
branding it a panacea was to fence against a straw man. The gold price was
relevant only to the gold shortage; other policy instruments to manage the
balance of payments would always be essential for securing the United States
its share of an adequate total gold supply.

The Sproul report had noted the possibility that a problem could arise from
excessive accumulation of reserves in dollars to meet international liquidity
needs. However, this problem was not seen as an impediment to correcting
the imbalance in the U.S. international accounts. Nor did the report mention
the words "gold shortage," although the thesis of a gold shortage had been
forcefully proclaimed at this time by Robert Triffin of Yale in *Gold and the
Dollar Crisis*. Triffin did not drive the point home, however, because he did
not argue that the gold shortage itself caused a U.S. deficit and gold drain.
Rather, he contended that "the real danger which we face is not that of a dollar
collapse. It is the fact that such a collapse can ultimately be avoided only
through a substantial slowdown of the contributions to world liquidity
derived in the last nine years from the persistent weakening of our net reserve
position. The solution of the dollar problem will thus involve a reopening or
aggravation of the world liquidity problem."

Apart from being optimistic about the correction of the dollar deficit,
Triffin saw the revaluation of gold and flexible exchange rates as "two false
solutions." Instead, he argued in favor of a modified version of the Keynes
Plan for reforming the IMF. As the quotas in the Fund had just been raised by
50 percent, however, his emphasis on a possible economic collapse due to a
general shortage of international liquidity did not convince official experts.
Thus, there was not a basic contradiction between the Sproul report and
Triffin's argument.

Nevertheless, Triffin's book contained the most forceful analysis of the
dollar problem that had been presented up to that time. My comments on it
have not been intended to belittle Triffin's contribution, but only to show why
his conclusions were not watertight. When he asked my opinion of the book at
the time, I told him that his argument really showed that the priority should
be on measures to reduce the U.S. deficit and that the consequences of such a
reduction for the growth of total reserves could not be given political urgency
until the growth of dollar reserves slowed down.[6]

Once in office, Kennedy sent a message to the Congress on "The United
States Balance of Payments and the Gold Outflow from the United States."
More a description of the problems than an analysis of them, the report
pointed out that the U.S. deficit had been allowed to grow too large and that

the remedy was to reduce it. The U.S. price of gold could and would be maintained at $35; protectionism and exchange controls on trade and investment abroad were ruled out; and national security and foreign aid programs would not be sacrificed.

A program of fourteen measures was set forth "to correct the basic balance-of-payments deficit and achieve longer-term equilibrium." Some of the measures—economy on military spending abroad, tying aid, and greater sharing of defense and aid burdens by foreign countries—were in line with those of the previous administration. An added idea was a cut from $500 to $100 in the duty-free allowance for U.S. tourists. However, the unpopular restriction on the number of dependents allowed to U.S. personnel abroad had been rescinded. There was much waffle in the program, and when I proposed listing the measures in the BIS Annual Report, my international staff objected to empty intentions being called measures. The program was regarded as disappointing by foreign opinion, mainly because it renounced controls on capital outflows; the domestic recession more or less precluded a reduction in such outflows by means of monetary policy restraint and high interest rates. However, the domestic economy remained relatively weak so that an improvement on external account was a reasonable expectation.

U.S. economic developments in 1961 allowed some optimism about the Kennedy program. The trade and current-account balances both improved, and the deficit on reserve transactions was sharply reduced. As domestic recovery gained some momentum and unemployment began to fall, however, the external deficit worsened again in 1962. By then it was evident also that, while the economies realized on defense expenditures abroad prevented the total from rising, they did not produce a reduction. And the gold drain in 1961 and 1962, although only half as much as in 1960, was still almost $900 million a year.

Despite the uncertainties on the external front, Kennedy proposed a tax reduction to the Congress in January 1963 to accelerate domestic recovery. The Congress showed no inclination to accept the proposal. Its reluctance, however, had nothing to do with concern for the balance of payments. Rather, many members did not accept Keynesian demand-management ideas and were not impressed by Kennedy's youth and popularity. Consequently, the Federal Reserve maintained an easy monetary policy. Money-market interest rates were not much above the discount rate of 3 percent, and mortgage money, for example, was at about 6 percent.

As interest rates abroad were significantly higher, there was a marked upward trend in U.S. capital exports, which were also affected by the high rate of economic expansion in many foreign countries. Hence, a second special balance-of-payments message was sent to the Congress by the White House in July 1963. Putting the best face on the existing situation and expressing optimism about longer-term improvement, Kennedy called for "more immediate and specialized efforts" to reduce the deficit and to defend the gold reserves. A show of action was to be made on a variety of fronts, with the crux of the new program an interest equalization tax, as an alternative to direct controls on capital outflows. The tax imposed a premium on purchases of foreign securities, both bonds and equities, by U.S. residents and U.S. citizens resident abroad. Direct investment abroad, bank loans to non-residents, security issues by less-developed countries on the U.S. capital market, and all loans to nonresidents with less than three years' maturity were exempted from the tax. This measure supposedly had the advantage over direct controls of easier administration and free pricing in the markets. Whatever inhibitions the tax may have imposed, total capital exports continued to rise in 1963 and 1964. Unintentionally, the tax gave a major boost to the Eurodollar bond market in which branches of American issuing firms participated fully.

Inventive Financial Arrangements

The defense of the dollar in the three years of the Kennedy administration, however, did not rest primarily on balance-of-payments adjustment measures. Under Roosa at the Treasury, Charles Coombs at the New York Federal Reserve Bank, and Ralph Young at the Federal Reserve Board in Washington, the dollar was defended, rather, by a variety of imaginative tactical arrangements and measures in the financial sphere. Through their expertise, frankness, and concern for the problems and opinions of other countries, these men established excellent working relations with their opposite numbers, Roosa in Working Party 3 of the OECD and Coombs and Young in the circle of the main central banks. All three managed to create a spirit of trust and cooperation in devising the new arrangements.

First, a gold pool made up of the main central banks that met monthly at the BIS was established to maintain dominance over the gold market. At its inception in late 1961, the objective of the eight participating central banks was to prevent the market price from rising above $35.20. Thus, it began as a selling pool, with the United States taking a half-share in the original $270 million of gold pledged for this purpose. The real effect of the pool was to cushion the immediate impact on the U.S. reserves of any gold sales to the market. Eventually, the United States would lose gold as the dollar receipts of other participants arising out of such gold-market support were converted at the U.S. Treasury. Early in 1962, the gold pool arrangement was broadened to include the buying of gold from the market. The normal state of affairs at that time was that new gold supplies coming onto the market exceeded non-monetary demand by a fair margin. To avoid a central-bank scramble for the excess, the participants in the pool agreed to buy the surplus jointly and not to deal individually with gold-producing countries. The maximum price to be paid was $35.08, and the purchases were to be shared out on the same basis as pledges to the selling pool. The gold pool arrangement maintained orderly market conditions for several years, but looked at objectively, the necessity for it was evidence that, in terms of value, the amount of new monetary gold was skimpy.

A second financial arrangement was the Federal Reserve swap network, begun in 1962 and frequently enlarged in subsequent years. These facilities were analogous to those used for the first time to support sterling in March 1961 and in their early stages were associated with support for the dollar in the forward exchange markets. Reciprocal credit facilities, which could be activated quickly to counter exchange-market pressures, were set up, initially on a modest scale, with the other central banks of the BIS group. It was agreed that drawings on the swap credit lines were always to be short term, with limited renewals. Often the money flows reversed themselves, allowing the swap credit to be paid off; if not, other means had to be found to liquidate the central-bank liability. The swap network proved to be a highly useful addition to the official financing facilities of the international monetary system, both for the United States and for other countries, as it eased the strain on reserves until the underlying situation could be evaluated correctly.

Other techniques that helped limit gold losses included advance repayments by other countries of official debts to the United States and the provision of exchange guarantees on some foreign official holdings of dollars through the issue to their holders of Treasury securities (Roosa bonds) denominated in the holder's currency.

The defense of the dollar was also bolstered by the General Arrangements to Borrow (GAB) in the IMF, first proposed by E. M. Bernstein in a speech at Harvard in 1958 and later repeated to the Joint Economic Committee of Congress. Although Kennedy had cited, in his first balance-of-payments message, the U.S. drawing rights in the IMF as an element in the basic strength of the dollar, the fact was that the IMF did not have the resources in usable currencies to meet a very large drawing by the United States. Moreover, its resources would be even more limited if Britain were to draw heavily on its large quota. This condition stemmed from the fact that it had not been anticipated at Bretton Woods that the United States might be an applicant for IMF credit. To correct this shortcoming, the 10 principal countries in the IMF—which thus came to be known as the Group of Ten—agreed to make available $6 billion of special resources that could be borrowed only by participants in the arrangement, and only with the agreement of the lending countries of the group. Switzerland (not a member of the IMF) subsequently became an associate member of the group.

Several of the European countries cooperating in these measures were skeptical of their effectiveness. They considered that the program to reduce the deficit of the U.S. balance of payments was weak, that the U.S. authorities were primarily concerned with avoiding the discipline of gold, and that financing the external deficit by the semiautomatic accumulation of dollar liabilities was basically unsound. The reserve-currency troubles of sterling between the wars demonstrated for them the dangers that lay ahead for the dollar.

The French authorities, who were particularly skeptical, proposed in 1964 that the Group of Ten set up a procedure for "multilateral surveillance" of the financing of the external imbalances of member countries. This surveillance was intended to give an early warning signal of dangerous situations and allow time for frank discussion of the responsibility for corrective policy measures. The United States accepted this proposal, a statistical reporting form was soon agreed upon by a group of experts, and the BIS began to receive monthly data on the financing of Group-of-Ten countries' payments deficits and surpluses, including changes in the external positions of the commercial banks, with minimum delay. With the help of these improved statistics, the situation was reviewed regularly by the central-bank governors in Basel and by Working Party 3 of the OECD in Paris on the government side. However, there were subjects, particularly exchange rates and the price of gold, that could seldom be touched on in such discussions because of their political sensitivity and the risk of leaks to the market. Such matters could be aired in limited confidential talks outside formal meetings. That the surveillance did not yield more positive results, therefore, was not for lack of information or opportunities for discussion; it was due to the political repercussions that strong measures could entail.

THE JOHNSON ADMINISTRATION

The balance-of-payments and gold situation inherited by the Johnson administration after the assassination of President Kennedy in November 1963 did not appear overly severe to U.S. officials, even though there was a constant erosion of the U.S. international liquidity position to worry about. The external deficit on reserve transactions had fallen to under $2 billion in 1963 from $2.7 billion the year before, while gold losses declined to $460 million from $890 million. The improvement continued in 1964, when the deficit declined to $1.5 billion; the trade surplus reached a peak of $6.8 billion, even though the economy was expanding under the stimulus of the tax reduction proposed by Kennedy, which Congress had finally passed at Johnson's request. It was an outstanding example of an adjustment process aided by price and cost stability and the competitive enterprise system.

Vulnerability of the Dollar

Behind these favorable signs, however, the outlook for the dollar was threatened by the fundamental disequilibrium of sterling. For whenever sterling might be devalued, confidence in the dollar price of gold could be expected to evaporate and a large rise in the market demand for gold, as well as in central-bank conversions of dollars for gold at the U.S. Treasury, could be anticipated.

After the sterling crisis erupted in October 1964 and the decision of the authorities of the United Kingdom to hold the parity of the pound had become known, I sought out Robert Roosa at the Treasury to urge decisive action by the United States. In the BIS background paper on the gold situation to the Group of Ten Deputies, which had met over the previous year to consider possible reform of the system, I had not emphasized the gold shortage in order to allow full scope for other constructive proposals to be brought forward (see also Chapter 8). But now I told Roosa that a year of G-10 discussions had shown that no agreement on the management of reserves could be negotiated that would be satisfactory to the United States. The ability of the Treasury to maintain the convertibility of the dollar was on a downhill course, which could only be reversed by bold action to raise the gold price. The monetary system depended for its functioning on the United States accumulating liquid external liabilities; but at the present price of gold, the United States could never be a net buyer of gold to support the growing volume of such liabilities. The devaluation of sterling, when it came, would produce a gold crisis for the United States. The cover of a large rise in the gold price would help the British authorities with the political problem of devaluing the sterling-dollar exchange rate and most likely a few other parity changes could be negotiated to make the whole affair an exercise of international monetary statesmanship. I stressed that the value of the United Kingdom as an ally in NATO would be eroded by any effort to cling to the pound at $2.80. As for the United States, it was right behind the eight ball blocked off by an antiquated gold price. I added that it was politically absurd for the United States to be dependent on Russian gold sales. The United States had to assert its sovereignty and show the capacity for constructive monetary leadership.

As Roosa listened to all this without indignation, I felt sure that my view of the situation did not come as a surprise to him. He said he felt personally that it was useful for a while to keep the nation under strict discipline. I asked for an appointment with the secretary; Roosa told me that the date for Dillon's resignation was already fixed and that it would be better to see Chairman Martin at the Federal Reserve. Bill Martin also listened to me without challenging my basic views. He felt, however, that while the situation might reach a point at which the gold price had to be changed, the time for such action was not yet ripe. I agreed that the judgment on timing was up to those responsible for the decision and volunteered not to talk with anyone else about the matter for the time being. It was misplaced discretion.

My sentiment was that the vulnerable position of sterling made quick action very desirable and that any adverse event could set off an explosion. Moreover, I thought the time was ripe because President Johnson had good relations with the Congress, and it seemed possible for him to achieve a rise in the gold price without a political backlash. The American people had no interest in gold or the price of gold, and whatever opposition might arise would be confined to conservatives, who would, in any event, be opponents of Johnson's policies. If the president were to say that he had had enough of selling off Fort Knox gold at a bargain price and that the excellent U.S. record on inflation demonstrated that U.S. gold losses were not caused by monetary and budgetary laxity, he would surely have carried the public and the Congress with him. And what could the opposition have said after the gold reserves started to rise again?

De Gaulle's Attack

In any case, whether the situation was ripe or not, there were soon signs of its becoming rotten. The French authorities had been telling the United States confidentially of their concern over the deterioration of the dollar's position. They aired their views in various meetings, including those of the G-10 Deputies. They were annoyed, too, by the negative attitude of the United States to their proposal on collective reserve units in the discussions on monetary reform (see Chapter 8). Having received little assurance from the United States, they announced in January 1965 that French policy on the composition of reserves would be changed so as to reduce dollar holdings to the amount needed for working balances and to convert the excess dollars into gold. The new policy was not revolutionary, as French reserves at the end of 1964 contained over $3.7 billion in gold and less than $1.4 billion in dollars. Nevertheless, as a start, the U.S. Treasury was asked to convert $300 million. Faced with this open challenge, the Treasury turned a blind eye and meekly converted the French dollars at $35 an ounce. No information has come forth that Johnson was advised to do anything else, although any expert who could not see that the days of $35 gold were numbered was short on expertise.

Announcement of the new reserve policy was followed up by a staged press conference by General de Gaulle in February 1965. He denounced the system of reserve currencies and called for a return to the gold standard. He did not mention the price of gold, but his ideas implied a large increase. Noting that this "reform" of the system would require the organization of international credit facilities, he announced that France was ready to participate in their negotiation. As the situation was not pressing, he added, it was a good time to undertake the reform objectively and calmly.

The substance of de Gaulle's attack directed at the dollar was that the accumulation of dollars by other countries gave the United States a privileged monetary position, enabling it to escape from balance-of-payments discipline and allowing a disequilibrium to persist. He charged, in particular, that the financing of the U.S. deficit by dollars meant that the buying-up of foreign firms by U.S. enterprises amounted to expropriation.

The case de Gaulle presented was obviously one-sided. He neglected to point out that the foreign accumulation of dollars up to that time had been largely voluntary and that the United States was a victim of an outdated price of gold and of the propensity of other countries in the aggregate to run a net surplus on their balance of payments. Nor did he mention the service rendered by the dollar to central banks and to the conduct of the world's business. Moreover, the tone of his remarks was aggressive and hardly designed to initiate an amicable, constructive negotiation.

Although the French viewpoint was well known to U.S. officials from the meetings of the G-10 Deputies, its public avowal by de Gaulle was a bombshell to Washington. The Treasury, always on the alert against itself, immediately issued a press release rejecting any notion of a return to the gold standard, which was quite impossible anyhow, and recommitting the United States to a gold price of $35 an ounce. This commitment now became a symbol to U.S. officials of the nation's international political standing. The door closed on any reasoned discussion of the problem.

The state of affairs was bizarre. France advocated a policy that gave the United States an escape route, and the United States chose to forego this option rather than lose face to de Gaulle. In fact, it was only a few officials who could have lost face. The prestige and strength of the nation would have been enhanced.

De Gaulle's press conference also had a considerable influence on other industrial countries. As it brought the gold question more prominently into the international political sphere, other countries were forced to choose between the United States and de Gaulle. Inevitably, they lined up with the United States, not only because de Gaulle's position was extreme, but because the United States was the bulwark of the NATO defense against the threat of Soviet aggression.

In Washington, de Gaulle's press conference was viewed as a kind of ploy to increase French influence. But its main purpose was to justify the change in French policy on the composition of reserves. From a practical standpoint, the French conversion of dollars for gold was to avoid losses when the dollar should be devalued—what Olivier Wormser has called "a measure of precaution." The Bank of France had done the same with its sterling balances in 1931. A high French official who was upset by the action on reserves was challenged by de Gaulle: Was the official able to give an assurance that the whole mess of sterling and the dollar would not lead to a breakdown? The official felt obliged to admit that he could not give him such an assurance.

A few days later, President Johnson sent to the Congress a review of the "International Balance of Payments and Our Gold Problem." In preparation for several months, the message was not a direct response to General de Gaulle's press conference. The fact was that the interest equalization tax had not slowed down the outflow of capital funds from the United States. This was primarily because medium- and short-term lending by the banks, which was not subject to the tax, had more than offset the effect of the tax on new foreign issues in the U.S. capital market. New bank lending exceeded $1 billion in the fourth quarter of 1964, and the total outflow of U.S. private capital jumped by more than $2 billion for the year as a whole.

Pledging a "firm determination to bring an end to our balance-of-payments deficit," Johnson's major proposal was for a voluntary limitation on bank loans to nonresidents, designed to hold the increase in foreign lending to about $500 million in 1965, as against almost $2.5 billion in the previous year. Other financial institutions were asked not to substitute for the banks in lending abroad and to hold their placements of liquid funds in foreign markets at their level at the end of 1964. Congress was requested to extend the interest equalization tax to the end of 1967 and to include all foreign credits of a year or more within the scope of the legislation. While a variety of other measures were announced, the administration's real answer to the external deficit was to tighten capital controls.

The Vietnam War Inflation

With the support of the new controls on capital exports, Washington officials seemed fairly confident about the position of the dollar in the spring of 1965. The trade surplus had reached a new peak the year before, price and wage increases were moderate, and gold reserves were still around $15 billion. But, in fact, a future crisis over the dollar price of gold was already in the making—even without the aggravation of the Vietnam war. Indeed, had the shortage of new gold not existed, there would have been no need for discussion of a reform of the system (see Chapter 8).

The situation was building up in a number of ways. First, sterling had no chance of a durable recovery at $2.80, and a devaluation of the pound was certain to precipitate a major disruption of the exchange and gold markets. Second, the reserve policy of France was indicative of a more general official skepticism about the price of gold, so that the U.S. loss of gold reserves in the first half of 1965 rose to more than $1.4 billion. Quite a few other countries were seeking protection and also believed that the United States should be subjected to the discipline of gold. Third, the statistical position of gold was quite weak and clearly showed a shortage of new supply relative to the total official demand. In 1964, despite Russian sales of $450 million, only $710 million of gold had been added to official holdings. At the same time, the high U.S. trade surplus in 1964 meant that a significant devaluation of the dollar in the exchange-rate structure was out of the question and that the problem was limited essentially to the supply of new gold itself.

In the summer of 1965, when President Johnson announced that U.S. military forces would actively enter the struggle in Vietnam, the problem quickly intensified. Large orders for military supplies and equipment were soon being placed by the Defense Department, and the economy responded to the double stimulus of the war and tax reduction. Although the size of the war spending was not yet known, William McChesney Martin, the chairman of the Federal Reserve Board, became concerned about the inflationary impact of Vietnam. He knew from previous experience that excess demand pressures were bound to come more quickly than expected, and he had information from contacts in industry that bottlenecks were already developing. The administration, however, considered that his fears were premature so that months slipped by without any restraining measures being taken. It was only in December that the discount rate and the ceilings on interest rates for time deposits, fixed under Regulation Q, were raised.

By the end of the year, Johnson was advised that the imminent prospect of excess demand required an increase in taxes.[7] But soundings in Congress suggested strong opposition to increased tax measures. The president procrastinated, probably because he had no desire to jeopardize his domestic spending program, particularly his "war" on poverty, or to stress the magnitude of the American involvement in Vietnam. Treasury Secretary Fowler later maintained that new tax increases could not have been obtained from the Congress anyway.[8] The budget put forward in January 1966 did not call for a tax increase, and no supplementary tax measures were requested in the following months when total demand in the economy had clearly become excessive. When a tax increase was finally proposed in the January 1967 budget, it was not approved by the Congress until the middle of 1968.

Thus, the task of restraining inflation was left to monetary policy. The Federal Reserve progressively tightened the money supply during the spring and summer of 1966 by restrictive open-market policy. Interest rates rose steadily, reaching new highs for the postwar period, and the banks drew heavily on the Eurodollar market to meet their commitments to customers and to make up for the drain of fixed-term deposits as U.S. money-market rates rose above the Regulation Q ceilings. As the autumn approached, the monetary squeeze on financial institutions was intense, obliging the Federal

Reserve to moderate its restrictive policy. Nonetheless, aggregate demand had been weakened significantly by declines in both housing and business spending on new plant and equipment, and the economy moved into a mild recession in the first half of 1967. With the continuing large budget deficit, however, recovery was quick in the second half, and strong expansion continued in 1968.

The escalation of the Vietnam war, and the excess demand that came with it, had immediate consequences for the position of the dollar—renewal of inflationary pressure and a reduction in the trade surplus. It is probable that, even without excess demand, the wage guidelines taken over from Kennedy's time would have weakened with the advent of the war. But under the influence of demand pressure, an inflationary spiral of prices and wages promptly took hold. From mid-1965 to the end of 1968, consumer prices increased by about 13 percent and hourly earnings by 20 percent. For those days, it was a sharp inflationary movement.

At the same time, the trade surplus declined drastically by more than $6 billion, to the modest level of $0.6 billion in 1968 and 1969. Besides the effects of relative price inflation on exports and imports, the trade balance was directly weakened by excess demand. Also important was the continued growth of the productive and trading capacity of other industrial countries. Rising imports in these years brought growing protests from U.S. domestic industries. Unfair competition from cheap labor in Japan, and in less-developed countries like Hong Kong, South Korea, and Taiwan, was the common complaint, which had strong political support from the trade unions. One after another, a series of industries was assisted by direct controls on imports, in some cases by legal quantitative controls and in others by voluntary agreements with the exporting countries. These controls on specified imports were protectionist, rather than general measures to help the balance of payments. However, from their proliferation it was apparent that the dollar had become overvalued against a significant number of other major currencies and that the balance of payments was in fundamental disequilibrium. U.S. losses of gold reserves during 1965-68 amounted to $4.6 billion.

At the same time, efforts were continued to convince the market that the situation was under control. Increases in the swap network, which was enlarged from under $1 billion in 1962 to over $10 billion in 1968, became part of the propaganda machine, and dubious practices were resorted to in the statistics of the reserve position to show less unfavorable results. For example, gold was bought from the IMF so that the statistics would show a smaller loss of gold reserves, even though the Treasury committed itself to return the gold at the IMF's request. Likewise, foreign central banks were induced to invest in 13-month paper, so that such dollar reserves would be excluded from the statistics of U.S. liquid liabilities that included only foreign holdings with an original maturity of up to one year. In addition, the counterpart in sterling of lending to Britain out of the swap line was counted in reserve assets; it was contended that sterling was a convertible currency even though it was not a liquid reserve holding that the United States could have used to intervene in the market at that time.

The resistance to adjustment in this period by Britain as well as the United States profoundly affected the sources of reserve creation. Apart from new gold, the growth of total reserves had previously come mostly from voluntary accumulation of foreign exchange, plus increased reserve positions in the IMF. But the larger disequilibria that arose in the late 1960s had to be financed more and more by the means of special official credit facilities (such as the swap network) outside the IMF. Thus the difficulties Triffin had foreseen from failure of total reserves to grow never came about; special credit facilities that helped individual countries meet their external financing problems also assured the growth of gross global reserves. But these were borrowed reserves whereas the need was for owned reserves. In 1967-68, special credit transactions supplied $9.2 billion of new reserves to the system, an amount much greater than the total increase in official foreign-exchange holdings of $6.9 billion during these two years.

The Gold Crisis

It was the increased tension in the gold market rather than a general flight from the dollar that first culminated in a major crisis. The uncertainties of the war in Vietnam produced a large rise in private demand on the gold market, with private absorption of new gold increasing by almost $600 million in 1965. As gold production had virtually leveled off, the amount left for net official purchases fell to $370 from $710 million in 1964, even with Russian sales to the market at the high level of $550 million.

The following year, however, the Russians made their last big sale of gold. Their practice had been to sell a substantial amount at a time, partly through offers to market dealers, but mainly to the BIS, which then resold to the gold pool. In the face of a large Russian offer in 1965, the market price was allowed to drop significantly below the price that had been prevailing. Press comments on the price fall were highly critical of the Russian selling methods although, in fact, it was the official gold pool that was managing the price movement between the limits of $35.08 and $35.20. The Soviet authorities, incensed by the public criticism directed at them, decided to sell no more Russian gold as long as the official price remained at $35. (This was not known for some months, until they told a Western central-bank governor when he was visiting Moscow.) As a consequence, private demand in 1966 absorbed almost the whole of the new supply to the market, and the gold pool was continually under pressure to make up for market shortages.

From January to September 1967, Western official gold holdings declined by $230 million, indicative of the supplies that the gold pool was obliged to feed to the market to hold the price to the $35.20 limit. In mid-1967 the French authorities withdrew from the selling pool, considering it senseless to dissipate their reserves further, and officials of several other countries informed the United States that they would largely recoup their gold-pool losses by converting dollars at the U.S. Treasury. Although the Treasury was advised by at least one U.S. official that the game was up, it still tried to weather the storm.

The next blow in this fragile situation was the devaluation of the pound in November 1967. The judgment that a sterling devaluation would put enormous pressure on the gold market, as well as on the dollar itself, was fully borne out by events. The last quarter of 1967 saw Western official holdings drop by over $1 billion. The high demand in the market continued in the early months of 1968, with a loss in official gold holdings of about $1.7 billion. Losses were particularly large after a public statement by Senator Javits proposing that the United States suspend convertibility of the dollar and that the gold pool stop supplying the market. Finally, the London gold market was closed on Friday, March 15, and a meeting of the contributing central banks in the gold pool was called for the next day in Washington.

Rigidity of the U.S. Attitude to Gold

The United States faced this crisis meeting with a viewpoint absolutely frozen against any idea of a rise in the dollar price of gold. After General de Gaulle's press conference in which he advocated a return to the gold standard, Johnson looked upon de Gaulle as a cross he had to bear. He never responded personally to French views. As the social and political disaster of the Vietnam war began to unfold, Johnson had neither the time nor the temperament to take a fresh look at the gold problem, and it is hardly likely that his top monetary advisors urged him to do so. Comments by the press on every French statement or action concerning gold emphasized the opposition between the United States and France and stressed its political character.

Early in 1967, Secretary Fowler told me he did not understand my views about gold and the dollar and asked me to put them in a memorandum. Taking this suggestion seriously, I wrote a lengthy paper explaining why the shortage of gold constituted a snare for the dollar and why it entailed a constant drain on our gold reserves.[9] There was no response from either Fowler or the Treasury. A Federal Reserve official acknowledged receipt of the paper; he said that the analysis contained important insights, but the conclusion that raising the price of gold was the only way out for the United States under the rule of fixed par values was unjustified; the problem could be solved by the proposed new reserve asset, Special Drawing Rights (SDRs) in the IMF (see Chapter 8).

Among economists outside the government circle, only a handful publicly advocated raising the gold price, in the face of the opposition of the establishment. The majority of private specialists was in favor of letting the dollar float, both on theoretical grounds and because they saw the reluctance of governments to accept required changes in par values under the fixed parity system. Others, who did not find it so easy to brush aside the problems that would attend floating, proposed one technical arrangement or another for bottling up official demand for gold and providing reserves by some new credit mechanism in the Fund. The idea of a plan for reserve creation was in the air, and it seemed somehow more rational and contemporary to these economists to dream up a plan than to seek an equilibrium in the existing system through a change of the price of gold. The Triffin Plan, the Stamp Plan, and the Bernstein Plan were only the best-known schemes among many that followed this path, with an unwarranted faith in the discipline and cooperation of nations to make the planning work. My experience in the game of international monetary cooperation did not give me such faith. Until my paper was circulated, it was not generally recognized that a behavioral characteristic of the system was to leave the United States with a payments deficit. The United States was constantly criticized for not adjusting its balance of payments, just as other countries had to do.

It was not difficult for the palace guard and other economists to invent arguments to support the U.S. opposition to a rise in the gold price. It was considered infamous that gold hoarders and speculators should benefit, though their only real fault was that they were right. Other arguments were that South Africa and Russia would reap rewards as the two largest gold-producing countries and that the gains from the increased value of existing gold reserves would go only to the richer countries holding reserves in gold. Besides, it was said to be a waste of productive resources to dig up gold to put into the vaults of central banks, and the vagaries of gold production were said to make gold unsuitable as a base for the system. It was also contended that a new gold price would not be a permanent solution as the price would have to be raised again in ten or twenty years owing to inflation and the demand effect of rising real incomes, as if there could ever be permanent solutions in the management of money and the monetary system.

What was wrong with all these arguments was that somehow the interests of the United States, the utility of a disciplined real adjustment process, and renewed public confidence in the dollar received scant attention. But clearly, had the United States decided on raising the gold price, it would have been even less difficult for officials and others to find arguments to support the action. The idea of equilibrium, central to economic thought, was largely ignored except by the advocates of floating rates. The focus of official measures and most public discussion was on *how to get along with disequilibrium*.

Various schemes were proposed to scare off gold hoarders and gold-holding central banks, on the underlying assumption that they were behaving irrationally. It was proposed, for example, that the United States put ceilings on the amount of gold it was prepared to buy from gold-holding countries so as to throw doubt on the liquidity of gold. Another idea was that the United States should threaten the world with floating of the dollar if its gold reserves were too heavily drawn upon, which would be unattractive to foreign monetary authorities. Fritz Machlup went so far as to propose that the United States announce a series of reductions in the price of gold, which he thought would discourage gold buyers.[10] Such ideas were quite out of touch with the deep premonitions about gold of both private buyers and central banks. And their premonitions were not wrongheaded. With more realism, Robert Aliber compiled "A Cost-Benefit Analysis of a Rise in the Price of Gold." It turned out that the benefits were monetary and the costs political.[11]

Sometime in 1966, I experimented with calculations of what the dollar price of gold should be to provide a continuous annual rise in U.S. gold reserves. The key target figure required for the model was a judgment of how much new gold, in value terms, it would be appropriate to add on average to total official holdings, including a residual amount to be bought by the United States. This amount, evidently, should be small enough to require adjustment of extreme surpluses by countries that accumulated reserves partly in gold, as well as monetary discipline by the United States to assure its increment of gold reserves, but large enough, given these other conditions, to prevent a drain on Fort Knox gold. I took this target to be an annual increment to official gold holdings of between $1.5 and $2 billion. The trend of private demand was derived from assumed rates of inflation and rising real incomes, both of which influenced private demand for gold. The final answer as to the new price depended then on the price elasticity of private demand and on the probable effect of a higher price on gold production and Russian sales. It turned out that, inserting reasonable values for these variables, a price of about $70 would be needed to reach the target. I did not allow for large-scale private dishoarding, as had happened when the price was raised in the depressed conditions of 1934, but assumed that Russian sales would be resumed and that a production increase in other countries would more than offset a possible decrease in South Africa.

By chance, I found out that Dolph Kessler of the Netherlands Bank had made similar calculations, using methods quite like my own. He came to a rather higher price, however, not because his model was very different, but because he took as his objective a 20-year period for the stability of the new gold price. I had used 10 years in order to limit the size of the required price increase. But the point is that neither of us had come across any similar exercises published by other economists, apart from those of gold-mining interests that made use of unconvincing assumptions and methods. Although it was a time of great activity in econometric work, there seemed to be an amazing lack of interest in the very idea of the equilibrium price of gold.

The Two-Tier System for Gold

Given the rigid attitude of the United States, there was little hope that a constructive solution for the system would come out of the Washington gold pool meeting of March 16-17, 1968, immediately after the gold market had been closed under crisis conditions. Martin, who had called the meeting, acted as chairman, while Fred Deming, under-secretary of the treasury, represented the United States. The other principals were O'Brien of the Bank of England, Blessing of the Bundesbank, Carli of the Bank of Italy, Stopper of the Swiss National Bank, Zijlstra of the Netherlands Bank, and Ansiaux of the National Bank of Belgium. Pierre-Paul Schweitzer, managing director of the IMF, and Gabriel Ferras, general manager of the BIS, were also present as observers.

After Martin had confirmed that the United States was determined to maintain the existing $35 parity for gold, he called upon Governor Carli. Carli repeated the proposal he had made at a previous discussion, namely, that the gold pool withdraw support from the market, that the market be left to find its own level for the price of gold, and that a separate circuit for official gold settlements be maintained at $35—regardless of the market price. Sales of newly mined gold would have to be disposed of on the market, and participating central banks would refrain from buying on the market at prices above $35. It was apparent from Martin's calling upon Carli to lead off with his scheme that the United States had come around to this way out of the crisis.

As an alternative solution to the problem, O'Brien proposed a substantial increase in the official price of gold. This proposal was strongly supported by Zijlstra and Ferras. Other governors, who confidentially believed that $35 was outdated, did not speak up on the matter, as their governments, which had the power over the gold parity, were not willing to oppose the United States. The basic reason for this was their reliance on the United States for defense against the Soviet Union. In fact, a majority of the governors of the Group of Ten and Switzerland had been for some time in favor of raising the gold price, although they were not free to say so publicly and, as far as I knew, did not press their views on the United States, even confidentially.

Martin said that as the price of gold could not be raised that weekend, it was necessary to come to a practical solution before the market opened on Monday. The day ended without agreement being reached either on the gold question or on a new support package for sterling, which Governor O'Brien had said was essential to enable Britain to maintain its new parity in the coming week.

When I had a chance to talk with Martin that evening, I told him it was evident that, without Russian gold sales, the market price must rise—even if it did not do so immediately because of the huge quantity of the metal that buyers had taken on recently. Any adverse news would set it off, and when the market price got to $45 or $50, the secretary of the treasury would be regarded as ridiculous by the public if he sold gold to other central banks at $35. In any case, a market price of even $40 would surely cause a massive run on the dollar and plunge the United States into another crisis. As Martin did not see any possibility of a change in the U.S. position, I said it would be far better for the United States simply to stop all U.S. gold sales and let the gold price float for a month or two. Although this would produce some disturbances in the foreign-exchange and gold markets, the underlying forces would give some sense of direction and build up an atmosphere conducive to a more solid agreement to stabilize the international monetary system. But Martin did not think this line would be acceptable to the administration and was not prepared to pursue it.

The next morning, the governors and their aides were treated to a surprise—an article in *The Washington Post* by Paul Samuelson on "Increasing the Price of Gold." He first revealed that he had briefed Kennedy during the summer of 1960 on the "sad facts of life concerning the true economic position of the dollar," but said he felt that Kennedy came to a judgment then and there that his margin of electoral support would not permit a drastic solution of the fundamental problem. Having sown the wind, we were now reaping the whirlwind of the gold crisis. Then, with a mixture of sarcasm and passion, Samuelson rehearsed the facts of U.S. gold losses and temporizing measures that had been used to deal with the basic disequilibrium. He rejected any idea of promoting an adequate export surplus by contriving a sluggish rate of economic growth and noted that the floating-rate solution advocated by academic economists had been unjustly greeted with smiles and a yawn by the authorities. Hence, he advocated that the long-term shortage of newly mined gold relative to the growth of trade be solved by an agreement doubling the price of gold overnight and that, at the same time, the overvaluation of the dollar against the currencies of surplus countries be adjusted by a 15 percent devaluation vis-à-vis those currencies. He passed over the various arguments against raising the gold price by choosing it as the best among evils, rejecting as invalid the argument that a general devaluation against gold would be inflationary. As he saw it, doubling the price of gold was a solution that would buy time that could be used to work toward a new regime of "paper gold." "But," he added, "I have no illusions that my advice is likely to be followed soon. As has been usually the case, we shall settle for the simplest, surest measure that will permit us to carry on for another six months."

Samuelson's argument was unanswerable, except that he did not tell the United States how to devalue by 15 percent against which surplus countries. But his predictions proved correct. The United States refused to budge from its position, and in the course of the day, the governors fell into line on the separate circuits for gold. After some hesitation, O'Brien agreed that the London gold market should remain closed for two weeks to allow the situation to calm itself. In addition, a further facility of $1.1 billion was put together to assist the Bank of England in its support of the parity of sterling.

Thus, the United States rejected the made-to-order opportunity of a gold-market crisis to initiate an adjustment process under conditions of *force majeure*. Parenthetically, it may be noted that since the end of 1949, only five countries had accumulated more than $1 billion of gold reserves: France $4.7, Germany $4.0, Italy $2.1, Holland $1.5, and Switzerland $1.1 billion. The gold reserves of South Africa and Canada, both producers of gold, had risen only about $500 million and Australia's only $100 million.

A draft communiqué was put before the governors, which not only set forth and justified the results of the meeting but aimed to promote confidence in the market. A key sentence stated that "as the existing stock of monetary gold is sufficient, in view of the prospective establishment of the facility for Special Drawing Rights, the governors no longer feel it necessary to buy gold from the market." This statement did not reflect the views of most of the governors, and they argued against the sentence heatedly. Clearly, it made sense only if it was intended that gold should be demonetized and that in the meantime the United States should not be called upon to fulfill its obligations of gold convertibility. But this was not the intention of most of the governors, as was evident from the fact that they resisted the idea of a "pledge," proposed by the United States, not to buy gold from the market.

The United States fought hard for the sentence as a contribution to confidence and finally got its way. U.S. officials also made clear to the other central-bank officials that confidence would be helped if there was a temporary let-up on the conversion of dollars for gold at the Treasury.[12] In fact, from this time on, many countries hesitated to call on U.S. gold reserves; otherwise, the climax would have come well before August 1971. Some countries felt a strong obligation to the United States, and more were wary of the consequences of a breakdown of the convertible dollar system. The new arrangement was called the two-tier price system for gold. If it was a system, it was not a sustainable one. As for the official price of $35, it was not a price in the sense of a value related to supply and demand—it was a law.

A sequel to the meeting was a second article by Samuelson three weeks later, which illuminated the intentions of at least some U.S. officials. He described how his telephone began to ring after the publication of his first article with protests from friends on his advocacy of doubling the price of gold. One can well imagine the pressure that was put upon him. But, he protested, he had not known that at the Washington meeting the gold-pool participants would announce that they "pledged themselves unilaterally to take a giant step toward demonetizing gold." Not only would they push ahead with the SDR facility, but they would "not buy or sell gold with anyone or any central bank who deals with the private market." (The quotes are Samuelson's words, not the communiqué.) Maintaining his position that the dollar was in fundamental disequilibrium, he said that "this is a matter of relative currency valuations and now, at least, we can divorce this whole problem from the problem of gold and of devaluation." While he found some reasons to expect the U.S. situation to improve somewhat in the future, he thought a residual overvaluation of the dollar would remain. If this were not corrected by other countries revaluing their currencies relative to the dollar, he considered that there was no better solution than a departure from the present inflexible parities.

This, then, was the weird position into which the United States had drifted. The gold par value of the dollar had priority, and the adjustment process was to be left to revaluations by other countries—which were thus supposed to reduce the price of gold in terms of their currencies. The idea of reducing the price of any commodity in short supply, the production of which was being subsidized in some producing countries, was certainly unorthodox economic doctrine. And indeed, as the United States was the seller of gold of last resort, revaluations of other currencies would thus tend to intensify and not to lessen the pressure on the U.S. gold stock. If this position were maintained, it could only lead to floating exchange rates, which at the time were equally opposed by the United States. Robert Solomon has called the feelers the United States put out to get a few other countries to revalue, while the dollar remained rigidly at $35 an ounce of gold, "The Reform that Failed."[13] He did not mention that the whole idea was politically and economically absurd.

The extent to which top U.S. officials saw the implications of their policy position was a mystery. Federal Reserve Chairman Martin published an article entitled "The Price of Gold Is Not the Problem,"[14] while the New York Federal Reserve seemed to believe that the adjustment process could be sidestepped by means of an expanding swap network. And Treasury Secretary Fowler's uncertain grasp of the subject was all too evident at the G-10 meeting in Bonn in November 1968. With his briefing book open, he pressed the German authorities to revalue the D-Mark, although they had previously announced a decision not to do so. Schiller, scarcely hiding his annoyance, asked Fowler why it was so necessary for the D-Mark to be revalued. The secretary responded that revaluation was needed because the large German surpluses on the balance of payments showed the D-Mark to be in fundamental disequilibrium. With an evident air of trumping this ace, Schiller demanded: Then how about the U.S. deficits? Do they not show that the dollar is in fundamental disequilibrium?

The fact was that the whole conception of curing the dollar's ailments by such tactics was impractical. Isolated currency revaluations would, at best, produce a marginal narrowing of the U.S. payments deficit. A significant adjustment could be obtained only if the United States itself took a strong and comprehensive initiative, but insistence on the fixed par value of the dollar foreclosed this possibility.

With the two-tier scheme, the die was probably already cast for a monetary system without gold, though it was left to the next administration to deliver the *coup de grâce*. For a time, the free gold price in London held to a fairly narrow range around the level of $40 while the market was digesting its high absorption of gold over the six months of crisis.

During this period, the South Africans became concerned about the longer-term problem of disposing of their gold output without depressing the market price. They wanted to establish their continued right to sell to the Fund as provided in the Articles of Agreement. So, in June 1968, they offered a token sale of gold to the IMF at $35, even though the market price was around $39. The matter was discussed by the governors at the BIS, but agreement could not be reached on meeting the South African request, against a hard-line U.S. position. The United States did not agree that the IMF had the legal obligation to buy gold, and it opposed the Fund purchase because it feared that once the precedent was established, South Africa might attempt to manipulate the price by holding gold off the market. Discussions of the matter continued all through the next year, and after the market price declined to $35 and South Africa was under pressure to cover a balance-of-payments deficit, an agreement was reached in December 1969, much helped by talks between Paul Volcker, the new U.S. under-secretary of the treasury, and the South Africans. In effect, the Fund was to maintain the floor price of gold, and South Africa was free to sell gold to the Fund to meet its balance-of-payments needs; for its part, South Africa was committed to maintain orderly marketing of its gold production so as not to put pressure on the market price.

THE DOLLAR CRISIS OF 1971

At the beginning of 1969, President Richard Nixon took office. While his election mandate was primarily to bring an end to the Vietnam war, he had inherited severe problems in the domestic economy that demanded forceful policy measures. An attack on excess demand and inflation could be expected to ease the external deficit, though it would not cure the fundamental problem of the dollar. Time was growing short for resolving this dilemma without a breakdown. The gold reserves stood at under $11 billion, and it was rumored widely that Congress would not allow them to fall below $10 billion.

The critical significance of the price of gold for the position of the dollar was recognized by the president's leading advisors in economic affairs: David Kennedy, the new secretary of the treasury; Arthur Burns at the White House; and Alan Greenspan, who had been close to Nixon during the election campaign. So there was some hope that a conservative administration, not tied down by the commitments of the previous officials, would take bold action.

Clearly, the only practicable alternative to a major rise in the price of gold was a floating dollar brought on under crisis conditions. This would be bound to produce a flight from the dollar, with unforeseeable repercussions. It was certainly not a conservative course to let this happen, particularly as the credibility of the U.S. authorities was being undermined by their evident reluctance to initiate an adjustment process. The price of gold was important, not to give gold a larger role or to restore the gold standard, but to maintain confidence in the system that revolved around the dollar.

Just before the new administration took office, David Kennedy was asked by the press about the intentions of the administration with regard to the price of gold. He replied that they wanted to keep their options open, which suggested that top officials had discussed the matter and had not ruled out raising the gold price. His response produced an outburst of headlines in the press, and the top officials were besieged by demands for clarification of the position. Under this pressure, Kennedy declared the intention of the administration to hold firm to the $35 official price. If ever there had been any possibility that the White House would face up constructively to the adjustment process, the opportunity was now passed over. Later events showed that in domestic affairs President Nixon was already concentrating on the next election.

To deal with excess demand and the price-wage spiral, the authorities imposed strong restraining measures. It was announced that budget expenditures would be cut by $4 billion, and Congress was asked to repeal the investment-tax credit of 7 percent dating from 1962 and to continue the 1968 income-tax surcharge at a reduced rate of 5 percent, although the latter proposals were not passed by Congress until December 1969. Nonetheless, as tax receipts were rising and outlays tapering off, the budget shifted into surplus in the first half of 1969.

At the same time, the Federal Reserve moved strongly toward monetary restraint. Having already raised the discount rate in December 1968, the Federal Reserve raised it again to 6 percent in April 1969. It also increased reserve requirements in order to squeeze bank liquidity. The proclaimed aim was to retard lending to large corporations without pressing down on savings institutions and housing, as had happened in 1966. To help in this objective, the Regulation Q ceiling on certificates of deposit was held at 6.25 percent. The effect was a rapid draining off of large deposits from the banks and a forcing up of interest rates in the money market.

After its 1966 experience with tight monetary policy, business was borrowing heavily to protect itself against a liquidity shortage, so that the banks came under great pressure for funds. They turned for relief to borrowing in the Euromarket through their branches abroad. By the summer, the prime rate was 8.5 percent, while three-month Eurodollar deposits moved to around 11 percent. The Euromarket borrowing by the banks for the first three quarters of the year exceeded $6 billion, and the total inflow of liquid funds was over $9 billion. Vigorous protests came from European central banks that were losing reserves through this flow of money to the United States, and in August, the Federal Reserve imposed a 10 percent reserve requirement on any further increase.

As a result of the money inflow, the U.S. balance on reserve transactions in 1969 showed a surplus of $2.7 billion. Even gold reserves rose as both France and Germany were obliged to sell gold to the Treasury to meet their needs for dollars. The trouble was that this anomalous result was bound to be reversed when monetary restraint was relaxed, a point often brought up in international meetings.

The restrictive fiscal and monetary policy in 1969 was slow to force a reaction on the economy owing to the counterweight of the prevailing inflationary psychology. But after the summer, it became evident that the boom was receding, and in the first half of 1970 the economy definitely moved into recession. Short-term interest rates began to decline at the beginning of the year, and their fall accelerated as the recession deepened. In the course of the year, money-market rates fell by more than three percentage points while the three-month Eurodollar rate dropped from over 11 percent to about 6 percent, and rates were still declining at year-end. While the Federal Reserve raised the Regulation Q ceiling in January 1970, so that the banks could compete for funds, it maintained the discount rate at 6 percent until mid-November and held the money supply to a moderate rise. Corporations, as a safety measure, began to borrow heavily on the capital market in order to reduce their indebtedness to the banks.

Under these conditions, the banks became increasingly liquid and, as had been foreseen, lost no time in repaying their higher-cost borrowing from the Euromarket and other foreign sources, as well as resuming lending to nonresidents. Although the recession in the economy improved the trade balance, the gain was swamped by the outflow of money. In all, the export of funds by the banks in 1970 amounted to $7.4 billion, of which $4.3 billion took place during the fourth quarter. Because much of these funds was going back into the reserves of foreign central banks, the surplus in the reserve position of the year before turned into an enormous official settlements deficit in 1970. At the beginning of the year, the SDR facility in the Fund had been activated for the first time with initial allocations totaling $3.4 billion, of which the U.S. share was $867 million. Even with this gain to the reserves, the official settlements deficit for the year reached $9.8 billion. Part of this loss reflected the elimination of sterling and French franc holdings as the Bank of England and the Bank of France repaid earlier drawings on their swap lines. During both the third and fourth quarters, the loss of gold reserves was around $400 million, and substantial swap credits in foreign currencies were drawn on several central banks to prevent the gold losses from being larger. Waning confidence in the dollar was apparent also from the rise in the market price of gold, which reached about $37.50 in the fourth quarter. Both the market and monetary authorities knew that an adjustment could not be long delayed.

A new feature of the situation was that the rate of wage-price inflation quickened as the recession deepened. From the start, the Nixon administration had proclaimed its opposition to wage guidelines or price surveillance on the doctrinaire grounds that they contravened the principle of free markets and that they always broke down sooner or later. This policy renunciation was an open invitation to organized labor to flex its muscles. And while the budget shifted to deficit and monetary policy was greatly eased, these impulses aimed at reversing the decline in economic activity were swallowed up in rising prices.

Leaning with the Wind

The deterioration in the position of the dollar accelerated sharply in the first quarter of 1971. The official settlements deficit rose to $4.7 billion from $3.1 billion in the fourth quarter of the previous year. The atmosphere was charged with the coming crisis, and there was a rush of covering transactions and outright speculation, which even affected trade movements. The flow of money to Europe centered on the D-Mark as an inevitable candidate for revaluation. To limit the reflow of funds from banks in the United States to the Euromarket, the U.S. authorities in the months from January to April sold special securities at favorable yields to the foreign branches of American banks. Previously, special arrangements had been made to "mitigate" U.S. gold losses caused by other countries' purchases of gold from the U.S. Treasury to pay the increase in their IMF gold-tranche subscriptions. As usual, inventiveness was forthcoming in financial arrangements and in presenting a bold front to the market, but the fetish of the $35 gold price ruled out inventiveness in the adjustment process.

The break-up started with the D-Mark. The flow of money into Germany became a flood in early May, and after the Bundesbank had bought about $1 billion in the first hour of business on May 5 to hold down the exchange rate, it withdrew from the market. The central banks of Switzerland, the Netherlands, Belgium, and Austria took similar action. To find some *modus vivendi,* Schiller, the German economics minister, proposed that the six Common Market currencies float jointly against the dollar. But Italy and France, whose currencies had not been subject to intense pressure in the exchange market, were not receptive to such a scheme because they felt that their currencies would be carried up to excessive levels through appreciation of the strong currencies, particularly the D-Mark. While the D-Mark and the guilder continued to float, the Belgian authorities relied on their divided exchange market to take the strain, and the Swiss franc and schilling were revalued by 7 and 5 percent, respectively. The yen was held within the upper margin of its par value.

All the hectic activity in the exchange markets produced changes in currency rates that were negligible from the standpoint of correcting the overvaluation of the dollar. The immediate upward movement of the D-Mark was less than 4 percent and appreciation reached 5 percent only after the Bundesbank began to sell dollars in order to absorb some of the excess liquidity that the previous inflow of money had created. Meanwhile, the guilder rose about 2 percent above par.

But the market understood well enough the state of the dollar. The free price of gold shot up to $41, and the flight from the dollar into other currencies also continued, now concentrating more on the yen. The U.S. gold loss in the second quarter was $456 million, and a further $300 million was to be lost in the third quarter. Thus, the notion that the United States could sit back and wait for the appreciation or revaluation of other currencies to restore equilibrium to the dollar was shown to be unworkable—which anyone should have known beforehand. Only by the administration in Washington was the U.S. policy considered, somehow or other, to make any sense. John Connally, who had been named as the new secretary of the treasury early in the year, still boldly proclaimed that the United States would neither devalue the dollar nor change the price of gold.

By that time, however, no candor remained in administration pronouncements. The outflow of money quickened in the summer, the news was filled with stories on devaluation, and the gold reserve was nearing the critical $10 billion level. A report by a subcommittee of Congress's Joint Economic Committee declared that the dollar was overvalued and should be devalued. The administration's policy on the domestic front was also a shambles. The wage-price spiral had worsened even though the recession had brought a further rise in unemployment. Arthur Burns publicly recommended the surveillance of wages and prices; the adamant official stand against wage guidelines had already been breached in the face of excessive wage increases in the construction industry. A final week of enormous selling of dollars in the exchange market brought matters to a head in mid-August, when the government was compelled to institute measures to meet the crisis.

Policymaking at Camp David

The crash program was announced by the president on August 15, following a weekend meeting of the administration's economic team at Camp David. On the domestic side, the program was intended to check the inflationary psychology and give an expansionary impulse to the economy. A three-month freeze was put on wages and prices and a wage-price council established to watch over developments when the freeze period ended. Projected federal spending was cut by $4.7 billion, and a 10 percent tax credit was proposed on business investment in new equipment of U.S. manufacture, together with the repeal of the excise tax on automobiles.

On the external side, the main action was the suspension of the convertibility of the dollar. This course had been recommended to Nixon by George Shultz, director of the Office of Management and Budget, who stood highest with Nixon on economic affairs at the time. In addition, a 10 percent tax was imposed on imports. Both measures, described as temporary, were justified by the kind of oratorical flights usual on such occasions. Speculators had been waging war on the American dollar, Nixon said; he neglected to give any explanation for their behavior. He observed that the import tax was needed because unfair exchange rates had placed American products at a disadvantage, again failing to mention the years of intensive resistance to devaluation of the dollar. The implication was that other countries were responsible for the unfair exchange rates, as Nixon said that, when the unfair treatment was ended, the import tax would end as well.

It has never been made clear what results were expected from these measures, if indeed there were clear expectations. A temporary suspension of convertibility might have been intended, after a period of floating, to promote a realignment of exchange rates. If this had been the objective, then the import tax was illogical because it was an obstacle to the rates floating fully to an equilibrium relationship. Or the label of "temporary" may have been just to soften the domestic political impact of the declaration of inconvertibility. Nixon said that the United States would cooperate in the IMF to reform the international monetary system, but it was not contemplated that the reform would rule out the norm of fixed exchange rates.

It does not appear that such issues were clarified in the discussions at Camp David. In the meeting, Arthur Burns expressed his opposition to the immediate suspension of gold convertibility on the grounds that the remainder of the program, including the domestic measures, should be adequate to restore confidence in the dollar. But Connally said that he was against allowing any possibility of further demands for the conversion of dollars into gold because it would leave the initiative with foreign countries for stopping the convertibility of the dollar. The taboo on any change in the par value of the dollar blocked a realistic conception both of equilibrium and of the kind of tactics required to bring it about. Robert Solomon, in discussing the exchange crisis, has confirmed that the United States did not have a "coherent plan for bringing about a broad and sufficiently large realignment of currencies"—even though that was supposed to be the "game plan." And with regard to the Camp David meeting, he has reported that Volcker and McCracken "were somewhat concerned that the 10 percent surcharge plus suspension of convertibility might constitute overkill."[15] And this with a U.S. payments deficit on current account running in the second half of 1971 at an unprecedented annual rate of some $4 billion!

It has been alleged that the United States allowed, or even encouraged, the crisis of the dollar by a policy of "benign neglect" toward its fate. The phrase had come from a private study group headed by Gottfried Haberler, which had prepared a report on balance-of-payments policy during the previous election campaign. But, in fact, policy had been aggressively interventionist, notably through repeated drawings on the swap network. No sooner was one batch of swaps cleared up by gold sales or drawings on the IMF, than new intervention was undertaken. In the last week before convertibility was suspended, new swap drawings amounted to more than $2 billion, and at the end, there was $3 billion outstanding, plus $2 billion of Roosa bonds.

The defense-of-the-dollar policy resulted in the unprecedented deficit on reserve transactions for July-August 1971 of over $11 billion and for January-August of more than $22 billion. Up to August 15, gold losses were $865 million and transfers of SDRs, which had a gold value guarantee, were $465 million. In reality, the defense did not defend; nor did the August 15 blitz settle the disequilibrium of the dollar.

7
The Smithsonian Agreement

The day after convertibility was suspended, Connally held a press conference to justify the Camp David program to the American public. At the conference, he reiterated the U.S. policy on the $35 price of gold for the dollar. Thus, from the start he gave up the initiative in the negotiations that culminated in the Smithsonian Agreement in December 1971. Although Connally was aggressive about the misdeeds of other countries, he left himself little in the way of policy action that he could use to secure a favorable adjustment. By the tactics of the import surcharge and the discriminatory investment tax credit, the United States infringed the GATT rules on trade practices and risked retaliatory measures; and by excluding the idea of a new parity for the dollar, the United States contravened the Fund's rules and left it to others to set the pattern for adjusting "unfair" exchange rates.

THE CRISIS ATMOSPHERE

The main exchange markets remained closed for a week following the August 15 announcement. When they reopened, most major currencies were allowed to appreciate somewhat against the dollar, but the flight from the dollar continued despite the oversold position that had built up over the previous months of crisis. The Bank of Japan alone continued to hold the old dollar rate until the end of August, when it too was overwhelmed by the flood of dollars and was forced to let the yen float. Throughout the autumn months, the central banks of some major countries intervened heavily in the markets to limit appreciation of their currencies, but they had to yield bit by bit. Speculators were given another round of easy profits. During the last four months of the year, the gross reserves of Germany, Japan, and the United Kingdom rose by $2.8, $1.7, and $1.4 billion, respectively, while the U.S.

official settlements balance showed a further deficit of $7.3 billion. With the unsettled atmosphere in exchange markets continuing, the official establishment saw floating as a crisis that had to be resolved.

An IMF Initiative

Pierre-Paul Schweitzer, the managing director of the IMF, took the initiative in dealing with the problem. In late August, he recommended that the members of the Fund seek a collective agreement on the exchange-rate structure, and he urged prompt action to avoid a snowballing of discriminatory measures. In addition, he said publicly that the United States should contribute by devaluing the dollar.

Earlier, Schweitzer had paid a courtesy visit to the new secretary of the treasury, John Connally, during the course of which he mentioned the fundamental disequilibrium of the dollar and the need for a devaluation. It was the first time that a top official of the IMF had spoken of the matter to the United States. Connally was furious, and Schweitzer was never able to establish good relations with him. After his public statement in August, Schweitzer was really in trouble with Washington. Subsequently, the United States blocked his reappointment as the IMF managing director, without, however, noting that Schweitzer had overstepped the IMF rules in publicly suggesting devaluation of the dollar.

It should be stressed that Schweitzer had never supported the necessity for a general increase in the price of gold—the "uniform change in par values" allowed for in the Fund's articles. Whatever his real beliefs, it would have been embarrassing for him as a Frenchman to have supported the French position on gold, against the United States.[1]

The IMF economists set to work on calculating a tentative set of exchange rate changes that would serve as a basis for a collective approach to end floating. These changes were presented to the Fund's executive directors in confidence, but somehow or other the numbers leaked to the press. As the figures were quite close to the rate changes finally adopted in the Smithsonian Agreement, the methods used to arrive at them are of interest. The objective was to calculate the appreciation or depreciation of every currency of the Group of Ten plus Switzerland required to adjust current-account balances to what was judged to be a reasonable figure in each case—not from what the balance happened to be at the moment but from what it would be if the total demand and output levels of each economy were at full employment. Hence, the starting point was the OECD estimates of countries' current-account surpluses and deficits at full employment. The exchange-rate changes required to adjust these surpluses and deficits to equilibrium levels were then calculated by means of a multilateral exchange-rate model worked out previously by the IMF staff.[2] The model allowed for five groups of goods and included demand and supply functions for each, specified from scrappy data on price elasticities. The rest of the world was treated as an additional "country," and allowance was made for adequate capital exports from the G-10 countries to the less developed world. The point of the model was that it took account of the effect of the change in each country's exchange rate on all the other countries and so yielded a multilateral solution.

As the work progressed, the IMF technicians showed officials of several of the surplus countries the size of the exchange-rate revaluations indicated for their currencies. The general reaction was astonishment and even laughter at what were taken to be very excessive figures. The IMF experts were shaken by this reception. While they were under no pressure to give it any weight, it added to the uncertainties they felt over the weak basic data and influenced the final results—in the wrong direction. They did not contact U.S. officials because of the strained U.S.-IMF relations occasioned by the earlier public statement of Schweitzer. But after the figures had been leaked, three economists from the CIA visited the IMF to obtain all the data of the model and the calculations. They did not say who sent them.

The IMF procedure had other shortcomings. For one thing, it was based on a static model that did not allow for changes already in progress in the pattern of trade flows and international competitiveness. Nor did it take into account the need for a pattern of exchange rates that would be convincing to the market, and that would thereby restore confidence. As the adjustment process in trade was expected to take several years, with some adverse initial effects, market confidence was essential if the crisis psychology was to be eliminated and a reflow of money to the United States secured. The IMF staff also did not address themselves to the problems of fundamental disequilibrium of the system and restoration of the convertibility of the dollar. It is doubtful whether the staff even considered these problems to be crucial for the future of the system they were meant to oversee; yet without a solution to them, no new structure of exchange rates could be durable.

As the G-10 ministers and governors were scheduled to meet in London in mid-September to exchange views on how to resolve the crisis, a preparatory meeting of their deputies was held in Paris early in the month. Because the crisis centered on the dollar, Paul Volcker, the U.S. deputy, led off by stating the American position. Washington had ruled out the idea of itself taking any adjustment initiative, so Volcker analyzed the change required in the U.S. balance-of-payments position without proposing fresh U.S. measures to bring it about. He argued that the United States required a current-account surplus of $9 billion a year for several years to cover capital exports of $6 billion to developing countries and to allow an overall surplus of $2-3 billion in order to restore confidence in the dollar. Since he projected the existing full-employment deficit at $4 billion, the target implied a swing in the current account of $13 billion, mostly on trade. Such a swing could be achieved by a combination of currency revaluations, reducing barriers against imports from the United States, and larger participations in joint allied defense costs, all to be carried out by other countries. In effect, Volcker was asking for a massive improvement in the U.S. balance of payments, combined with a minimum policy contribution from the U.S. authorities.

Volcker's conception of the adjustment mechanism was met by European demands that the United States participate through some devaluation of the dollar. Although they cited a few technical reasons for a U.S. contribution to a new pattern of exchange rates, the Europeans also claimed that it was essential from a political standpoint—they would be charged at home with submitting to dictation by the United States if the United States did not make such a contribution. The Europeans stressed that a moderate devaluation of the dollar and revaluation of a few other currencies would leave the average price of gold expressed in leading currencies almost unchanged.

In taking this position, the Europeans accepted in essence the IMF assumption that a viable exchange-rate structure could be established without correcting the fundamental disequilibrium in the system or restoring the convertibility of the dollar. At the same time, they clearly thought that the payments swing suggested by Volcker was much too large for their countries to bear. They feared that it would recreate a situation of dollar shortage for many countries, and they did not believe that allocations of SDRs could effectively fill the gap.

By the time of the ministerial meeting in London, the Common Market ministers had come to a joint view. Speaking for the group, the Italian minister Ferrari-Aggradi maintained that the aim of the United States to shift its balance of payments into surplus was too ambitious to be achieved within a short period of time. He also insisted that, in the selective realignment of parities to correct the fundamental disequilibrium, both surplus and deficit countries (that is, the United States) should share the burden of adjustment. Ferrari-Aggradi justified the first point by saying that too sudden an adjustment would impose serious sacrifices on countries in terms of employment and output, and on the second point, he referred to the idea of the average price of gold remaining unchanged. The latter point was spurious since the official price would be a fiction if the United States did not return to gold convertibility.

A Three-Stage Approach To Solve the Crisis

Schweitzer, who was called upon to give the views of the IMF staff, observed that the conference was faced with more issues than could be settled in a single package in one negotiation. He suggested a three-stage approach. In the first stage, agreement should be reached on the realignment of exchange rates, on temporarily wider margins of fluctuation around the new parities, and on removing the U.S. import surcharge. In the second stage, the question of restoring some form of convertibility for the dollar, as well as any additional measures to improve the U.S. balance of payments, could be taken up. In the third stage negotiations should deal with more fundamental reform of the international monetary system, including the extent to which reserve currencies should continue to play a major role in reserves or should be replaced by international assets (SDRs). Schweitzer stressed that floating had not produced a satisfactory pattern of exchange rates and that it was not likely that such a pattern could be found as long as the United States refused to accept its share of the responsibility. He put the necessary improvement in the U.S. balance of payments at $8 billion, without explaining the figure, and stated that a decline of the dollar in terms of other currencies of approximately 10 percent on a weighted-average basis would be required to bring it about. Edwin Stopper, the president of the Swiss National Bank, was the only participant who spoke of the need for a devaluation by the United States as a means of restoring confidence in the dollar. He stressed that the United States itself had declared the dollar overvalued, and he said it would remain so in the eyes of the world if the United States failed to take action. Stopper suggested that an impartial individual might be chosen to visit all the Group of Ten countries to see what sort of exchange-rate changes might be negotiable.

Connally, who had intervened in the discussion to answer various points that other ministers had raised, took the floor again at the end of the meeting. He said that he did not want any misunderstanding of the U.S. position. The United States was not going to devalue the dollar or raise the price of gold. The United States, he insisted, had taken its measures and now wanted to see what action would be taken by other countries. Predictably, the other countries did not do anything in the way of formal action to resolve the dilemma. They just continued to intervene in the exchange market to limit the appreciation of their currencies. And the United States did not do anything to oppose such intervention. But this logjam began to loosen when the Group of Ten met again later in September during the annual meeting of the IMF and the World Bank. While none of the ministers made any concessions on matters of substance, the procedure previously suggested by Schweitzer was taken up. The decision made was to concentrate on the problems he had singled out for the first stage of negotiation, namely realignment of exchange rates and removal of the U.S. import surcharge.

The way the wind was blowing was evident when Arthur Burns took up Stopper's suggestion. Burns asked Governor Zijlstra, in his role as president of the BIS, to consult with the various governments as to what might be a negotiable structure of exchange rates. Clearly, Burns was prepared to see the dollar devalued as part of a general settlement. While this approach gave the other countries the upper hand in fixing the relative depreciation of the dollar, it was an outcome predestined by the U.S. refusal to take any initiative of its own. The United States at no time suggested that there should be a limitation on the use of the dollar as the intervention and reserve currency of the system.

Two months later, at the next ministerial meeting in Rome, the United States fought a rearguard action on the amount of adjustment to be sought in the U.S. balance of payments and in the dollar's exchange rate. Governor Zijlstra had circulated a secret report based on his talks with the various countries. The report was comprehensive in scope, covering the realignment of currencies and removal of the U.S. surcharge, other trade measures and burden-sharing in the areas of defense and aid, as well as future convertibility of the dollar and the longer-term reform of the system. Interest naturally centered on the current problem of the realignment.

Zijlstra stressed that the information he had gathered illustrated the great difficulty of securing multilateral agreement on a simultaneous realignment of the Group of Ten currencies. The least controversial figure, he said, was the aggregate current-account surplus of the Group of Ten, which had been running at $11 billion annually in the recent past, and was assumed to remain at that level for the time being. But the estimates made by the various countries of their own current balances for the coming year (1972) yielded a collective surplus of only $5.5 billion. By contrast, the current-account targets of the countries, based on their broad balance-of-payments objectives, added up to $16.5 billion; "the difference is, therefore, a seemingly 'unaccountable' overall adjustment of $11 billion; unaccountable, because the adjustments should, of course, add up to zero. This difference might be called a 100 percent deviation from a consistent outcome."

According to Zijlstra, the $13 billion saving sought by the United States was too great, and should be reduced at least by $2 billion, the amount which the United States had allowed for accumulation of reserves. The minimum U.S. adjustment should be taken as $8 billion, the figure calculated by the OECD and the IMF, so that "putting the target at more than $8 billion but not more than $11 billion, the spread for seeking a solution has been marked." Zijlstra explained that the 10 percent change in the relative position of the dollar against the other Group of Ten currencies was calculated to yield an improvement in the U.S. current account of more than $8 billion, that some additional effect could be expected from trade measures and burden-sharing, and that widening margins to 2 or 2.5 percent would also be helpful. He then proposed the following changes in par values or central rates[3] from their pre-May levels: devaluation of the dollar in terms of gold by (about) 5.5 percent; revaluations of the D-Mark by 6 percent, the Swiss franc by 7 percent, the yen by 9 percent, the Belgian franc and Dutch guilder by 3 percent each. Britain, France, Italy, and Sweden were to hold their par values unchanged. It was assumed that the Canadian dollar would continue to float.

I told Zijlstra that his exchange rates would not produce the result he had indicated and also that he could not expect an effective stabilization of the situation without a large increase in the official gold price. As he had supported such action for many years, I believe he agreed on this point. But he felt, correctly, that the issue of the gold price was outside his assignment and that the exchange rates were about the best that could be negotiated. While I believed it would then be better to stay with floating for some time longer, he considered that to be too dangerous from the standpoint of opening the way to trade and payments restrictions and that he could not in any case go against the general desire for a settlement.

At the Rome meeting, Connally asked the other Group of Ten countries what they would do if the United States were to devalue the dollar by 10 percent. His question made it clear that, at long last, the United States was prepared to devalue the dollar.

As many other currencies of the world were sure to remain pegged to the dollar at their existing exchange rates, some of the ministers were not prepared to accept so large a relative appreciation of their currencies in terms of the dollar. Others, however, were ready to accept a larger total appreciation. But because the details of all the currency relationships could not be worked out on the spot, particularly the cross-rates among the Common Market countries, the meeting was adjourned without reaching an agreement.

With the next ministerial gathering scheduled for Washington in mid-December, President Georges Pompidou of France sought out a meeting with President Nixon. The French government was determined to keep the gold parity of the franc unchanged, and on that basis, Pompidou wanted to arrange for a devaluation of the dollar satisfactory to France. The two presidents and their ministers met in the Azores on December 13 and reached an agreement, the details of which were kept confidential. In fact, Nixon agreed to devalue the dollar by 7.9 percent, which meant a rise in the official dollar price of gold to $38 an ounce.

The Final Settlement

The meeting at the Smithsonian Institution in Washington, D.C., a few days later quickly settled down to a bargaining session over the new exchange rates between the United States and the other countries. The ministers were primarily concerned with what they imagined would be the impact of the new rates on the trade position of their countries. Connally tried to cajole the others into accepting larger revaluations, while they sought to protect the competitive position of their exporters and domestic producers. My impression was that few of the other ministers saw that the United States would be condemned to a continued payments deficit, and I did not hear that Connally stressed this point in the sessions where ministers alone were present.

Under the agreement finally reached, the dollar was devalued by 7.9 percent, while the revaluations were 7.7 percent for the yen, 4.6 percent for the D-Mark, and 2.8 percent for the guilder and the Belgian franc. Britain and France held to their existing parities, while Switzerland kept the parity it had fixed in May, when it had revalued by 7.1 percent. The inadequacy of the whole realignment was capped when Italy and Sweden both devalued their currencies by 1 percent on the grounds that their balance-of-payments positions could stand a dollar devaluation of 6.9 percent, but not one of 7.9 percent. Canada resisted the pressure put upon it to fix a new rate. The agreement also included a temporary increase in the allowed margins of fluctuation for currencies on either side of parity to 2.25 percent (from the 1 percent in the IMF's Articles) and the removal of the U.S. import surcharge.

The most important aspect of the Smithsonian settlement, however, was that the other countries fixed the exchange rates of their currencies to an inconvertible dollar. This constituted a fundamental change in the monetary system itself, and it remained to be seen whether fixed exchange rates among the Group of Ten could be maintained on that shaky foundation. The communiqué on the agreement stated that discussions should be undertaken promptly to consider a longer-run reform of the system. "It was agreed that attention should be directed to the appropriate monetary means and division of responsibilities for defending stable exchange rates and for ensuring a proper degree of convertibility in the system."[4]

THE BREAKDOWN OF THE SMITHSONIAN AGREEMENT

The IMF calculated that the effective devaluation of the dollar against all other currencies was 9 percent; that is, the multilateral change in exchange rates would have an effect on the U.S. balance of trade equivalent to a unilateral devaluation of the dollar of that magnitude. While the effective revaluation of the yen was estimated at 11 percent, the largest other effective revaluations were only 5 percent for the D-Mark and the Swiss franc. For the other countries, the effective changes were negligible.

If any of the ministers had doubts about the solidity of their work, they gave no signs of dissatisfaction. Several governors had serious misgivings, though the majority seemed to feel that the agreement was viable. American officials, including Connally, believed that the effective adjustment of the dollar rate had been too small, but this view seemed not to have been very strongly impressed on President Nixon, since he congratulated the ministers and governors on "the most significant monetary agreement in the history of the modern world." In fact, given the magnitude of the disequilibrium, the agreement could hardly have been worse.

Failure to Restore Confidence

First of all, the Smithsonian settlement failed to convince a large majority of financial institutions and traders in the market. The devaluation of the dollar by 7.9 percent was considered too small a corrective for its serious and long-standing fundamental disequilibrium, particularly by comparison with the 15 percent devaluation of sterling in 1967. This judgment was reinforced by the fact that a 7.9 percent devaluation was substituted for the 10 percent import surcharge. Nor did the market believe in a devaluation of the dollar that failed to reestablish convertibility.[5] It could not understand a rise in the official dollar "price" of gold to $38 an ounce when the market price was at $43. The market also believed, from the experience of other cases, that devaluation required the support of restrictive policy measures to lay a foundation for the new parity by an immediate reflow of hot money. But the United States took no restraining measures, 1972 being an election year, and the direction of policy until late in the year was toward expansion. The state of confidence was evident from the fact that the market price of gold started to rise at once, reaching $48 in February 1972 and $60 in May. Another sign was the spurt of almost 10 percent in January in the indexes of world-market commodity prices, even though the currencies of most primary-commodity-producing countries had remained pegged to the dollar.

As the U.S. official settlements deficit in 1971 had been a gigantic $30 billion, the leads and lags in international payments were exceptionally adverse to the dollar; that is, in anticipation of the upset of exchange rates, payments in foreign currencies had been speeded up and those in dollars had been slowed down. In addition, protective and speculative positions in various currencies had been increased by purely financial transfers. The United States expected that the devaluation would induce some reversal of these abnormal positions, though officials were cautious about the size of the reflow of money that might take place. The dollar was, in fact, quoted well above the new central rates immediately after the Smithsonian Agreement. But this phase lasted only a few weeks, and the dollar weakened from the latter half of January 1972 into March. Thereafter measures taken against money inflow by the strong-currency countries provided some respite. Germany, in particular, imposed the "Bardepot" charge, a special penalty on borrowing abroad by German corporations, and in addition exhibited a determination to hold the dollar exchange rate of the D-Mark. Even so, for

1972 as a whole, there was a net outflow of money from the United States rather than an inflow, and the official settlements deficit came to $10.3 billion.

Larger Devaluation Necessary

Besides the failure to restore confidence, there was a failure in basic adjustment that showed itself quite soon. The objective of the exchange-rate realignment was a large improvement in the U.S. current account, particularly in the trade balance. While the initial effect of devaluation might be adverse because of higher prices of imports and a lag in the expansion of exports, the adjustment effects on trade volumes were expected to show up in the second half of 1972. These expectations were disappointed. The trade deficit, which had widened from $200 million to $1.4 billion between the third and fourth quarters of 1971, increased further to $1.8 billion in the first quarter of 1972 and hardly fell below this level in the rest of the year. For 1972, the trade deficit totaled $6.4 billion, as against $2.3 billion the year before and a surplus of $2.6 billion in 1970.

This sharp deterioration of the trade balance occurred despite a $5.6 billion or 14 percent increase in exports. The devaluation was not a major factor in the export expansion because it had not been large enough to give U.S. exporters much new competitive edge. Rather, the export expansion reflected exceptional shipments of grains and cereals because of bad harvests abroad, a rebound in shipments after the dock strikes in the late months of 1971, and a normal response to cyclical upswing in foreign countries. For imports, however, the rise of $10 billion or 22 percent in 1972 was exceptional, particularly after the large increase of $5.7 billion the year before. A major factor here was the rise in the dollar price of imports due to the devaluation and to the general advance in primary commodity prices. These price effects accounted for about one third of the increase in the value of imports. Most notable, however, was the rise in imports of manufactured goods by 27 percent, following their 20 percent rise in 1971. It was evident that industry abroad was making major price adjustments and marketing efforts to enlarge its share of the U.S. market and that both consumers and business in the United States, expecting the price of imported goods to increase further, were being stimulated to purchase such goods immediately.

At a meeting of Working Party 3 in early September 1972, I asked Christopher Dow, the OECD director of economics, whether he intended to introduce a discussion on the failure of the Smithsonian accord. He and others protested that it was too early to make such a judgment—the adjustment process had to be given more time to overcome the initial adverse effects of the devaluation of the dollar. It was enough, I replied, that there had been no reflow of money to the United States. In addition, the statistical data for the first six months of the year gave absolute proof; whereas the aim had been an improvement in the U.S. current-account balance of $8 billion, implying a $6 billion surplus, the data were indicating an $8 billion deficit. There could be no expectation of a turnaround of $14 billion just by waiting. In his discussion of the situation later in the meeting, Dow said that the pre-Smithsonian estimates had probably not taken sufficient account of the rate at which the U.S. balance had been worsening and that the improvement would therefore be about $2 billion less than had been foreseen. In fact, the current-account deficit for 1972 turned out to be $10 billion; this was an $8 billion change, but the sign was a minus instead of a plus.

During the IMF annual meeting in Washington at the end of September, I sought out Arthur Burns and repeated my views on the inadequacy of the Smithsonian realignment. I argued that a further devaluation of the dollar was essential to prevent a breakdown. Burns was not one to give anything away in chance conversation; but while he did not contest the gravity of the situation, he did not consider immediate action feasible. As the U.S. presidential election was only two months away, I assumed that the obstacle was political. In that case, I told him, we could expect a major blowup soon. The government should be well prepared to act and should not, as in 1971, have to improvise in the midst of a crisis. In the event, this was precisely what it had to do.

Further Turmoil and a New Dollar Devaluation

An uneasy calm prevailed in the exchange markets until the second half of June 1972. Then new trouble started with a flight from sterling. After an outflow of money from London equivalent to $2.8 billion, the British authorities decided on June 23 to let the currency float. The dollar, in turn, then came under heavy selling pressure, amounting to about $5 billion in the next three weeks. Barriers against the inflow of money were strengthened by the continental countries. Germany prohibited the sale of D-Mark bonds to nonresidents and the Swiss imposed negative interest rates on increases in nonresidents' bank deposits. On July 18, the finance ministers of the Common Market affirmed their intention to continue support of the Smithsonian exchange rates, and the next day, the Federal Reserve resumed operations to support the dollar for the first time since the previous August. The pressure against the dollar and toward the European currencies then ceased, although the money flow into yen remained quite strong in the months that followed. The U.S. balance on reserve transactions showed a net deficit of $5.6 billion in the third quarter, but this narrowed to $1.5 billion during the fourth quarter, actually $0.5 billion less than the deficit on current account.

The lull on the exchange markets lasted until late January 1973, when new breaches in the fixed-rate structure appeared. From the fourth quarter of 1972, Italy had been subjected to a large flight of money prompted by political uncertainty, and in January announced measures to stop the losses. The permitted leads and lags on international commercial payments and receipts were narrowly fixed, and a divided exchange market was adopted with a floating rate for capital transactions. These actions incited a flow of money into Switzerland and, as the Swiss authorities were struggling with inflation, they decided to let the franc float so as to preclude unwanted increases in domestic liquidity that would result from purchases of dollars by the central bank.

Over the next week, the Swiss franc rose by 3 percent against the dollar, which also weakened against other currencies. Then in early February, doubts about the dollar's prospects in view of the continuing payments deficit triggered a fresh currency crisis.

Within a week, the principal central banks had bought about $8 billion, the Bundesbank alone accounting for $6 billion; the exchange markets were closed on the following Monday (February 12). After consulting with its Group of Ten partners, the U.S. authorities announced a new devaluation of the dollar by 10 percent on February 13. By agreeing to this unilateral dollar devaluation, the other countries made it quite evident that they realized they had bargained too narrowly on the Smithsonian exchange-rate structure. But without a strong support program, the new devaluation alone could not restore confidence. On the next day, the yen and the commercial lira were allowed to float.

The exchange markets were relatively quiet during the week that followed, and the Bundesbank was able to sell almost $1 billion out of its previous large purchases. This reversal was more technical than fundamental, however. The basic lack of confidence in the dollar was shown by the rise in the price of gold from $65 to $85 and the floating up of the Swiss franc and the yen. The U.S. Treasury seemed totally oblivious of the problem of confidence. George Shultz, the new secretary, issued a statement saying that the rise in the dollar price of gold had no significance, that the United States undertook no obligation to intervene in the market to support the dollar, and that the U.S. intention was to dismantle the controls on capital exports at the end of the year. The dollar weakened again in the last week of February, and the pressure came to a head on March 1, when the Bundesbank alone had to buy $2.7 billion to hold the D-Mark-dollar rate. The exchange markets were again closed to give an opportunity for discussions in Europe. The Common Market countries, apart from Italy, decided to maintain stable exchange rates among themselves, with margins of 2.25 percent, but to let their currencies float vis-à-vis the dollar. The deterioration in the U.S. net reserve position in the first quarter of 1973 amounted to $10 billion.

Thus, the international monetary system arrived at two main blocs of currencies. One revolved around the dollar, the other around the Common Market arrangement of fixed cross rates. Several currencies—notably sterling, the yen, and the Canadian dollar—were allowed to float individually. Not only had the fixed par-value system broken down, but the way in which the authorities had fumbled matters left the market with an indelible impression that they did not have the will to control events. More speculators became prepared to back their own judgments on exchange rates against the official propaganda line. At the same time, the circle of gold hoarders and speculators was widened, making a return to gold as the basis of par values increasingly impracticable.

8

Monetary Reform

When President Kennedy rejected any change in the par value of the dollar in 1961, the United States was left with only two methods of dealing with the progressive disequilibrium of the system. The first was to defend the existing par value both with measures to limit the balance-of-payments deficit and with financing arrangements to hold down the loss of gold reserves; these have been described in Chapter 6. The second was to change the international monetary system—"reform." The U.S. objectives in reforming the system altered considerably with time. Initially, the aim was to maintain fixed exchange rates, but this proved hopeless, and the United States embraced the *fait accompli* of a floating dollar. The reform effort suffered from U.S. reluctance to define the issue clearly and to confront the other countries with realistic options.

Robert Triffin's book, *Gold and the Dollar Crisis,*[1] stimulated economists to investigate the problem and to propose ways and means of averting the prospective crisis. But the diversity of the economists' views was even greater than that of the officials'. For example, Jacques Rueff, an advisor to President de Gaulle, advocated a return to the gold standard, facilitated by a rise in the price of gold. Roy Harrod, on the other hand, proposed a rise in the gold price to provide adequate gold reserves and to protect the viability of the reserve currency system.[2] Milton Friedman argued for floating exchange rates as a way to free the adjustment process and to eliminate the need for growing reserves. Other economists proposed various plans for providing for the growth of reserves while relying less on gold and dollars. Triffin's own plan, for example, called for gold and reserve currencies to be centralized in the IMF and for reserve growth to be provided through lending or open-market operations by the IMF. The Posthuma plan[3] was for countries to hold a given share of their reserves in a variety of currencies and thereby limit the monetary demand for gold. The Bernstein plan, referred to below, had a similar objective. The Stamp plan[4] proposed that the IMF issue to underdeveloped countries "Fund Certificates," which, when spent, would

169

constitute a growth of reserves to countries in surplus. There were many variations on the theme, and a whole literature grew up around attempts to identify the problem and put forward solutions.

REFORM BY A SUPPLEMENT TO GOLD

The first official proposal on monetary reform was made at the 1962 annual meeting of the IMF by Reginald Maudling, then chancellor of the exchequer in Britain's Conservative government. Maudling proposed the creation of a mutual currency account at the IMF that deficit countries could use to meet certain needs for external finance. The surplus countries would benefit from a gold-value guarantee on their assets in the account, and the system would benefit from a crisis-proof mechanism for the growth of reserves. The Maudling plan, which was along Keynes-Triffin lines, was opposed by Roosa and was looked upon by the surplus countries as a scheme devised mainly to aid sterling. Consequently, it received little support.

By the following year, however, the discussions between Roosa and officials in other countries had resulted in the realization that a serious study of the problems of the system was in order. In October 1963 Douglas Dillion, the U.S. secretary of the treasury, issued a statement on behalf of the Group of Ten:

> In reviewing the longer-run prospects, the Ministers and Governors agreed that the underlying structure of the present monetary system—based on fixed exchange rates and the established price of gold—has proven its value as the foundation for present and future arrangements. It appeared to them, however, to be useful to undertake a thorough examination of the outlook for the functioning of the international monetary system and of its probable future needs for liquidity.

The statement also affirmed that the "removal of the imbalances still existing in the external accounts of some major countries was the most important objective to be pursued over the near future," and added, to avoid alarming the market, that "the present national reserves of member countries, supplemented as they are by the resources of the IMF, as well as by a network of bilateral facilities, seemed fully adequate in present circumstances to cope with possible threats to the stability of the international payments system."

Framing the problem in this fashion started the whole official consideration of monetary reform off on the wrong foot because it buried the basic problem of the system, namely, the disequilibrium between dollars and gold in global reserves. Moreover, the directive to the Group's deputies (who were charged with carrying out the study) specifically put the two key measures of floating rates and a rise of the gold price outside the terms of reference. Albert Hahn, a German monetary economist, commented satirically on these limitations in a newspaper column, noting that the study could not get any place because consideration of the only two possible solutions of the system's problems were ruled out by the terms of reference.

Hahn's view jolted me, but after thinking over the situation, I believed it was overly pessimistic. For one thing, the U.S. balance of trade had made a substantial recovery, and the external deficit was still declining. It seemed that a further adjustment was feasible and, in fact, the U.S. external position improved further in 1964. For another, the supply of new monetary gold was increasing through large Soviet sales and a steady rise in gold production. The increase in official gold holdings in 1963 turned out to be $840 million. On this not negligible base, I was fairly confident that the Group of Ten would be able to arrive at some cooperative plan or arrangement by which the gold-holding countries would share out the available new monetary gold without continually drawing down U.S. reserves. As my work since 1950 had been in the area of international economic and monetary cooperation, I had seen its successes; Henry Wallich's article, "Cooperation to Solve the Gold Problem,"[5] struck a responsive chord.

When the meetings of the deputies got under way, the other countries waited expectantly for Robert Roosa to present the U.S. plan. But it turned out that the United States did not have a concrete proposal upon which a negotiated settlement could be based. Instead, Roosa floated a rather amorphous scheme, suggesting that the surplus countries retain the dollars they received as the counterpart of their surpluses. The quid pro quo he offered for this passive acceptance of dollars was that the United States would accept other convertible currencies into its reserves when its balance of payments was in surplus. The system therefore would become one of multiple reserve currencies, implying a reduced demand for gold reserves.

Roosa did not attack the gold problem directly or suggest that an agreement on gold was essential. In a paper presented by the U.S. delegation to the group, it was stated that the system could be weakened by "excessively large gold movements" and by "competitive efforts to accumulate gold and raise gold ratios in the face of moderate annual global additions to world gold reserves." While the paper asserted that an increase in gold reserves "through a change in the price of gold is clearly ruled out," it did not provide an alternative way out of future weakness of the system. In the interest of avoiding the risk of conversion into gold of official dollar balances, it stated that the dollar, as a reserve currency, "must especially eschew the more extreme measures that on rare occasions may be resorted to by other countries, that affect the value or convertibility of its currency."

Predictably, Roosa's idea of enlarging the number of reserve currencies was not acceptable to most other participants. Apart from the British, who were already saddled with it, the other countries did not want the complications and the responsibilities of a reserve currency. Nor did they want to be relieved of balance-of-payments discipline. Most of them thought that the accumulation of dollar reserves was going too far and that it was up to the United States to stop it by imposing more effective adjustment measures. The United States got some support from Sven Joge, vice-governor of the Bank of Sweden, who explained why Sweden held most of its reserves in dollars. He demonstrated that interest earnings gave a better return than would be obtained from gold reserves by a moderate rise in the gold price. But the other deputies expressed no interest in this bait; the central banks were more concerned with safety than with earnings.

Collective Reserve Unit

Other countries and the BIS also presented papers to the group so that there was ample material to talk about, but the discussion lacked focus until a French paper was submitted. The French put forward a concrete plan for the creation of a reserve instrument to be used in settlements jointly with gold and to substitute for dollar reserves. Its name soon became Collective Reserve Unit, or CRU.

The CRU idea was based on a proposal that had previously been formulated by Edward M. Bernstein. As Bernstein summarized his plan[6]: "The functioning of the gold exchange standard requires another source of foreign exchange reserves and an agreement among the gold-holding countries to standardize their holding and use of gold and foreign exchange as reserves. The best way to do this is for the large industrial countries (the 10 Paris Agreement countries and Switzerland) to enter into an agreement to establish a Reserve Unit and to hold a minimum amount of such reserve units relative to their holdings of gold. The reserve units would be created by having each participating country deposit its own currency with the IMF, acting as Trustee, to an amount equal to its pro-rata share of the reserve units to be created. The currencies held by the Fund as backing for the reserve units would be guaranteed against exchange depreciation. The participating countries would be obliged to convert official holdings of their currencies into gold and reserve units in a minimum proportion—say, two thirds in gold and one third in reserve units. At the end of the fiscal year, adjustments would be made by transferring gold for reserve units from the countries with a deficiency of reserve units to those with an excess of reserve units." Bernstein did not think that other countries would voluntarily assume a reserve-currency function, and he conceived of this system as the means to "avoid a scramble for gold and provide an equitable means by which all eleven countries would share in supplying national reserves held in the form of reserve units.

It will be apparent that the operational success of the Bernstein plan (which was subsequently refined) depended on the U.S. balance of payments, like that of other countries, being able to fluctuate between surpluses and deficits, once the dollar ceased to be the sole source of growth in nongold reserves. In fact, his system contained an element of discipline upon the United States in the form of gold reserve losses to assure that the United States kept control over its deficits. The French plan for the CRU seized upon this element and magnified it significantly. It recommended that a limit be put on the maximum amount that the United States could borrow through accumulation of dollar reserves by foreign central banks, together with swaps and Roosa bonds; beyond that, it would be up to the United States to draw on the conditional resources of the IMF. Any further expansion of the fiduciary (that is, nongold) element in global reserves should take place through the creation of reserve units. Creation of reserve units would take place among a limited group of countries by their unanimous decision. Units would be allocated in proportion to countries' gold reserves and would be used in settlements along with gold in the ratio of gold to reserve units of all members combined. As only gold-holding countries could participate, the appropriate agent for the scheme was considered to be the BIS—as it had been in the EPU.

The apparent extreme rigidity of the French plan no doubt reflected a bargaining strategy. The French believed that the price of gold should be raised to facilitate the substitution of gold for dollars in reserves. Even so, the CRU plan was based on a one-sided view of the system in that it failed to recognize that the intervention and reserve role of the dollar was of great benefit to other countries. A tight plan like the CRU would soon have had to be modified—even if the price of gold had been doubled.

Given the unfavorable view of the role of the dollar that lay behind the French proposal for the CRU, the United States promptly rejected the plan. Roosa was so shocked by the scheme that in subsequent meetings he did not suggest alternative ideas for reserve units or other means of dealing with the dollar-gold problem. Even though the group as a whole did not support the French position, quite a few felt that the U.S. lack of discipline and the growth of dollar reserves were the basic threats to the stability of the system. The various views were aired as the discussions continued, until the time came to submit a report at the end of May 1964.

The completed report revealed the widely divergent views within the group.[7] For simplicity of presentation, the positions of the deputies were divided into two main groups. One group stressed the disadvantages of linking the creation of reserves to the balance-of-payments deficits of the reserve-currency country and the need for an effective adjustment process for the United States. Accordingly, they favored a close watch over the means used to finance payment deficits and the creation, if necessary, of an additional reserve asset to provide for adequate growth of owned reserves. They did not believe that the problems of the system could be solved by an increase in credit facilities, such as an enlargement of IMF quotas.

The second group believed that the system needed only to be reinforced, particularly in the sphere of credit facilities, and that it was important to preserve flexibility in the creation of dollar reserves. They thought the emphasis on excessive foreign-exchange reserves to be exaggerated, that the import of inflation from the reserve center was a myth, and that the U.S. balance of payments was clearly improving.

Deadlock on Reform

Negotiations had thus arrived at an impasse. It was therefore proposed that further study be made of the problems. Working Party 3 of the OECD was asked to examine the adjustment process, while officials from the Group of Ten countries were to study the possibilities for the creation of reserve assets. As a gesture to collective discipline, a system of multilateral surveillance of the financing of deficits and surpluses was set up (see Chapter 6).

According to the Group of Ten's report, there was complete agreement that "gold will continue to be the ultimate international reserve asset and common denominator of par values" and that "we cannot prudently expect new gold production to meet all liquidity needs in the future." But what seemed clear after a year spent in discussion was that a reform to assure the stability of the system within the limits of available new gold could not be negotiated. A group of countries believed that the United States was basically responsible for its deficits and gold losses, and they did not accept, in any real sense, responsibility for their own surpluses. Roosa's proposal for a multicurrency reserve system had fallen flat, the reserve unit scheme had been rejected (it was not intended to help the United States anyhow), and the strong attachment to gold and national sovereignty over the composition of reserves was apparent. The deadlock was fundamental; it forced me to the conclusion that the United States, with its responsibility for the reserve currency of the system, had to take the matter into its own hands by raising the price of gold to end the shortage, in terms of value, of new monetary gold.

The year that followed was one of marking time on possible reform. Rinaldo Ossola of the Bank of Italy was named chairman of the study group on the creation of reserve assets, but as the country participants were officials below the level of the deputies, the body was not expected to produce recommendations. At Ossola's request, I prepared a summary paper as a means of focusing the discussion on the similarities and differences of the various proposals for creating reserve assets, but I could not succeed in gaining acceptance of the definition of the reserve shortage in terms of net reserves—that is, gold.

George Willis of the Treasury and Robert Solomon of the Federal Reserve, who were the American participants, took somewhat different views on reserve creation. For months, Willis resisted any suggestion that the United States would ever accept any form of collectively created reserve unit, and with his ability to outsit all other delegates in lengthy meetings, he made sure that his position was clearly reflected in the draft. Claude Pierre-Brossolette, the participant from the French Treasury, said to Willis one day at lunch that he could not understand why Willis opposed the idea of reserve units so completely, since some day the United States might want to adopt it. Willis did not respond to this attempt at humor.

The report of the Ossola study group, completed in the late spring of 1965, owed much to the energy and grasp of the chairman.[8] It made clear that many varieties of reserve creation were possible, depending on whether participants were a limited group of countries or the full IMF membership, whether the scheme was to be within the IMF or to use the BIS as its agent, whether new reserves were to be used for settlements in conjunction with gold or independently, whether unanimous or majority decisions would be required, whether there would be reserve units or drawing rights on a fund, and what the conditions should be for use and acceptance of the created reserves. Having set out these various possibilities, the Ossola group handed the whole matter back to the deputies.

A Shift in the U.S. Attitude

Even as the report was being written, it appeared that the U.S. view on reserve creation had become more positive. The primary impetus behind the change came from Robert Roosa, who had left the Treasury and was now a private banker at Brown Brothers, Harriman. Originally, he had been opposed to the CRU and in favor of new international credit facilities, but now, after time for reflection, he argued that the real question was the conditions that would govern the use of the new monetary facility—whether it be called reserve units or credit facilities. In a series of lectures at the Council on Foreign Relations, published under the title *Monetary Reform for the World Economy,* Roosa observed that "the area that most needs to be probed in exploring the potentials for major innovation is that of creating additional reserve assets through group action." He indicated that he favored setting up "what might be called a 'Fund Unit Account,' " but that what really counted were not matters of technique but the fundamental questions of the location, participation, use, and decisionmaking of the reserve creation scheme.

The change by the United States to a positive attitude toward new monetary arrangements became official with a statement by Secretary Fowler in July 1965. Then, in the course of the annual IMF meetings in September, the Group of Ten asked its deputies to continue with the examination of improvements needed in the monetary system and arrangements for reserve creation as a matter of "contingency planning." What was the contingency?

The group's communiqué stated "that the deficit in the U.S. balance of payments which had for years been the major source of additional reserves for the rest of the world is being corrected and that the U.S. has expressed its determination to maintain equilibrium in its balance of payments." The contingency, therefore, was "to ensure that future reserve needs of the world are adequately met." By the time the communiqué was issued, however, the United States was actively in the Vietnam war, its trade surplus in the first half of 1965 was sharply lower than in the previous year, and the prospect of balance-of-payments equilibrium was quite remote. Moreover, the loss of U.S. gold reserves had sharply increased, and it was this which really posed the need to consider the future mechanism of reserve creation.

The discussions of the deputies' group during 1965-66 were once again complicated by divergent views on the problems to be faced. In fact, the principal protagonists in the debate on reserve creation had reversed positions. The French had turned against their own CRU proposal after de Gaulle had declared himself in favor of a return to the gold standard; the United States, with its gold reserves dwindling, had turned in favor of the idea of deliberate creation of reserves. As the differences could not be resolved by compromise, the next report of the deputies, distributed in July 1966 on a restricted basis, reflected the fundamental split.[9]

In its introductory section, the report identified three actual or potential problems of the system: insufficient effectiveness of the adjustment process; strains on the system arising from shifts in the composition of reserves from reserve currencies to gold; and the potential need for reserve creation because of the shortage of new gold and the undesirability of a further large growth of dollar reserves arising from U.S. deficits.

With regard to the adjustment process, the report stressed the necessity of speedier action in dealing with persistent large deficits as well as more effective efforts by surplus countries toward reaching equilibrium. On the harmonization of reserve policies, it noted that a proposal had been made that high-gold-ratio countries should tend to settle deficits in gold and accumulate surpluses in other reserve assets, whereas low-gold-ratio countries should do the opposite. But the proposal did not find general acceptance within the group. Some members thought that its administration would raise practical difficulties and "that it would therefore interfere unduly with the freedom of choice of monetary authorities as regards the composition of their reserves."

The report noted that "several members were, however, of the opinion that some understanding with regard to the composition of reserves would become necessary in the longer run in order to adjust reserve policies to the decline in the relative share of gold in total reserves which will inevitably come about." From the standpoint of the disequilibrium of the system, this statement was the most pertinent in the report, although it was not treated as such.

Much of the report dealt with deliberate reserve creation. It was surrounded with the usual officialese about the global need for reserves, though clearly the U.S. interest in the new facility was to supplement not total reserves but the gold component. Indeed, an earlier paragraph was devoted to the shortage of new gold, though with the injunction added that continued "large U.S. deficits must be ruled out as a source of reserves for the rest of the world." On this slender basis, the conclusion was drawn that the supply of reserves from gold and reserve currencies was "unlikely to keep pace with legitimate demands, at any rate in the long run." France was the only country to oppose "contingency planning."

Five schemes for the creation of new reserve instruments that had been proposed during the meetings of the group were described in an annex. The main differences among the proposals were whether the participants would be a limited group or would include all members of the IMF and whether the conception should be one of reserve units or drawing rights. The IMF too had been studying the possibility of reserve creation and had naturally favored universal schemes. The United States proposed, as a diplomatic gesture to non-G-10 countries, that reserve units be created by a limited group while additional drawing rights be created by and distributed to all IMF members. The Common Market countries, apart from France, favored a scheme limited to countries with convertible currencies, which could also be available for use in international short-term-assistance operations.

Although disequilibrium in the system involved only a limited group of countries, consisting of those that accumulated substantial reserves in gold, this fact was deliberately obscured by the formulation of the problem in terms of a potential shortage of global reserves. If the growth of global reserves had actually been too small, there would have been no good reason why all countries should not participate in the handout of the new form of reserves. But, of course, there was good reason. The potential shortage of global reserves never became a reality. The system worked in such a way as to leave the United States with a deficit because the rest of the world combined had a net surplus, and there was no point in boosting global reserves by distributing fiduciary reserves to countries that would quickly spend them, while leaving the imbalance between gold and dollars to worsen.

The report was considered by the Group of Ten ministers and governors in

July 1966. Michel Debré of France, then minister of finance and a fervent supporter of General de Gaulle, took a hard line against the U.S. His attack on the U.S. deficit and the accumulation of dollars in reserves, as well as his demand that gold be restored to the central position in reserves, had such political overtones that it alienated the other ministers. None of them was prepared to join France in opposition to the United States, so that France remained isolated in its stand against contingency planning. But the ministers were unable to resolve the basic issues. Their principal recommendation was that the deputies should hold joint discussions with the executive board of the IMF to see what common ground could be found on a scheme for reserve creation.

The first joint meeting at the end of November effectively killed any idea of a plan based on restricted participation. The executive directors from outside the Group of Ten obviously resented their exclusion from the earlier discussions and insisted that, whatever the scheme, it must be based on full participation of all IMF member countries. Alexandre Kafka of Brazil was particularly effective in making this case. The deputies of the Ten had two difficulties in arguing for a restricted scheme. In a face-to-face confrontation with representatives of the less-developed countries, it was impossible to insist on an exclusive clublike arrangement. Moreover, as the problem was cast in terms of the global need for reserves, the logic behind restricted participation was bound to look weak. The idea that a group of rich countries would band together to create reserves for themselves alone seemed iniquitous to the executive directors from the poorer countries. Otmar Emminger, who had been prepared to advocate the Common Market view that created reserves required the backing of strong convertible currencies, put his paper aside and took a more compromising line. Speaking for the United States, Frederick Deming presented the American proposal of separate and parallel creation of units and drawing rights in a more tentative way. The drift toward a universal scheme also killed off the idea that the new reserve assets should be used in some ratio with gold because the developing countries held only minimum quantities of gold.

Further joint meetings, as well as sessions of the Group of Ten, were required to iron out the details of the scheme for reserve creation and the prerequisite conditions for its activation. The Common Market ministers were anxious that France participate in the arrangement in the interest of European unity. Points of drafting and even of minor substance were put forward by them as compromises to gain French acceptance. The French kept insisting that the proposed scheme was a credit facility rather than a system for the creation of reserve assets. As a compromise, the arrangement was called special drawing rights rather than reserve units, while drawings in excess of 70 percent of a country's cumulative allocation were made subject to a repayment obligation. An 85 percent majority vote in the Fund was to be required for activation of the scheme and for any subsequent decision to allocate additional drawing rights. Also, individual countries were given the right to opt out of a particular activation decision. There was no real difference between "reserve units" and "special drawing rights"—except possibly in their public relations effects. In either case, an actual use of the facility involved surplus countries designated by the Fund making reserves available to deficit countries in return for a transfer to themselves of SDRs.

France, steadfast in its opposition, argued that the gold problem had to be considered. To meet its demand, a special G-10 working group on the gold problem was set up, with Dolph Kessler of the Netherlands Bank as chairman. Dewey Daane, a governor of the Federal Reserve Board, was the hatchet man for the United States, and his constant and heated interventions at the group's meetings made it very clear that the United States would not allow a factual examination of the gold-dollar disequilibrium and its implications for the price of gold. The whole effort was a failure, and Kessler had to report it as such to the governors.

The Birth of SDRs

The SDR facility, as it was originally conceived with the limited function of supplementing the flow of new monetary gold, was a useful idea. It seemed possible that a gradual buildup of SDRs in the system would help to limit the official demand for gold as the central banks developed familiarity with and confidence in the SDR. Good management of the facility would be essential to assure such confidence. But after the Group of Ten yielded to the pressure for full IMF participation in the allocations of SDRs, the probability of the new facility gaining the confidence of surplus countries was considerably lessened. The reason for this was the fear that quite a few countries with persistent balance-of-payments troubles would use their SDR allocations quickly and not take seriously the obligation subsequently to wipe out their debtor positions. If this happened, the countries capable of holding large creditor positions in SDRs, surely less than 10, would soon become unwilling to take in more and more SDRs because they would see no prospect of such positions ever being diminished and because the ultimate debtors were financially weak countries.

Another defect of the SDR was that it was given a full gold-value guarantee, which could be changed only by amendment of the IMF Articles. This guarantee was actually fuller than the one which had applied in the EPU or the one applying to ordinary IMF drawings. Paul Volcker had been opposed to the gold guarantee provision, but he believed he had to give way under pressure of several G-10 countries in order to get an agreement on the

SDR scheme as a whole. I tried to convince the group of deputies that the guarantee would block the use of the SDRs any time there was a threat to the price of gold. Moreover, the aim of a good supplement to gold should be to wean the system away from overattachment to gold.

But the most serious flaw was that in the course of the negotiations the concept of the SDR as a supplement to gold was changed to its being a supplement to gold *and* reserve currencies—that is, dollars. As there was no shortfall in the growth of dollar reserves requiring supplementation, this was a weird conception. I suppose the idea behind it was to de-emphasize the gold problem. But as it was explained, an allocation of SDRs would simultaneously relieve the shortage of new gold and limit the excessive growth of reserves in dollars. It was imagined that this latter effect would happen because central banks would look upon an allocation of SDRs as equivalent, unit for unit, to an earned increase of gold and dollar reserves and that surplus countries would take measures to reduce their earned increase in reserves to offset the amount obtained from an SDR allocation. The idea was pure fantasy because the incentive to surplus countries to adjust generated by small SDR allocations, which were not even part of the money supply, would be negligible.

The strategic decisions in the design of SDRs were taken at two ministerial meetings in London in July and August 1967. The final details were ironed out at another meeting in Stockholm at the end of March 1968. Only the French refused to accept the plan, even though a few additional changes were made in the draft to meet some of their objections. The IMF drafted amendments to the Articles of Agreement to embody the concept. Then the new Articles were submitted to the member countries for legislative approval. By the time of the IMF annual meeting in September 1969, the SDR scheme was approved by a sufficient majority of IMF members. French minister of finance Valéry Giscard d'Estaing then announced that his country too would participate in the arrangement.

Once the SDR was legally approved, a plan for its early activation was worked out. Belief that activation would be appropriate was strengthened by the impact of the U.S. credit squeeze in 1968-69 (see Chapter 6), which created a short-lived surplus on official settlements in the U.S. balance of payments. The total allocation was to be $9.5 billion, over three years, with $3.5 billion in the first year and $3 billion in each of the two following years. The Group of Ten deputies met in July 1969 and agreed that their countries would support the plan when it came up in the IMF. I tried to get them to reconsider the matter on the grounds that the SDR would almost surely be discredited if it were activated before the prevailing fundamental disequilibrium was adjusted. That danger was all the greater because of the gold-value guarantee. I pointed to the precedent of the IMF itself, which the United States had wisely decided to keep inactive until the postwar disequilibrium had had some chance to be adjusted; otherwise, the institution might have lost favor with the legislatures that had to approve any enlargement of its resources. This argument had no effect, although some of the participants agreed with it, including Ossola, the chairman. Volcker told me that the allocation of SDRs might help the adjustment process. It seems that after three years of negotiations on SDRs most of the ministers did not want to come to another IMF annual meeting without a positive result.

The proposal to activate was put forward by Pierre-Paul Schweitzer. It was accepted quickly by the member countries, and the $9.5 billion of SDRs was distributed in three annual lots, starting at the beginning of 1970. The activation of the SDR neither produced any evident strengthening of confidence in the dollar nor slowed up the crisis that came to a head with the suspension of convertibility in August 1971.

THE SEARCH FOR A NEW SYSTEM

After the dollar became inconvertible, neither the IMF nor the European members of the Group of Ten asked the United States to conform to the Articles of Agreement by restoring convertibility. Instead, they sought only U.S. participation in a realignment of exchange rates. Gold par values lost their substance, and IMF operations came to a standstill. Member countries would not engage in transactions with the IMF that involved gold-value guarantees or repayment in gold at the official price when the price was under suspicion and when they could not get gold at that price. It was evident that the IMF Articles would have to be revised, if only to take account of the new situation.

The Common Market ministers had recognized this need at the first pre-Smithsonian meeting of the Group of Ten in London in September 1971. Speaking on their behalf, the Italian minister had set out several principles to guide the reform of the system, calling for fixed parities, a new form of convertibility, and a reduced role for the dollar. But as he contended at the same time that the adjustment sought by the United States was too large for the other countries to bear (see Chapter 7), the principles of reform and the aims of the realignment were contradictory.

At the IMF annual meeting shortly afterward, the full board of governors adopted a resolution instructing the executive directors to study the problems of reform. And the Smithsonian communiqué in December stated, "The Ministers and Governors agreed that discussions should be promptly undertaken, particularly within the framework of the International Monetary Fund, to consider reform of the international monetary system over the longer term."

The U.S. Treasury evinced little interest in the IMF's study of reform, and its negative attitude drew criticism from other countries. As my own view of several years' standing was that the dollar detached from gold would be unstable, and as I had even less faith than the Treasury in the solidity of the Smithsonian exchange-rate structure, it seemed to me that the Treasury's lack of interest in longer-term reform was quite justified. I thought that Paul Volcker, at least, was reconciled to a floating dollar.

Arthur Burns, in a speech in Montreal in May 1972, gave a surprise impetus to serious consideration of the reform problem. Burns did not lay out a full-blown scheme for a reformed system, but rather presented 10 guidelines for the construction of a new system. His guidelines included strengthened international cooperation, sound domestic financial policies, more prompt adjustment of exchange rates in cases of disequilibrium, the responsibilities of both surplus and deficit countries in the adjustment process, and appropriate levels of reserve assets and official credit facilities. He also stressed that gold should be retained in the system, that SDRs should become a larger part of aggregate reserves, and that the use of the dollar as a reserve currency had advantages both to the United States and to other countries. In addition, he proposed reestablishment of some form of convertibility for the dollar, although he qualified this point by saying that it was not more important than the other aspects of reform.

While Burns's views were too vague to be considered the blueprint of a workable system, his initiative was widely welcomed by other countries. Following the resignation of Connally in the same month and the appointment of George Shultz to the Treasury, the official attitude of Washington toward reform became more receptive.

The Committee of Twenty

A critical question was how the new reform discussions should be organized. The Treasury, after having had to yield on the devaluation of the dollar in the Smithsonian negotiations, was fed up with the Group of Ten and believed it could not rely on sympathetic reception of its views in that circle. Moreover, countries outside the Ten were insisting that all IMF members be represented in the new discussions on reform. As a result, an ad hoc Committee of the Board of Governors on Reform of the International Monetary System and Related Issues (to be known as the Committee of Twenty) was established by the IMF with the same constituencies as the Fund's executive board. The committee members, most of them finance ministers, were permitted to name two associates who could participate in the meetings. A corresponding committee of deputies was established to prepare the work of the committee. It was an unwieldy group, one which increased the diversity of views about the objectives of monetary reform. Ali Wardhana, finance minister of Indonesia, was chosen as chairman of the committee, and Jeremy Morse of the Bank of England was named as chairman of the deputies.

When the deputies began their substantive work late in 1972, the international monetary situation was not propitious. The U.S. trade deficit was running at over $1.5 billion a quarter, and the deficit on reserve transactions for 1972 was heading toward a total of more than $10 billion. A breakdown in the exchange markets was certain unless the Smithsonian rate structure was quickly adjusted. Moreover, U.S. official reserve liabilities were about $60 billion, compared with $17 billion at the start of 1970, while reserve assets (with gold valued at $38 an ounce) amounted to only $13 billion, including SDRs. Apart from the serious complication posed by this overhang of dollars, the discussion on reform had to deal with the demand by the developing countries for a link between allocations of SDRs and development assistance. As the major industrial countries were manifestly unable to summon up the realism and cooperative frame of mind to deal with the current problems of the system, it was hard to imagine that they could both create some sort of reformed system and suddenly find the will to make it work.

The deputies had as background a report on monetary reform from the IMF executive directors, which had been issued in August 1972. They accepted from that report that "stable but adjustable par values" and convertibility were the two basic features to be retained in a new system. These objectives raised the questions of what was to replace gold as the common denominator of par values, how countries were to fulfill their obligations, and what reserve assets were to support convertibility of the dollar.

The U.S. Reserve Indicator Plan

In the light of the failure of the SDR to ward off the dollar crisis, the United States had lost all confidence that further allocations of SDRs would promote an adjustment process for imbalances in international payments. Furthermore, in order to reassume the obligation of convertibility, the United States wanted assurance that an active adjustment process would extricate it from its persistent deficit position. Thus, it proposed that a series of reserve indicators be made a feature of the new system. Under this scheme, changes in a country's reserves beyond a certain point would be taken as "objective indicators" that effective adjustment measures by the country were required. Countries failing to adjust would be subject to censure by the IMF.

While the U.S. plan left the choice of adjustment measures up to the country in disequilibrium, the ultimate adjustment instrument was, of course, a change of the par value. The United States saw in the reserve indicator plan a means of making the pressure for par-value changes more symmetrical and nonpolitical. Excessive gains of reserves would constitute a presumption for revaluation by surplus countries, while excessive reserve losses would provide a justification for devaluation of the dollar, as well as of other currencies. In this strange reversal of roles, the United States became the leading advocate of an effective adjustment process. The conception that a reformed system of stable par values required such a mechanism to ensure greater exchange-rate flexibility ignored the likelihood that large changes in reserves would be signals (objective indicators!) to the exchange market and precipitate currency instability.

The U.S. plan never had a chance of acceptance because the surplus countries were unsympathetic to it. They contended that excessive changes in reserves were often due to temporary factors or to forces unrelated to the basic balance of payments, and that such changes, even though their character might be recognized fully in official discussions, were nevertheless likely to induce speculative movements of funds that would aggravate the situation. More fundamental, however, was the fact that balance-of-payments policies and changes in par values were political acts and that few countries were attracted to the idea of objective indicators that pointed out that they were evading their responsibilities. The considerations that had prevented the IMF from defining fundamental disequilibrium in the past were still pregnant with meaning from a political standpoint.

As their counter to the American plan, the surplus countries insisted that restoration of convertibility of the dollar must be the primary objective of any reform. Convertibility was considered essential to subject the United States to balance-of-payments discipline and also to provide the surplus countries with reserve assets that would not suffer a loss of value in the event of a devaluation of the dollar. The surplus countries also were in favor of some obligatory settlement of deficits in reserve assets so as to prevent the continuous rise of foreign-exchange reserves in dollars. Other deficit countries were obliged to use reserve assets when they intervened in the market to maintain their currencies at par, and asset settlement of deficits by the United States was looked upon as a technique that would make the reformed system more symmetrical. In addition, the limitation on dollar reserves would enable the IMF to manage more effectively the growth of global reserves in the system. It was recognized that the United States would have to be protected against demands for conversion of the large outstanding volume of dollar reserves, and it was thought that provision for consolidation of the overhang could be made within the IMF framework.

Although the United States did not immediately reject these ideas, it insisted that they were not feasible without an assured mechanism of adjustment to allow its balance of payments to fluctuate between deficits and surpluses like the payments balances of other countries. Because agreement on such an assured adjustment mechanism could not be obtained, the U.S.

response had the effect of ruling out agreement on convertibility. From the U.S. standpoint, the demand for dollar convertibility was simply a demand for an exchange-value guarantee on the fiduciary instruments that financed its deficits, while surplus countries retained the freedom to allow their surpluses to pile up.

In essence, the convertibility discussion was artificial because it presumed that the United States would come into possession of adequate reserve assets to support it and also to restore confidence in the dollar. The gap between the market price of gold and its official value made it impossible for the United States to gain gold reserves. And since it was also presumed that the new system would limit dollar reserves, the deputies were swept along by the idea that the SDR*would become the main reserve asset of the reformed system. The developing countries were attracted to this idea also, as they hoped to secure a link between allocations of SDRs and development assistance. Supporters of the link argued that creditor positions in SDRs arising from their use by developing countries to finance imports would be a perfect substitute for new gold in its function of creating a net surplus for the system. At the same time, many countries considered that it was up to the United States to compete for its share of this net surplus; in addition, in some versions of the link the United States would be receiving its annual allocation of SDRs to help it support convertibility.

The Failure of Reform

The atmosphere of fantasy in the discussions stemmed from the fact that the right questions did not come to the fore. To start with, the deputies did not recognize the likelihood that the dollar divorced from gold would be unstable. Most of them, in addition, did not face up to the fact that a U.S. deficit was a fundamental characteristic of the system, although the reason for it had been demonstrated in the Smithsonian negotiation and was evident again in the rejection of the reserve indicators.

Then, too, there was little foundation for faith in the SDR. There were only a few surplus countries in a position to accept SDRs on a significant scale, and they did not really believe they should have to pay a toll in the form of the link to development assistance. Nor did they welcome the prospect of accumulating an ever larger proportion of their reserves in SDRs against a deficit SDR position of weak-currency countries. As the SDR did not have intrinsic value, like gold, to make it acceptable, it would have to be considered as international fiat money by countries and their central banks. But few countries even affected to believe that the Board of Governors of the IMF was a sovereign power with the capacity to create money and invest it with an assured quality of legal tender. Likewise, on the critical issue of the sovereign power over reserves, "paper gold" (as the SDRs were often called) was not the equivalent of gold.[10]

After the breakdown of the Smithsonian exchange-rate structure in March 1973, the public had no confidence in the ability of the authorities to reestablish "stable but adjustable par values," and the governments were in basic disagreement on the major issues concerning the adjustment process, convertibility, reserve assets, and the link. To be sure, the deputies worked hard in producing draft after draft to try to effect a compromise, but the failure of reform could not be disguised. Finally, the added confusion in the international monetary situation brought about by the rise in the price of oil by OPEC gave a pretext for the decision to wind up the attempt at reform. Meeting in Rome in January 1974, the Committee of Twenty decided that its report on reform to the IMF Board of Governors would be completed in June but that implementation of the essential provisions would have to be postponed to a later date. The "Outline of Reform" was submitted in mid-June and was published by the IMF together with several annexes, the reports of various technical groups, and related documents.[11] At that juncture, the Committee of Twenty was dissolved and was succeeded by an Interim Committee of the Fund's Board of Governors with similar membership and with advisory functions.

One may well ask why the Bretton Woods Agreement was negotiated with success while the Committee of Twenty discussions on reform failed. As explained in Chapter 1, Bretton Woods was a quite simple agreement, confining itself to a few ground rules and negotiated by a small group of like-minded countries, with the United States having the decisive voice. Second, the agreement took as the core of the international monetary system an instrument that already existed, namely, the dollar convertible into gold, which commanded universal confidence and acceptance. The instrument did not have to be created by going outside tradition and by acts of faith.

In contrast, the reform discussions of 1972-73 were carried out by a large group of countries with very divergent positions and objectives. On the face of it, the basic purpose seemed to be "stable but adjustable par values." But in fact, the first objective of the United States was an assured adjustment mechanism, while other advanced countries put the priority on convertibility of the dollar, and the developing countries wanted the monetary system to be an engine for increasing economic assistance.

The discussions also were complicated in various respects by the injection of several general notions that reflected dissatisfaction with the previous evolution of the system. One such was that the system should be made more symmetrical—symmetrical as between the dollar and other currencies with regard to asset settlement, and symmetrical as regards the adjustment obligations and policy instruments of surplus and deficit countries. Another notion was that of fairness, which came out in the preference for SDRs as a reserve asset over gold or dollars.

The critical difficulty, however, was that there was not an accepted core on which stable par values could be based. Without gold, the only core left was the dollar. The crux of the discussion revolved around the refusal of many countries formally to accept a dollar system in which the United States was not pledged to discipline. The aim was thereby pushed beyond reform of the system to the creation of an entirely new system, the core of which was the universal acceptance of the SDR. But that effort failed, as it was bound to fail, because such a system, with no roots in accepted practice, could not hope to rally the confidence of all monetary authorities or the general public. By the end, of course, inflation had been let loose on so large a scale that the authorities had no inclination anyhow to consider a return to fixed rates between the dollar and the Common Market snake.

The Common Market Snake

The snake was the outcome of a quite different line of reform to facilitate the adjustment process that had begun to be discussed informally, and largely unofficially, in the early 1960s. Because U.S. opposition to any change in the par value of the dollar was well known, the idea of joint floating by a Common Market bloc of currencies against the dollar and the many currencies in the dollar bloc was talked about informally. Initially, it was considered an arrangement that would be feasible only after monetary integration within the European Economic Community had been achieved. The possibility of a flexible exchange-rate system between two currency blocs had been considered in the 1963 Brookings Report on the U.S. balance of payments.

When the dollar became inconvertible in August 1971, joint floating of the Common Market currencies was proposed by Germany at a meeting of the EEC ministers (see Chapter 6). But it was not accepted at first because the starting point for the fixed cross rates between EEC countries was not considered appropriate by several ministers. France, in particular, was concerned that the franc would float up with the D-Mark. The Belgian and Dutch authorities alone agreed to limit the fluctuations between their currencies to margins of 1.5 percent on either side of the parity.

The Smithsonian realignment, however, set up a new exchange-rate structure, on which a monetary arrangement in the Common Market could be based. The EEC countries felt that the wider margins for market fluctuations against the dollar would allow possible changes in cross rates among their own currencies that could distort the competitive situation in their own agricultural and industrial trade. The band vis-à-vis the dollar of 4.5 percent could allow a change of 9 percent in the relation between any two EEC currencies, apart from the guilder and the Belgian franc. Consequently, in April 1972 the Common Market Council of Ministers adopted a scheme to limit the bands of fluctuation between their own currencies to 2.25 percent. As the band against the dollar for the currencies as a group was 4.5 percent, the arrangement became known as "the snake in the tunnel" (of the dollar). Although the narrower band of the snake was in principle to be maintained primarily by market intervention in the EEC currencies themselves, intervention would be in dollars when a particular EEC currency found itself at the upper or lower limit vis-à-vis the dollar. The debtor positions arising from intervention in snake currencies were to be settled normally at the end of every month. Settlements out of reserves were to be made by pro-rata use of the various assets in the country's total reserves, including gold at its official value. Britain, Denmark, Norway, and Ireland joined the scheme in May 1972.

From the standpoint of stable trade relations, the snake scheme was a constructive reform for the closely interrelated economies of Western Europe. A country's adherence to the snake was dependent on its having sufficient control over inflation to maintain confidence in its competitive position—as would be necessary for adherence to any fixed-rate arrangement. Sterling was the first victim of a loss of confidence. As described earlier, it was sold heavily in mid-June 1972 and was allowed to float against both the snake and the dollar. Denmark withdrew from the snake at the same time but rejoined in October. In addition, Italy was temporarily exempted from the hypothetical obligation to use gold in settlements. With the continued weakness of the lira, Italy also withdrew from the snake in February 1973.

The exchange-market crisis in February 1973, and the failure of the second devaluation of the dollar to stabilize the exchange-rate structure, confronted the Common Market countries with a new situation. Arrangements were made in March for a joint float against the dollar by Belgium, Holland, Germany, France, and Denmark. When the plan began to operate, Norway and Sweden also decided to participate, and Austria later adhered to it informally. A European Monetary Cooperation Fund was established in April and began operating in June to support the arrangement and to facilitate the multilateral settlement of debtor-creditor positions.

The Jamaica Agreement

After the Committee of Twenty had been replaced by the Interim Committee, the objective of a reformed system based on "stable but adjustable par values" was retained for a time. But as the United States had renounced the instruments essential to maintaining a par value, and as it had no confidence that surplus countries would participate actively in the adjustment process, it reached the conclusion in the course of 1975 that its only viable policy was to continue with the floating dollar. Generalizing this insight, it put forth the thesis that the aims of a country's exchange-rate policy were more important than any specific exchange-rate obligation. The principal opposition again came from France, which considered that floating should be reserved for exceptional situations. While some of the other G-10 countries shared the French view, they were unable to devise a practical plan that gave a reasonable assurance of successful operation. Finally, the futility of further wrangling was recognized, and agreement was reached on a radical revision of the IMF Articles at Jamaica in January 1976.

The agreement abolished the obligation of member countries to maintain par values and allowed them to adopt a floating rate or a fixed rate as they saw fit. A par value in gold was prohibited. The way was left open for establishing a general system of par values in the future should conditions make it feasible, but this provision of the agreement was only a diplomatic sop to the French view. Countries were enjoined to cooperate with the IMF to assure orderly exchange rates and to avoid exchange-rate manipulation, while the Fund was given the responsibility to exercise surveillance over exchange-rate policies and to "adopt principles for the guidance of all members with respect to those policies."[12]

The other main provisions of the Jamaica Agreement concerned gold. The official price of gold and the use of gold as a unit of account for declaring the par values of currencies were abolished. So was the use of gold in members' dealings with the Fund. The Fund was to dispose of a third of its gold stock by returning one half of this amount to countries that had paid it in as part of their quota subscriptions and by selling the other half in the market and using the profits (namely, proceeds over and above the previous official book value) to establish a Trust Fund for the benefit of less developed countries. Within the Group of Ten, it was agreed that for a period of two years no effort would be made to peg the market price of gold and that the level of the Group's combined gold stock, together with that of the IMF, would not be increased. Evidently, gold had become the villain of the monetary system, at least to the United States. In place of gold, the unit of account of the system and the unit for expressing par values was to be the SDR. As the valuation of the SDR had been changed from one gold dollar at $35 an ounce to the weighted value of a basket of currencies, any par value that might henceforth be declared would be denominated in a unit that was itself floating.

It has usually been said that the Jamaica Agreement at any rate recognized the situation that had come about in the monetary system. In actual fact, it went a good deal farther. It effectively denied that gold could serve any useful purpose in the system, and it officially enshrined the idea that domestic financial policies should not be constrained by specific international rules with regard to exchange rates.

9

The Floating Dollar and the OPEC Surplus System

After the breakdown of the Smithsonian exchange-rate structure in February 1973, a further devaluation of the dollar failed to stop the exchange turmoil and, in early March, the markets were again closed. When they reopened, the authorities of the European countries whose currencies formed the snake arrangement had agreed, as stated in the previous chapter, to float jointly against the dollar. Since many currencies remained pegged on the dollar, it was in the main a bloc floating system, though some currencies floated independently. The opportunity to observe how this bloc floating would work out under reasonably normal conditions, however, lasted little more than nine months because the international monetary situation was drastically changed by the huge increases in the price of OPEC oil at the end of 1973.

THE FIRST TEST OF FLOATING

At first, fluctuations in the exchange market remained within a narrow range around the rate pattern established by the devaluation of the dollar in February. Some unwinding of oversold dollar positions and abnormal leads and lags in payments more than offset the basic distrust of the dollar; the Bank of Japan sold over $3 billion and the Bundesbank $1 billion in the second quarter of 1973 to finance the reflow of money to the United States. The Swiss National Bank, on the other hand, bought $850 million, even though it allowed the franc to float up about 5 percent. In all, the reflow of money into dollars was quite small relative to the earlier flight out of dollars, an indication that confidence was far from restored.

This initial phase did not last long. Starting in mid-May 1973, the dollar underwent two violent shifts, first down and then up, in the space of seven months. Although the U.S. trade balance was improving significantly, the dollar began to weaken, apparently because the previous corrective process on short-term money flows had run its course. But once started, the dollar's depreciation quickly accelerated following the sharp tightening of monetary policy in Germany. The German authorities seemed to believe that floating had removed the external constraint on the use of monetary weapons to counter inflation, but as confidence in the dollar was still weak, the result was a flight into D-Marks. By the end of June the D-Mark had risen almost 14 percent against the dollar since March. In the process, the other snake currencies were pulled up, obliging the Bundesbank to acquire DM 4.5 billion of the joint float currencies. At the end of June the German authorities revalued the D-Mark in the snake by an additional 5.5 percent. This move did not strengthen confidence in the dollar. On the contrary, the D-Mark continued to climb in a disorderly market. From March to July 6, it showed a cumulative appreciation of 25 percent against the dollar. The rise of the Swiss franc—the other currency into which investors of short-term capital funds were attracted—was even more pronounced. All in all, over this four-month period, the effective exchange rate of the dollar (the weighted average of its exchange rate relative to the currencies of the United States' principal trading partners) declined by almost 9 percent, that is, by the same amount as it had done at the Smithsonian and February 1973 devaluations, even though on this occasion the dollar exchange rates of the currencies of Japan and Canada, the chief trading partners of the United States, had not altered.

The situation was reviewed at the BIS meeting in July, and the governors issued a statement stressing that arrangements were available for official intervention to restore order to the market. The Federal Reserve swap network was increased from $11.7 billion to $18 billion, and the Federal Reserve together with the Bundesbank supported the market with about $600 million during the rest of the month. These exchange-market tactics were reinforced by some easing of monetary policy in Germany and some tightening in the United States.

The dollar thereupon strengthened rapidly during August and again in October, and continued to gain ground until late in January 1974. The market was influenced by the recovery of the U.S. trade balance, which shifted from a deficit of $6.4 billion in 1972 to a surplus of almost $1 billion in 1973. While this direction of change was consistent with the post-Smithsonian depreciation of the dollar, a number of factors other than the exchange rate dominated trade movements. Booming demand abroad gave a strong impetus to exports, and shipments of U.S. farm products rose dramatically as a result of crop failures in various countries. In 1973, exports of agricultural products reached a record $18 billion, after the already high figure of $9.5 billion the year before. On the other hand, U.S. imports increased only moderately following the flood of shipments in 1972. Despite appreciation of the yen, for example, the dollar value of imports from Japan in 1973 was only slightly above the level of the previous year.

However, the major reason for the dollar's strength was the outbreak of war in the Middle East in October, and the beginning of the oil crisis stemming from the OPEC oil export embargo and price rise. The dollar gained because the United States was considered a strong and stable nation in uncertain political conditions and therefore a safe haven in which to maintain funds. In addition, the market assumed that the U.S. payments position would not be so adversely affected by the oil difficulties as those of other industrial countries more dependent on imported oil. The effective exchange rate of the dollar advanced 14.4 percent during this phase from late July 1973 to late January 1974, not only making good the decline of May-July 1973, but also reversing a large part of the February 1973 devaluation. The D-Mark and the Swiss franc declined to about 20 percent below their previous high points in terms of the dollar, and the yen, which had been pegged to the dollar at 265, was allowed to depreciate to 300. (See Figures 2 and 3 at the end of this chapter.)

Thus, within less than a year, the dollar's effective exchange rate first fell and then recovered by about 15 percent. This was exchange-rate flexibility with a vengeance. The market proved unable to establish any kind of lasting equilibrium in exchange rates or even to resist erratic or excessive movements of rates. The risks were simply too great to permit foreign-exchange firms and commercial banks to take large open positions. Central banks were obliged to intervene to keep some order in the market and to try to limit the "follow-the-crowd" behavior invited by floating.

In explaining this condition, E. M. Bernstein[1] has drawn on the concepts of stable and unstable equilibrium, first developed for a single market by Alfred Marshall. Stable equilibrium means that in the face of some temporary disturbance to supply or demand, "there will be instantly brought into play forces tending to push it back to that position." But the dollar exchange market was liable to be in a position of unstable equilibrium, like "an egg . . . balanced on one of its ends [which] would at the smallest shake fall down, and lie lengthways."[2] This case applied to the exchange market because basic payments flows were generally unbalanced, and when the exchange rates moved, large-scale covering and speculation accentuated the fluctuations.

The most damaging impact of the exchange-market turmoil was the strong impetus it gave to inflation and inflationary psychology. This effect was not an inherent consequence of floating but occurred for two reasons: the particular circumstances of the early 1970s and the fact that the dollar was the key currency in the breakdown. In 1970, there had been an outburst of very high wage demands, particularly in Italy, Germany, Britain, and Japan, which continued in the following two years. In most industrial countries, the annual rate of wage increase reached double-digit proportions and in a few was over 20 percent; average pay increases were maintained around the 6 percent level only in the United States. In addition, most countries were pursuing expansionary demand policies. As regards the specific role of the dollar, large increases in some countries' money stocks arose out of the flight from the dollar in 1971-72. Thus, the international economy was in a situation of boom and inflationary pressure.

The monetary breakdown in early 1973 gave a further strong impetus to the inflationary forces; many traders and investors felt that the world economy had become unhinged and that many currencies were unsafe assets to hold. A buying wave for hedging and speculative purposes resulted in a violent upsurge of commodity prices; *The Economist's* and Reuter's indexes, neither of which included oil or gold, almost doubled over the twelve months of 1973. In their post-mortem analysis, "The 1972-75 Commodity Boom,"[3] Richard Cooper and Robert Lawrence concluded that the demand-supply situation could explain only part of this upsurge and that exchange-rate uncertainties accounted for much of the exceptional price rise. A clear indicator of market psychology at the time was the rise in the price of gold from $65 to over $120 an ounce in the first half of 1973. In the autumn, the fever in commodity prices diminished, but it began again after the October oil crisis and continued until demand and output were significantly reduced by the recession of 1974-75. It was in these conditions of soaring commodity prices that the OPEC cartel announced the sharp rise in the price of oil at the end of 1973.

THE OPEC SURPLUS SYSTEM

The boost in the OPEC oil price to four times the pre-October 1973 level imposed a tremendous shock on the international economy. It not only directly affected consumer prices and oil costs in the production process, but it strengthened the inflationary psychology that had already been dominant for several years. In this heated atmosphere, the wage-price spiral accelerated, sometimes via indexation and more generally on expectation of further inflation. Wage increases in 1974 were around 25 percent in Britain, Italy, and Japan and 12 percent or more in other industrial countries. Price increases were of a similar order of magnitude.

In addition, the rise in the oil price helped to bring on a recession in economic activity because it drained off purchasing power to the OPEC countries and caused uncertainties that disrupted spending patterns. There was an obvious effect, for example, on the purchasing of automobiles and other oil-using equipment. The recession deepened as monetary restraint was widely intensified as a means of combating inflation.

Equally important was the fact that OPEC's action profoundly changed the structure of the international monetary system. The world was highly dependent on OPEC oil for its energy requirements, and could not develop substitute sources of energy for a considerable time or reduce its oil imports substantially without intolerable economic disruption. The OPEC countries, on the other hand, were unable, for the time being, to spend a major share of their combined increased revenues on much greater imports. Hence, a disequilibrium of major proportions necessarily remained in the world balance of payments. The international monetary system had formerly operated with a net current-account surplus for all countries combined, equal to the inflow of new gold reserves to the system. Starting in 1974, however, the non-OPEC world had to operate on the basis of an aggregate current-account deficit equal to a huge OPEC surplus.

This net deficit was seen at once to be the dominant feature of the monetary system. A few optimists believed that substitute energy sources for OPEC oil would be developed quickly and that the OPEC cartel would founder as soon as this happened. But the official opinion was that the adjustment period would be long and difficult. In the meantime, there was no alternative to financing the deficit, perhaps partly out of reserves, but mostly by borrowing. This meant that the system required intervention in foreign-exchange markets.

Moreover, the fact that there were floating exchange rates, largely between the dollar bloc and the snake, could not help an overall adjustment of the oil deficit since that deficit had no connection with exchange-rate distortions. If an individual country tried to adjust its own oil deficit by exchange depreciation, it would at best only pass its own deficit on to other oil-importing countries; if many countries indulged in this game, the result probably would be an intensified downward spiral of output and employment.

Various official groups discussed how best to deal with the situation. As early as January 18, 1974, the communiqué of the Committee of Twenty issued at its session in Rome stated:

> They [the members of the committee] recognized that the current account surpluses of the oil-producing countries would be very greatly increased, and that many other countries—both developed and developing—would have to face large current account deficits. In these difficult circumstances the Committee agreed that in managing their international payments countries must not adopt policies which would merely aggravate the problems of other countries. Accordingly, they stressed the importance of avoiding competitive depreciation and the escalation of restrictions on trade and payments . . . They recognized that serious difficulties

would be created for many developing countries and that their needs for financial resources will be greatly increased; and they urged all countries with available resources to make every effort to supply these needs on appropriate terms.

The committee went on to observe: "They also received a report on the Deputies' preliminary discussion of conditions and rules for floating in the reformed system." The first draft contained the statement that, "Members of the Committee recognized that in the present situation the establishment of guidelines for floating would be an important interim step," but it was eliminated in the final text because some countries, including the United States, did not want the IMF staff to embark on such possibly embarrassing policing at that juncture.[4]

The role of official facilities in financing the net oil deficit was discussed at other meetings, particularly in Working Party 3 of the OECD and at the IMF. The result that emerged, against much opposition from weaker deficit countries, was that, in the main, countries would have to rely on their ability to borrow from the private financial system of international banks and bond markets. The critical issue for official lending was not financial soundness, but the sheer political difficulty of assembling a large pool of resources from the limited number of surplus or moderate deficit countries available, and of distributing it on some kind of equitable basis. Due to the persistence of its managing director, the IMF was able to set up the first oil facility in 1974 to help with the financing problem. But most of the financing was undertaken by the international banking system, which began to make loans to sovereign borrowers on an unprecedented scale.

While the global deficit vis-á-vis OPEC had to be accepted for the time being, monetary experts believed that the financing burden would be eased if it were shared among the oil-importing countries, perhaps in proportion to their higher import costs for OPEC oil. The initial international policy line, therefore, was that all countries should eliminate their nonoil deficits and surpluses. However, because of differences among countries in rates of inflation, in adherence to discipline and in success in exporting, the actual nonoil imbalances became larger in the years that followed, and some non-OPEC countries remained in surplus on current account. As before, these surplus countries, such as Japan and Germany, were opposed to any adjustment measures that risked an increasing rate of inflation and, in any case, they believed that the responsibility for adjustment rested with the high-inflation countries.

The U.S. Policy of Nonintervention

In the face of the OPEC surplus, monetary authorities generally accepted that they would have to intervene in the exchange market to finance their oil deficits and to manage their balances of payments so as to minimize nonoil deficits and surpluses. Moreover, the experience of 1973 had shown that official intervention would be required to maintain an orderly exchange market and prevent bandwagon pressures on exchange rates. The United States, however, was reluctant to assume responsibility for its own balance of payments or the movement of the dollar in the exchange market. With reference to an earlier period, Guillaume Guindey, formerly general manager of the BIS, commented that "the partners of the United States, at the very moment they engaged in the enterprise of the International Monetary Fund, had to wonder whether the Americans really acepted that the rules of the game should apply to themselves."[5] The same doubt arose again with respect to managed floating under the OPEC surplus system.

The reason that the United States could even contemplate nonintervention as a policy was that the dollar was still, by common practice, the reserve currency of the system. The U.S. oil deficit, which was to increase by $16 billion in 1974, would automatically be financed so long as OPEC accumulated its surplus in dollars. Other countries in deficit could not contemplate nonintervention since their currencies would certainly have foundered in the exchange market, setting off a depreciation-inflation spiral.

An important influence on U.S. policy was the reaction in Washington to the earlier years of turmoil, which left the authorities fed up with the external monetary and payments problem. The heavy U.S. use of swaps and other credits to hold off the breakdown of 1971 had involved significant losses after the dollar was devalued. The support operations were criticized at that time, and officials were reluctant to engage in new support of the dollar that would be dependent on large-scale borrowing of foreign currency.

A great complication in supporting the dollar, of course, was the fact that the United States had virtually no usable reserves. It was incensed about the whole problem of gold and opposed to any ad hoc arrangement that could have made gold reserves usable; in fact, it really wanted to exclude gold entirely from official settlements, as soon became evident.[6]

This passive attitude to the exchange markets took an absurd turn in October-November 1973, when the dollar was rapidly appreciating. At a meeting of the governors in Basel, the Bundesbank urged the United States to buy D-Marks in the market so as to hold the dollar down and prevent erosion of the gain in the U.S. competitive position achieved by the February devaluation. This suggestion was very sensible because the devaluation obviously had been necessary. The New York Federal Reserve Bank favored such action, and would have been happy to accumulate a stock of D-Marks against future needs, but the Treasury in Washington refused to budge.

In the uncertain state of the balance of payments and the dollar exchange market, Secretary Shultz announced in late January 1974 that all controls on U.S. capital exports were removed. This objective had been stated several times before, even by Connally. It had been said that the political pressure for decontrol was difficult to resist and that the controls were not effective because ways around them were easy to find. Certainly, the controls would have had to be adapted to the need for recycling any excess of the OPEC surplus placed in the New York money market. But the complete abolition of controls on all money and capital outflows was an extreme measure. It rested on the faith that free floating would reflect underlying forces and solve the external problems of the dollar. If the defenders of the dollar suffered a defeat when convertibility was suspended in August 1971, abolition of capital export controls in January 1974 demobilized the army. But it turned out that the war was not over.

THE SLIDE OF THE DOLLAR

The dollar began to decline immediately after the removal of capital export controls, and by October 1975 had been subject to four large swings. Both domestic and external forces lay behind these swings in a combination difficult to disentangle, but the bandwagon exchange-market psychology was a force in itself—as it had been in 1973.

Even though industrial output in the United States began to fall with the announcement of the OPEC oil price advance, wages and prices increased sharply throughout 1974, narrowing the gap between U.S. and other countries' inflation rates. A high wage award to end the strike in the coal-mining industry set the tone; average hourly earnings rose 12 percent in the course of the year—about double the rate in 1973. Spurred on by higher costs and expectations of more to come, wholesale industrial goods prices soared by 20 percent while consumer prices advanced at about the same rate as wages. The Federal Reserve imposed severe monetary restraint to break the grip of the inflationary psychology, sending short-term interest rates up into double figures. Finally, output declined sharply from October 1974 to April 1975, bringing the economy its deepest recession of the postwar period: from 5.1 percent of the labor force in the first half of 1974, unemployment rose to an average of 8.5 percent in 1975.

With respect to the balance of payments, the gain of 10 percent in the quantity of exports in 1974 exploded to almost 40 percent in value because of higher prices. But higher prices abroad, in particular the price of oil, sent up the value of imports even more, despite a small decline in volume. Hence, the trade balance went into substantial deficit, and the current-account balance worsened by $4 billion. On capital account, meanwhile, the rest of the oil-importing world's huge financing needs induced a vast outflow of both short- and long-term funds from the United States, particularly through the banks. These outflows substantially exceeded the autonomous foreign placement of dollars in the U.S. market. The deficit on official reserve transactions amounted to $8.3 billion.

The payments situation was drastically reversed by the major recession in the following year. As the recession came more slowly in some other industrial countries, U.S. exports in 1975 increased by a further 10 percent. But imports fell in both volume and value so that the trade balance moved into a surplus of $9 billion and the current account to a surplus of $12 billion. This current surplus, however, was once again more than offset by capital outflows, mainly through the banks, so that official reserve transactions showed a deficit of $3.5 billion.

In the exchange market, the dollar depreciated about 16 percent against the snake currencies from late January to early May 1974. On a trade-weighted basis, it fell more than 10 percent. The movement then reversed itself, and the dollar rose about 8 percent against the European snake over the summer. U.S. monetary policy was very tight in these months, and the failure of the Herstatt Bank in Germany weakened the D-Mark. In the autumn, a fresh decline of the dollar began, and over the next six months, its depreciation against the snake currencies was again about 14 percent, despite U.S. intervention of more than $1 billion to support the currency. As the large U.S. surpluses on trade and current account emerged in 1975, the course of the dollar was again reversed: between April and September, it appreciated against the snake by about 15 percent, particularly in the third quarter, almost coming back to the exchange rates of March 1973. The Swiss franc alone maintained a large appreciation over the dollar. These exchange-rate swings cannot be explained simply by underlying economic conditions. Speculative attitudes and feelings were a major factor that not only exaggerated the movements but helped to cause them.

Wider Currency Disturbances

In 1976 the scene of violent exchange-rate movements switched to Europe. After having been subjected to very large budget deficits and to wage increases of some 45 percent in two years, first the lira and then sterling depreciated abruptly. Between January and April 1976, the lira dropped against the dollar from around 690 to 915, as the virtual exhaustion of reserves forced an end to the previous policy of maintaining almost rigid stability in the rate. Strong measures were taken in May to bolster the currency. Purchasers of foreign currency were required to deposit 50 percent of the equivalent in lira at the Bank of Italy, and export earnings had to be converted within seven days. The lira recovered about 10 percent during the summer but tailed off again later in the year, after which an anti-inflation program allowed stabilization of the exchange rate.

Massive pressure against sterling, including a large reduction of sterling balances of OPEC countries, sent the pound down from more than $2.00 at the beginning of March 1976 to $1.70 in early June. The decline, originally triggered by official selling of sterling in the exchange market, was halted during the summer with the help of a short-term credit facility of over $5 billion from the Group of Ten central banks and the BIS. At the end of October, despite cumulative exchange-market intervention totaling $6 billion since March, and despite increases in the Bank of England's minimum lending rate to 15 percent, the dollar rate of the pound was down to $1.55. It was time for a strong stabilization effort, which was put together with the help of a firm stand by the IMF on reducing the budget deficit substantially and on setting definite limits to the expansion of bank credit. At the same time, a Third Group Arrangement was set up to assist sterling, although without much enthusiasm, by the major central banks and the BIS to provide resources of $5 billion. Sterling rebounded to $1.70 in the last quarter and was held around that rate in the first half of 1977 in the face of a large reflow of money to London, as the authorities took in dollars to recoup earlier reserve losses.

Rapid wage-price inflation in France also caused confidence in the franc to deteriorate in the first months of 1976 and the trade account to shift into substantial deficit. After the reserves had been drawn down by $3 billion, the franc was detached from the European snake in mid-March and allowed to depreciate gradually until July; its decline against the dollar was about 5 percent. In the face of demands for increased wages, profit margins, and prices from many organized groups, prices and wages were subjected to direct controls. From the autumn on, the authorities were able to hold the franc stable in terms of the dollar.

While these upsets to other currencies were going on, the dollar itself remained much steadier than in the previous two years. Its exchange rate on a trade-weighted basis held within narrow limits, with the help of moderate intervention by the Federal Reserve, from the last quarter of 1975 up to the spring of 1977. Against the snake currencies, however, the dollar depreciated about 8 percent, all in the second half of 1976, so that the stability of the dollar really resulted from averaging the weak and the strong currencies on either side of it.

The seesaw of a gain in the balance of payments combined with a slump in domestic activity was, however, in the process of tilting the other way. As early as the second quarter of 1975, the inventory cycle in the United States began to reverse itself and a strong economic recovery occurred in 1976. On the external side, the trade balance swung from a $9 billion surplus in 1975 to a deficit of the same size in 1976. In the face of slower economic expansion abroad, U.S. exports increased only $7.6 billion whereas imports jumped $26 billion. While imports of oil, at its high price, accounted for $7.6 billion of this increase, the percentage rise of other imports was equally large, particularly industrial materials and automobiles and other consumer goods. Thanks mainly to increased investment income, the deterioration of the current-account balance was less severe; the surplus of $11.5 billion in 1975 shifted to a deficit of $1.4 billion in the following year. With continued large capital outflow, much of it channeled through the Euromarket and the Caribbean branches of U.S. banks, the U.S. official settlements deficit amounted to $8.7 billion, largely matched by the increase of $7.6 billion in the net foreign claims of the banks. No doubt the government was concerned about the turn of events, but the only action it took was to implement a recommended change in the presentation of the balance-of-payments statistics, eliminating any idea of an overall balance and permitting each analyst to choose whatever he considered to be a meaningful measure.[8]

The Carter Administration

At the start of 1977, a new administration under President Carter came into office. It aimed to promote economic expansion and to reduce unemployment, without much concern for the external deficit. While the main stimulative measures it first proposed in the budget did not find favor with Congress and were withdrawn in May, the economy continued to respond to active business investment and consumer buying. Unemployment dropped from 7.8 percent in December 1976 to 6.4 percent a year later, even though the total deficit of the government sector, on a national accounts basis, actually declined for the year.

The impact on the external accounts came quickly. Imports rose sharply in the first quarter of 1977 while exports were stagnating; the trade deficit increased to $7.1 billion from $3.6 billion in the last quarter of the previous year. With exports remaining on a plateau of about $30 billion a quarter and imports rising further, the trade deficit reached $31 billion for the year, against $9.4 billion in 1976. This huge deterioration may be accounted for in part by lagging recovery abroad and perhaps by some weakening of the competitive position of U.S. industrial goods. In addition, the usual lag of six months or more in the adjustment of trade flows to the depreciation of the dollar was a factor in 1977. But from a broader perspective, the turnaround in the U.S. trade balance pointed to the fact that the rest of the world could not support a trade deficit vis-à-vis the United States on top of its deficit toward OPEC. With many countries' balances of payments under pressure from the OPEC surplus, and with consumer price inflation continuing at average rates of 8 percent or more in the OECD area, trade flows seemed to have become less sensitive to the relative price changes resulting from exchange-rate movements.

The response of total U.S. imports to increases in the GNP was substantially magnified after 1973 by the combination of higher oil prices and the increased share of the U.S. economy's oil needs being met from imports. But even nonoil imports retained the higher income elasticity that had come about in the years of the Vietnam inflation (see Figure 1). Foreign goods found ready buyers in the U.S. market, and in a lagging recovery, foreign producers made special efforts to use spare capacity by exporting to the United States, in some cases as a matter of national policy. On the other hand, U.S. exports were adversely affected by the adjustment programs of countries in large deficit, by the tightening of import controls in countries short of foreign exchange,[9] and even by the resistance of the private business community, in some instances, to competition from cheaper American goods. American firms with substantial production facilities abroad did not readily push exports from the United States to the detriment of their foreign output. Trade practices in many countries were affected by high unemployment and by heavy foreign borrowing that entailed a much increased debt-servicing burden on the balance of payments.

In Washington, the failure of U.S. exports to rise was attributed to slow economic growth abroad and to the stronger competitive position of foreign industrial goods at the exchange rates prevailing in the spring of 1977. As the administration did not consider a slowdown in U.S. recovery to be an appropriate policy, it believed that an adjustment process should be brought about by the surplus industrial countries applying greater stimulus to economic expansion and allowing exchange-rate appreciation to reduce the strength of their competitive position. These measures would tend to increase imports and to decrease exports of the surplus countries and thereby help reduce the deficits of other countries, including that of the United States. U.S. officials, notably secretary of the treasury Blumenthal, called upon Germany and Japan to lead the way.

Finance ministers of the OECD issued a communiqué in late June 1977, which stated that surplus countries were "ready to see a weakening of their current account positions and an appreciation of their currencies in response to underlying market forces." Secretary Blumenthal said in July that he was perfectly prepared for the dollar to depreciate further; he would like to see free floating and would allow the dollar exchange rate, vis-à-vis the yen and the D-Mark, to settle down wherever market forces might take it. "Whether or not that point has been reached, time will tell, and I would be quite happy to live with whatever the result is."[10]

Heavy Selling of Dollars

The exchange market readily understood that appreciation of strong currencies meant depreciation of the dollar, and starting in mid-June 1977,

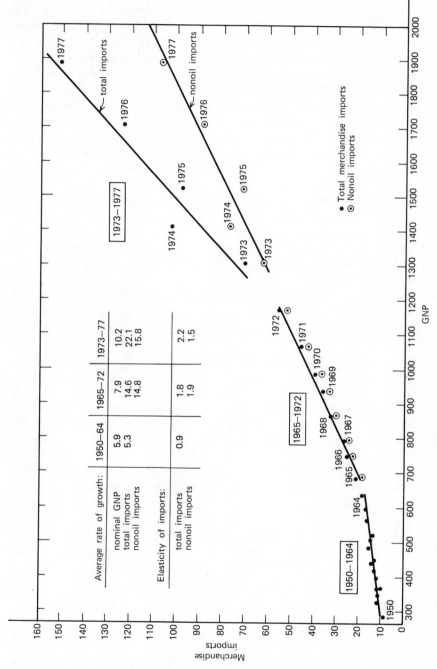

Figure 1. United States gross national product and merchandise imports (in billions of current U.S. dollars).

there was heavy selling of dollars for about a month. The yen, which had already gone up about 5 percent in the first quarter, rose a further 3 percent, while the D-Mark and Swiss franc gained about 4 percent. After heavy buying of dollars by the Japanese, German, and Swiss central banks, and U.S. statements affirming the importance of a strong dollar, the slide of the dollar petered out and partially reversed itself. But confidence, which was still a critical factor in the system of managed floating, had been badly shaken. It was not customary for a finance minister to speak openly about exchange rates in a way that implied his own currency should depreciate.

The tactic of stimulating the economy had no appeal for the German authorities, who had been opposing this advice more strongly than ever since the bulge of exports in 1974. The budget deficit was already large, and keeping a check on the money supply was a continuous problem because of the inflow of funds from abroad. Having gotten control over two-digit inflation, the authorities did not want to risk starting it up again. At the same time, in such major European countries as Britain, Italy, and France, the direction of policy was toward restraint in an effort to reduce the rate of inflation and keep a hold over the balance of payments.

In the autumn of 1977, with the huge U.S. trade deficit continuing, a new wave of dollar selling began, on a larger scale than in June-July. Secretary Blumenthal at the IMF annual meeting estimated the current-account deficit for 1977 at $16-20 billion, and private forecasts indicated a larger deficit in the coming year. The administration's energy program was stalled in Congress, and little action was likely before the congressional elections in 1978. In addition, the official line was that intervention in the exchange market would be limited to counteracting disorderly conditions, but not to resisting underlying economic forces. The widespread belief was that the United States wanted the dollar to depreciate. Over the winter, the condition of the market verged at times on panic. Many investors had been and were unloading portfolios of dollar securities, the leads and lags in payments were very adverse to the dollar, and indeed, its slide had become an underlying economic force.

In the fourth quarter of 1977, the dollar fell against all the principal currencies except the Canadian dollar and the Swedish krona despite large buying of dollars by the main central banks and $800 million of intervention in D-Marks by the Federal Reserve, drawn on the swap line with the Bundesbank. A striking feature of the situation was the decision of the Bundesbank to intervene in the dollar exchange market on a large scale for the first time since March 1973. The increase in the gross monetary reserves of the Group of Ten countries in the fourth quarter came to $20 billion. Despite this, the decline of the dollar in the fourth quarter amounted to 7 percent on a trade-weighted basis, to 10 percent against the D-Mark and the yen, and to 15 percent against the Swiss franc. Although U.S. officials, including the president, were seriously concerned by this time, they seemed unable to gird themselves to take strong moves to manage the floating dollar. In a sorcerer's-apprentice kind of situation, the disorderly fall of the dollar continued in 1978.

The widely held belief in the exchange market was that the large U.S. trade deficit implied a fall in dollar exchange rates. In these circumstances, the extent to which central banks, including the Federal Reserve, were prepared to buy the volume of dollars offered in the market against creation of the currencies being demanded was of crucial importance. As the flight from the dollar built up, and the United States showed itself unwilling to share the responsibility for full-scale intervention, other major central banks limited their own intervention and allowed dollar exchange rates to fall. In fact, the selling pressure was even intensified by some central banks switching exchange reserves out of dollars.

While the United States intervened to some extent against disorderly market conditions, it did not keep to its pledge of preventing them, and it repurchased the foreign currencies whenever there was a let-up in the market pressure. The U.S. authorities were also ambivalent about the concept of allowing the exchange rate to reflect underlying economic forces. They were not prepared to say at what dollar rate this condition would be satisfied or to arrange full support for the dollar at any such rate. In practice, the United States considered unrestricted capital outflows and the banks' foreign lending to be underlying economic forces, whereas the other principal countries conceived of underlying forces more in terms of current-account transactions.

International monetary cooperation deteriorated in the face of these differences in viewpoint. In its annual report issued in January 1978, the Council of Economic Advisors, while noting that "rate changes have sometimes led to actual changes in underlying variables" and that "rates are buffeted by the flow of commercial transactions and buy and sell orders of traders whose time horizon is measured in days or at most weeks," concluded that "the evolution of the system of market-determined exchange rates has been a major achievement of this decade." What else could it say?[9]

Growing Criticism of Free Floating

But more generally, there was growing criticism of the behavior of the floating-rate system both at home and abroad. In Europe, the complaint centered on the unwillingness of the United States to share adequately in intervention to control the sharp decline of the dollar. In the United States, the complaint centered more on the failure of the floating-rate system to induce adequate adjustment of large current-account surpluses and deficits, particularly the U.S. deficit. Although the large increase in the trade deficit since the start of 1977 was extraordinary, it was not inherent in a system of managed floating exchange rates. Rather, it can be attributed to the behavior of other oil-importing countries faced with added demands on the balance of payments arising from the OPEC surplus.

As already remarked, the oil-importing countries were involved in a negative-sum game, the negative sum being their aggregate current-account deficit with OPEC. With many other oil-importing countries struggling to limit the growth of their external indebtedness, an exceptional share of the aggregate deficit gravitated to the United States. A persistent basic deficit of the United States had been a feature of international payments for the previous two decades; with the added impact of the oil disequilibrium, it had become difficult for the United States to avoid a deficit even on visible trade. Nor was the temporary disappearance of the OPEC surplus in 1978 sufficient to alter this fundamental tendency in the international system.

However that may be, the situation was aggravated by the fact that the United States gave up all efforts toward a balance-of-payments program. In the OPEC-surplus condition of the system, which demanded deliberate financing of deficits, the United States more or less gave up intervention in the market. Capital-export controls had been dropped at a time when many other countries were eager to indulge in excessive borrowing, while attempts to secure economies in oil imports were hampered by domestic political opposition. The order of the day was to leave the adjustment process to the exchange market in the belief that depreciation of the currency would strengthen the trade balance and that surplus countries would in any event hold their reserve gains in dollars. Thus, the dollar went down after the middle of 1977 because the U.S. authorities wanted it to go down.

As criticism of the free-floating policy mounted from late 1977 onward, statements alleging the administration's concern over the decline of the dollar began to come out of Washington, even from the president. But the Treasury apparently continued to believe that the market would find its own floor for the dollar and that a further dose of depreciation would start a process of substantial balance-of-payments adjustment. Such optimism was misplaced. It ignored not only the obstacles to trade adjustment mentioned above, but also the fact that the decline of the dollar intensified the inflationary psychology inside the United States. The 1978 report of the Council of Economic Advisors noted that the effect of depreciation of the dollar on the cost-of-living index, through the rise of import prices, was fairly moderate. But it overlooked the impact on the price of import-competing U.S. products, and also took no account of the effects of the flight from money into real assets, like housing, or of the widespread fear that the drop in the dollar was a reflection of inflation, against which large wage demands and other compensatory and protective actions were justified. In short, the notion that a favorable shift of the trade balance to match a deficit on capital account would be brought about by a fall of the exchange rate did not apply to a situation in which there was a full-scale flight from the dollar.

After the long strike in the coal-mining industry was finally settled in January 1978 by a 13 percent wage increase, despite President Carter's plea for moderation, the exchange market was convinced that the year would be one of high inflation, and the heavy selling of dollars continued. On the basis of comparative prices, the dollar clearly became undervalued against the strong currencies, but the consequence was to accelerate inflation rather than to adjust the deficit/surplus positions in international payments. Under the fixed-rate system, the priority in national policies had to be shifted at times from measures prompting domestic expansion to those aimed at controlling inflation and the external balance. Experience in 1977-78 showed that floating did not provide the dollar with an escape from the clash of domestic objectives with external necessities. Indeed, compared with the position under the gold-dollar system, the clash for the United States was intensified in some respects.

In August 1978, President Carter asked Secretary Blumenthal and Federal Reserve Chairman G. William Miller to prepare a program to help the dollar. But very little came of it because the authorities were cautious about slowing down the economy and were not prepared for full-scale intervention in the exchange market to put a floor under the currency. Chairman Miller, while contending that the dollar was undervalued on the basis of fundamental factors, said that the government was not going to "start using sledge-hammers." Apparently the sledgehammers were to be left to the market to use. In fact, the dollar was so flat that it looked as if the bear attack had been with a piledriver. By the end of October, the D-Mark had risen to 1.74 against the dollar, the yen to 177, and gold to nearly $245.

Gold Hoarding and Speculation

The gold market, for its part, had become gradually more volatile ever since the crumbling of the Smithsonian exchange-rate structure five and a half years before. As the February 1973 crisis of the dollar approached, investment and speculative demand for gold increased sharply and pushed the market price to nearly $90. With the weakness of the dollar in mid-year, the price reached a new peak of $127. It then drifted downward until after the outbreak of the Middle East crisis in the autumn. A strong new buying wave struck the market in late November, and by February 1974, the price had doubled to reach $185. (See Figure 4, page 230.)

As gold no longer had any official standing in the United States, there were demands to restore the freedom of American citizens and residents to buy and own gold. The secretary of the treasury gave his support to this idea in May 1974, and legislation was soon enacted to allow private gold trading at the start of the following year. The price of gold had been falling prior to this legislation, but now the market anticipated large American demand, and the price went up to almost $200 at the end of 1974. Shortly before that, the U.S. Treasury had announced that it would sell moderate amounts of gold by auction—partly to limit U.S. imports of the metal and partly as a step toward its ultimate aim of ending the official monetary role of gold. In the event, there was no rush by Americans to buy gold in the months after they regained legal freedom to do so, and the price weakened. At the first Treasury auction on January 6, 1975, only 23 out of the 62 tons offered were actually sold, at prices ranging from $153 to $185 per ounce. Americans with an interest in gold had already found ways of participating in the price rise of the metal through one dodge or another, and it had been quite legal for them to buy shares in foreign gold-mining companies.

Between the end of 1974 and late August 1976, the gold price declined sharply to $103. The greater part of this fall took place in the twelve months beginning in September 1975, under the impact of the IMF Interim Committee's Agreement (see Chapter 8) to eliminate gold from the IMF articles and to auction off one-sixth of the Fund's gold stock, or about 778 tons, over a four-year period. Forward selling by speculators contributed to pushing the price down. Then followed a rapid reversal that at first owed much to the covering of short positions taken up in previous months, but was subsequently sustained by heavy buying from the Middle and Far East and wider investment demands as the U.S. trade deficit increased in 1977. The gold price reached $153 in late March 1977, before dipping to a little under $140 in June. Thereafter the flight from the dollar gathered momentum and the gold price in dollars (though not in other currencies) resumed a strong upward trend. In July 1978, it passed the previous peak of just under $200 and at the end of October exceeded $240, despite an increase in market supplies from 1,140 tons in 1975 to 1,755 tons in 1978. Although Western gold production was quite flat, the market was fed by a large rise in Soviet sales, as well as by IMF and U.S. Treasury gold auctions.

The End of Free Floating

On November 1, 1978, the U.S. authorities took a real plunge. It was announced that a $30 billion package of foreign-currency resources had been put together to provide support for the dollar. Germany, Japan, and Switzerland would be sharing in the stabilizing operations. In addition, the Federal Reserve raised the discount rate by 1 percent to 9.5 percent and increased reserve requirements applying to large time deposits, both measures of monetary restraint aimed at dampening inflation and attracting funds to the United States. While commitments about future intervention policy were left indefinite, it was emphasized that for the next few months the dollar would not be allowed to depreciate freely.

It was an end to official faith in free floating and also to the belief that domestic expansion could be allowed to run on in the face of the rapid depreciation of the currency. Inflation was said to have become the number-one problem but the restrictive monetary policy also meant restraint on economic activity. The need for these changes in policy could have been recognized about a year earlier, when the Bundesbank decided to resume large-scale market intervention in dollars. Delaying the change only added to the inflationary atmosphere, as was apparent from the large increase in the OPEC oil price at the end of 1978. The delay also meant that much larger intervention was needed to bring some stability to the exchange market.

Thus, an analytical description of events that began with the introduction of free floating ends with the authorities having to give it up. What the new policy conspicuously lacked, however, was any measure directly aimed at reducing the balance-of-payments deficit, apart from what an economic slowdown or recession might produce.

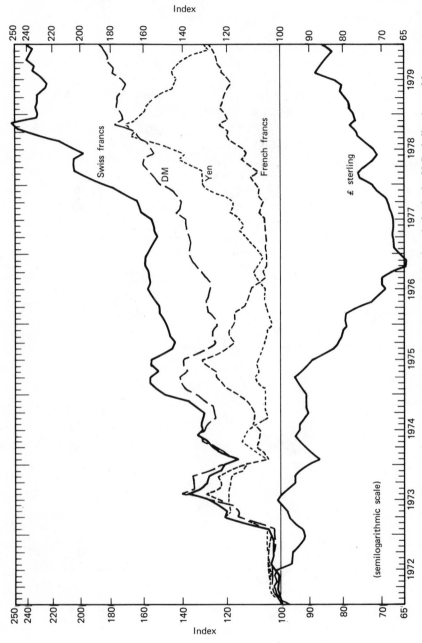

Figure 2. Nominal exchange rates: spot quotations for selected currencies vis-à-vis the U.S. dollar (monthly averages; indices: December 21, 1971 = 100).

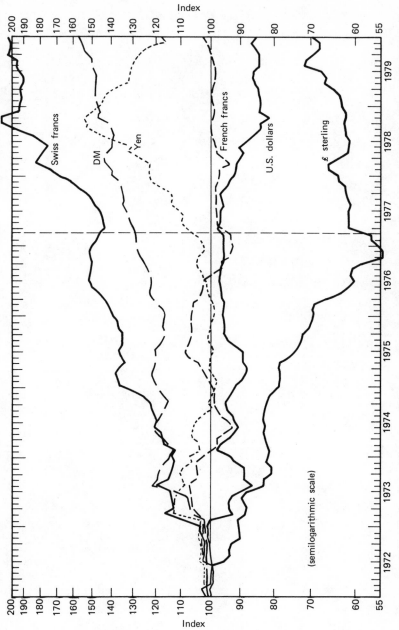

Figure 3. Effective post-Smithsonian exchange rates (monthly averages; indices: December 21, 1971 = 100). Dashed vertical line indicates break in data: as of March 1977 the series was put on a new basis by extending the coverage from 11 to 21 currencies and updating the trade weights from 1969 to 1972. (Source: Bank of England)

211

Part IV

10

Summary
and Conclusion

This account of international monetary developments from the end of World War II to the mid-1970s has focused on the adjustment process that was necessary to meet the balance-of-payments difficulties encountered by a number of industrial countries and to manage the evolving disequilibrium in the international monetary system. Adjustment measures undertaken have been surveyed to permit appraisal of their efficacy. Experience has shown that successful adjustment cannot come merely from good intentions or the pronouncement of desirable goals; appropriate policies have to be designed to meet a particular situation, and these policies must be reinforced by sufficient political will to carry them out.

Gold and the Breakdown of Fixed Rates

The major industrial countries of the West set themselves three basic economic objectives: sufficient growth to maintain high employment, reasonable price stability, and balance-of-payments equilibrium. During a long stretch of the postwar period, they managed a rapid rate of economic growth and high employment. Despite persistent inflationary tendencies, prices, until the late 1960s, were also held in reasonable check. Given the political tensions, wars, and social conflicts of the period, the record was reasonably good. As for the balance of payments, even here severe difficulties were encountered by only a few countries; nevertheless, official policy management failed, and this failure was reflected in the breakdown of the international monetary system hinging on the dollar.

Various rationales were developed to shift responsibility for the failure and to explain it away. The most bizarre notion, supported even by U.S. secretary of the treasury William Simon, was that the United States could not undertake an adjustment process because the dollar was "locked in" by the

Bretton Woods Agreement. This thesis was maintained even though Secretary Connally had refused to accept the IMF's own proposal to devalue the dollar when the dollar was declared inconvertible in August 1971. Other countries indulged in the myth that the adjustment process for the dollar was the same as it was for their currencies, even though these same countries then protested against the belated adjustment sought by the United States in the Smithsonian negotiations. It is important to clear the air of such pretenses because they hide certain vital characteristics of the monetary system that remain of relevance to the problems of the 1980s.

The gold-dollar system formalized at Bretton Woods functioned, in fact, on the basis of the dollar. Only the United States attempted to maintain its currency directly convertible into gold. Other countries maintained their par values by pegging their currencies to the dollar, and accepted the dollar without question as a reserve asset because of its gold convertibility and because the United States allowed free placement of foreign funds in the New York money market. Thus, the dollar had a unique role in the system, and as a result, the conception of equilibrium applicable to it and the adjustment process it might require were also unique.

Two conditions were necessary for efficient operation of the system. First, maintenance of liberal trade and payments practices required that the volume of official reserves expand in a reasonable relationship to that of international transactions. This condition was met chiefly by a U.S. payments deficit that supplied dollars for the growth of reserves in order to supplement the modest inflow of new monetary gold. Without the U.S. deficit, the competitive struggle of other countries for an acceptable balance in external payments would have been too intense to permit the simultaneous maintenance of fixed rates, liberal external trade and payments practices, and the growth of transactions. Hence, other countries had a stake in the U.S. deficit and in part determined it.

The second condition was the maintenance of harmony between gold and dollars, the two principal reserve assets of the system. A substantial margin of gold production over and above the amount purchased by private buyers was necessary for the United States to secure, with appropriate monetary discipline, a growth in its gold reserves sufficient to support the rise of its foreign official dollar liabilities. Without this condition, the gold convertibility of the dollar was bound eventually to be called in question. Because of the inflation during World War II and the transition period immediately following, this condition could not be met with gold at a price of $35 an ounce. However, the United States started with huge gold reserves, enabling the system to work reasonably well for quite a few years.

Following the widespread devaluations against the dollar in 1949 and the subsequent expansion of the export potential of other countries, the United

States began in the late 1950s to lose reserves to nations that traditionally held part of their reserves in gold. The eruption of the market price of gold in 1960 was a clear signal that the United States was being squeezed between the continuous rise of its dollar liabilities to foreign official institutions and the shortage of new gold available for reserves. Thus, a rise in the official price of gold was becoming essential for the United States to maintain adequate gold reserves.

It is necessary to reemphasize that a persistent U.S. deficit was, within certain limits, a characteristic of the system and required a different policy approach from the payments deficits of other countries. This state of affairs arose because the rest of the world taken as a whole considered a reasonable surplus on external payments to be a normal equilibrium feature of their economies. The years 1961-65 showed that, for the United States, strengthening the trade balance and holding back inflation were not enough to end the external deficit and gold losses. As a result, controls were put on U.S. capital exports; these worked to some extent, but could not overcome the need of the system for rising reserves. A significant devaluation of the dollar relative to other currencies was not an alternative to a substantial increase in the gold price, because there were just not enough countries with large surpluses to devalue against. Even at the time of the Smithsonian negotiation, the dollar deficit could not have been eliminated simply by exchange-rate adjustments. Attempts to fine-tune the exchange-rate structure could not work because a low rate of reserve growth would have soon brought the Triffin dilemma to the surface and led to devaluations of other currencies and reemergence of a U.S. deficit. If the deficit had not come on capital account, it would have come on trade account, because a dollar shortage would have led to additional trade restrictions or devaluations in the rest of the world.

The possibility that raising the gold price would be necessary was foreseen at the time of Bretton Woods—the IMF Articles of Agreement provided for such a rise. Although the United States had, in practice, full power over the official gold price, it shied away from use of this obvious adjustment mechanism. Its refusal was not the result of objections by other countries or because Congress stood in the way—the president could have readily created a situation that would have overcome any such obstacles. Nor was the lack of action caused by blind misunderstanding.

Rather, the U.S. position crystallized as a result of short-term reactions to specific political situations, both domestic and international. Attention first focused sharply on the issue when the market price broke loose during the election campaign of 1960. Kennedy, in the heat of the campaign, felt obliged to pledge that he would not raise the price of gold if elected, and he reaffirmed this pledge when he became president. His narrow election victory made him wary of any monetary experiments that would create political controversy.

When French policy on the composition of reserves was moved further in favor of gold during Johnson's administration, the United States converted the dollars offered by France into gold without protest, although the ultimate consequence for the dollar's convertibility into gold at $35 an ounce was evident. Following de Gaulle's open advocacy of a return to the gold standard, U.S. policy on the $35 price of gold became rigid. Somehow, official pride was concentrated on maintaining the existing price of gold rather than on maintaining the gold reserves at Fort Knox.

An adequate adjustment of the gold price would have stopped U.S. gold losses and led to an increase in its reserves, but the idea of such an adjustment encountered many hostile arguments. For example, one objection held that a rise in the price would not work because it would increase both official and private demand for gold. It was an argument in reverse logic. The United States was losing gold because the price was too low. Demand for gold would be increased by a price rise only if the rise was so small as to generate expectations of a further increase in the foreseeable future. In the absence of such expectations, a higher price would induce a shift of reserve preferences away from gold and, by enlarging the annual inflow of new monetary gold to the system, would lessen pressure on the U.S. international liquidity position to act as a net supplier of reserves to the rest of the world.

Another argument was that Russia and South Africa, as the chief producing countries, would be the main beneficiaries of the increased price of gold. But this was at best a matter of postponement. Holding down the official price could not indefinitely freeze the market price so that, in the end, Russia and South Africa were able to market their gold very favorably, while the United States was the main loser. Still another argument claimed that raising the price of gold would break faith with the countries holding dollar reserves. But dollar reserves earned interest for the countries holding them, and the United States was not obliged to give a gold guarantee on dollar holdings in addition to paying interest. A central-bank governor naive enough to believe he could enjoy the best of both worlds was in the wrong job.

Officials who made up such arguments were not cynics: they were taken in by their own propaganda. In the end, the United States professed to believe that gold was an outmoded form of reserves and that the discipline of gold was unnecessary. This attitude neglected the fact that to millions of people in the world confidence in the dollar was bound up with its gold convertibility. More important, it neglected the fact that increasing liabilities alone had never exerted much discipline on the United States. It was amazing that when a conservative Republican administration took office in 1969 it followed the same line of policy against adjustment and allowed the system to break down instead. Gold was only a constitutional monarch in the monetary system, but that did not save it from the guillotine.

A favorite contention is that raising the gold price would not have brought a permanent solution—as if there could be such a thing!—because the trouble would have arisen again with the inflation of the 1970s. It is specious reasoning. For one thing, the 1970s would not have thrown up the same problems if effective adjustment had been achieved in the 1960s and if the huge increases in the world money supply that originated in the flight from the dollar had not been let loose. But more fundamentally, it cannot be right to excuse the political interference with sound adjustment policy toward the growing monetary crisis in the 1960s by pointing to the possibility that such policy would have been ineffective in the face of a different set of problems that were not yet even known about. Such apologetics merely help to strengthen the tendency to give way to political expediency when new problems arise, as happened in the oil crisis. No doubt, the stability of the monetary system could not have been so dependent on unrestricted gold convertibility of the dollar forever. But countries should have been weaned away from gold slowly, not under crisis conditions with the dollar itself in fundamental disequilibrium.

The breakdown of the system has been frequently attributed to widespread and persistent rigidity of exchange rates in the face of fundamental disequilibrium. But the only two major currencies experiencing large and persistent deficits were sterling and the dollar. Britain was able to delay adjustment only because the United States provided heavy support for the pound in order to avert a crisis in the gold market. In 1949, the United States was able to urge devaluation of sterling because its own gold position was strong; by 1964, however, the United States feared a similarly necessary devaluation of the pound because U.S. gold reserves had dwindled. In the case of the dollar, where the devaluation relative to other currencies had in any case to be selective, no feasible devaluation could have been successful without a large rise in the price of gold. This was demonstrated by the selective—and unsuccessful—devaluations of the dollar in 1971 and 1973.

Rigidity of exchange rates in large surplus countries was also infrequent. The important cases were, first, Germany and a few smaller countries and, later, Japan. Criteria for the rapid adjustment of such surpluses were not developed in the formative stages of cooperative discussions; nor was it made very clear what size surplus constituted fundamental disequilibrium. By the time American policymakers became interested in revaluation as part of the adjustment process in the late 1960s, the fixation against devaluation of the dollar was strongly entrenched. The idea that a few other countries should revalue while the parity of the dollar remained fixed was a political nonstarter with surplus countries and would not have cured the problem of the dollar in any case.

The breakdown of the system is also attributed to what were called destabilizing capital flows. But such flows were in reality flights of money induced by increasing awareness on the part of the international business and financial community that a fundamental disequilibrium existed and that par values were sure to be upset. Since the private sector's information on these matters could come only from official statistical sources, the authorities were to blame for delaying action until capital flight had been needlessly provoked. In the critical case of the dollar, the American authorities themselves had known for several years that a fundamental disequilibrium existed. Yet they failed to take corrective action as month after month and year after year passed, and the time drew nearer when a flight from the dollar would force their hands under crisis conditions.

In 1972, the experiment was tried of fixed exchange rates, with wider margins, on the basis of an inconvertible dollar. Even if the dollar devaluation at the Smithsonian had been larger, the inconvertible dollar system would probably have proved unstable, both because it did not command confidence and because the United States was not prepared to undertake the kind of effective measures required to support it. But in addition, the Smithsonian realignment fell far short of what was required to ensure a major strengthening of the dollar. U.S. officials knew that further adjustment would be necessary, and the international business community knew it too. The sharp worsening of the U.S. trade balance in 1972 was due not only to the usual initial adverse effects of devaluation but also reflected the foreign trade community's expectation of a further devaluation of the dollar. The Smithsonian rates were held until early 1973 only because of the heavy support which central banks in Europe and Japan were prepared to give, trying to prove that the Smithsonian agreement had not been a mistake. The stage was set for the experiment of the floating dollar.

What was gained by the dogged effort to hold the gold price constant? In a world of even moderate inflation and rising real incomes, the gold price set in the 1930s was bound sooner or later to increase. The unwarranted refusal to raise it after the mid-1960s simply brought adverse repercussions in terms of loss of confidence, flight from the dollar, gold hoarding, and inflationary impact that are still being felt. The vast dollar outflow from the United States in 1970-73 boosted the money supply in many countries and was a significant stimulus to inflation and inflationary psychology. In addition, the succession of exchange crises, involving particularly sterling, the D-Mark, and the dollar itself, that had been allowed to drag out meant blow after blow to public confidence and the credibility of the authorities. The low state of confidence was reflected in the gold market and in the extreme flare-up of commodity prices in 1973. Worse still, the boom in commodity prices provided the backdrop for the OPEC decision to boost oil prices fourfold at the end of 1973.

TABLE 5 Global Reserves (in millions of U.S. dollars)

Amounts Outstanding

	end-1949	end-1950	end-1951	end-1952	end-1953	end-1954	end-1955	end-1956	end-1957	end-1958	end-1959
Gold	32,898	33,232	33,413	33,416	33,810	34,425	34,857	35,692	36,963	37,639	37,607
Foreign exchange	10,954	13,332	13,469	13,994	15,352	16,462	16,730	17,771	17,051	17,105	16,110
IMF reserve position	1,658	1,672	1,713	1,777	1,891	1,845	1,880	2,278	2,313	2,557	3,250
Total reserves	45,510	48,236	48,595	49,187	51,053	52,732	53,467	55,741	56,327	57,301	56,967

	Changes 1950-59	Yearly Average Changes
Gold	4,709	471
Foreign exchange	5,156	516
IMF reserve positions	1,592	159
Total reserves	11,457	1,146

Amounts Outstanding

	end-1959	end-1960	end-1961	end-1962	end-1963	end-1964	end-1965	end-1966	end-1967	end-1968	end-1969
Gold	37,607	37,765	38,594	38,969	40,007	40,490	41,526	40,776	39,392	38,730	38,923
Foreign exchange	16,110	18,493	19,130	19,896	22,692	24,217	23,993	25,605	29,313	32,544	33,021
IMF reserve position	3,250	3,570	4,159	3,795	3,940	4,155	5,377	6,331	5,748	6,488	6,726
Total reserves	56,967	59,828	61,883	62,660	66,639	68,862	70,896	72,712	74,453	77,762	78,670

	Changes 1960-69	Yearly Average Changes
Gold	1,316	131
Foreign exchange	16,911	1,691
IMF reserve positions	3,476	348
Total reserves	21,703	2,170

TABLE 5 Global Reserves (in millions of U.S. dollars)   continued

Amounts Outstanding

	End-1969	End-1970	End-1971	End-1972	End-1973	End-1974	End-1975	End-1976	End-1977	End-1978
Gold[a]	38,923	36,990	38,993	38,660	42,958	43,535	41,579	41,065	43,015	46,445
Foreign exchange	33,021	45,432	81,376	104,162	122,430	154,595	160,239	185,679	243,007	287,689
IMF reserve position	6,726	7,697	6,895	6,867	7,441	10,828	14,778	20,606	21,973	19,333
SDRs	-	3,124	6,379	9,430	10,624	10,845	10,260	10,057	9,879	10,566
Total reserves	78,670	93,243	133,643	159,119	183,453	219,803	226,856	257,407	317,874	364,033

Yearly Changes

		1970	1971	1972	1973	1974	1975	1976	1977	1978
Gold[a]		-1,933	2,003	-333	4,298	577	-1,956	-514	1,950	3,430
Foreign exchange		12,411	35,944	22,786	18,268	32,165	5,644	25,440	57,328	44,682
IMF reserve position		971	-802	-28	574	3,387	3,950	5,828	1,367	-2,640
SDRs		3,124	3,255	3,051	1,194	221	-585	-203	-178	687
Total reserves		14,573	40,400	25,476	24,334	36,350	7,053	30,551	60,467	46,159

[a] Valued at official prices: $35 an ounce until end-1971, $38 at end-1972, and $42.22 in 1973-78.

Disenchantment with Free Floating

Soon after the Smithsonian exchange-rate structure broke down, U.S. official opinion coalesced on permanent floating of the dollar. The effort at reform of the system through the creation of Special Drawing Rights by the IMF had failed because it ignored the real difficulty of the gold-dollar disequilibrium. And the later attempt at reform by the Committee of Twenty was no more successful. The committee produced a paper plan, but it could not reconcile the diverse objectives of stable exchange rates, convertibility, adjustment rules, and the claims of developing countries to real resources.

Although the floating dollar behaved about as well as could have been expected in 1973, subsequent experience turned out much worse than anticipated. One reason for this is that the American authorities had not considered how a floating dollar might need to be managed. Indeed, reaction against the policies of the 1960s led them to renounce any efforts to manage the balance of payments. Controls on capital exports were given up and so, more or less, was intervention in the exchange market. Thus, the fate of the dollar was left to other countries and their policy with respect to holding reserves in dollars, while the adjustment process was left to floating exchange rates.

Fixed rates and floating rates have usually been discussed in terms of their desirability as a system. But from a practical standpoint, the question of a fixed or a floating rate depends on the particular currency involved and on the particular situation in which it happens to be. Floating, at least temporarily, is a useful expedient in special circumstances; but to float the reserve currency of the system is something else again because of the importance of the dollar exchange and money markets and the danger of precipitating capital flight, particularly out of the large volume of U.S. securities in foreign hands. There is, after all, a vast difference between floating and sinking.

The other major factor which upset the floating dollar was the domination of the international payments system by the large net deficit of oil-consuming countries, corresponding to the OPEC (or OAPEC) surplus. In this negative-sum game for the non-OPEC world, once deficit countries began to feel the limits of their foreign credit potential and had to economize on nonoil imports, there was bound to be heightened pressure on the United States, forcing it toward payments deficit.

For a while, the difficulties of other oil-importing countries took the strain off the dollar. But the surplus registered in U.S. trade in 1975 soon proved more than the rest of the world—faced with high oil payments, a growing burden of interest and amortization on foreign debt, and the significant surpluses of some nonoil countries—was able to bear. In the nature of things, other deficit countries were forced to adopt measures to restrain demand and strengthen their external payments.

The upshot was that the U.S. payments deficit had become very large by the first half of 1977, and there was an enormous deficit in its trade account. The trade deficit could be explained to some extent by lagging recovery abroad from the recession of 1974-75 and undervaluation of the currencies of a few surplus countries, particularly Japan and Germany. But the trade patterns of many other countries were also determined by increasing restrictions, bilateral arrangements, and export credit facilities—designed not only to help the balance of payments but to protect domestic employment. In a number of countries, many business firms acted to maintain traditional trade channels, despite the availability of cheaper goods from depreciating-currency countries; even consumers were reluctant to buy foreign goods that displaced workers at home. In addition, pushing exports to the vast U.S. market was attractive, as always, to bolster capacity utilization. Americans, on the other hand, did not have a strong buy-American sentiment, and export promotion by some U.S. firms was blunted by a need to sustain activity in their production facilities abroad.

The Carter administration, trying to foster Keynesian demand policy in a post-Keynesian world of cost-push inflation, was reluctant to slow down domestic economic expansion to reduce the trade deficit; instead, it emphasized the necessity for surplus countries to adopt a two-pronged policy of stimulating internal expansion in order to boost their imports and appreciating their currencies in order to restrain their exports. It was an appeal to Bretton Woods exchange-rate policies in a post-Bretton Woods world of resistance to trade adjustment. The surplus countries, having gained control over the inflation outburst of 1973-74, did not want to give a greater stimulus to domestic demand and thereby risk a renewal of inflation. Nor did they want their currencies to go up and up against the dollar and suffer an excessive loss of competitiveness in world markets. To participants in the exchange market, it seemed clear that depreciation of the dollar was U.S. national policy and heavy selling of dollars was the inevitable consequence. In the autumn of 1977, the decline of the dollar accelerated, and a speculative selling wave developed. Heavy intervention by the Bundesbank was a sign of widespread disillusion with free floating.

The authorities in Washington, however, continued to rely on the possibility that the exchange market could find its own equilibrium. The Federal Reserve Bank of New York provided an exception to this mode of thinking and advocated taking a firm stand to stabilize the dollar. Yet while official statements proclaimed an intention to maintain the strength of the dollar, official intervention was only marginal, and the market was still left to find its own floor. So the slide of the dollar continued in 1978, despite large interventions by foreign central banks and several half-percent discount rate increases by the Federal Reserve. The movement of the dollar much surpassed the decline that might have been required to correct for higher U.S. costs and prices, but the trade deficit was slow to respond; at the same time, the floating down of the dollar was bolstering U.S. inflation because of higher prices of imports and import-substitutes and also because the flight from dollars into real assets pushed up the latter's value. Dollar depreciation fed inflationary psychology and inflation encouraged further depreciation.

In the face of this spiral, the United States finally announced in November 1978 that intervention facilities equivalent to $30 billion had been mobilized and that the dollar would be supported to whatever extent was necessary to prevent further depreciation. The discount rate was raised by one full point, and a special reserve requirement was imposed on large time deposits to help curb inflation and to strengthen confidence in the currency. Thus, the new policy priorities were to put a damper on inflation and to hold the exchange value of the dollar.

The Need for a Stable Dollar

As the dollar remains the principal reserve currency of the monetary system, so its stability is still the central pillar on which the soundness of the system must rest. Although other countries may look upon their currencies largely as microlinks in the network of the system, the United States is obliged to take a more global or macromonetary view. The critical macro-identity of the monetary system, without any gold being added to reserves, is that the sum of payments deficits is equal to the sum of surpluses, including the OPEC surplus. The financing of surpluses, together with the growth of international transactions, requires a continued increase of reserves, and the long years of experience since 1958 have demonstrated that a U.S. deficit is essential to meeting the system's need for rising international liquidity. For a nondollar currency that had suffered comparable exchange crises and depreciation, the appropriate aim of the authorities would be to impose stabilization measures in order to secure a basic external surplus and rising reserves to restore confidence in the currency. But the dollar's unique place in the system would soon frustrate any attempt by the United States to secure a lasting surplus along these lines.

Far from having such an objective, of course, the United States allowed a huge deficit to develop—a deficit much beyond the system's reasonable need for liquidity. Although many firms in the United States and abroad reacted to the large depreciation of the dollar in 1977-78, the reactions were, for a time at least, double-edged. Not only was a headlong flight from the dollar precipitated, but foreign buyers of U.S. goods limited purchases while the dollar was dropping. The U.S. trade deficit in 1978 amounted to $34 billion, and the official settlements deficit, for the second year in succession, was over $30 billion.

With an imbalance of this size, the weak link in the policy pursued after

November 1978 to maintain stability of the dollar was the absence of a complex of measures directly aimed at a substantial reduction of the deficit itself. Without an effective policy program to assure this critical objective, the danger remains that the burden of foreign-currency support for the dollar may become unmanageable. While the expectations of the U.S. authorities were obscure, they seemed until late 1979 to be relying on a convergence of growth rates in the main industrial countries and the lagged effect of depreciation in order to bring about sufficient adjustment.

Effective policy measures are obviously measures that work in the situation being confronted. Moderate steps can be effective when they are taken promptly, whereas indecision and delay in the face of accelerating disequilibrium will, in the end, demand much more potent and painful measures. All too often official procrastination caused by the political timetable or by fears of an adverse political reaction has resulted in accelerated inflation and external deficits. The worsening of the U.S. balance of payments in 1976 should have been an ample warning signal of growing disequilibrium, which demanded a higher priority for the external sector and a no-risk policy against renewed inflation. But the initial policy attitude of the Carter administration was just the reverse, which all but guaranteed the need for much more forceful measures later.

The usual instruments called upon to support exchange stability after depreciation of the currency are restrictive monetary and fiscal policy, with the intention of moderating economic activity so as to reduce inflation, improve the balance of payments, and restore confidence. This adjustment process has often been effective and, indeed, must produce results if pushed to the limit. The U.S. authorities relied on this type of policy to support the return to exchange stability in the late months of 1978 and sought, in addition, to impose voluntary guidelines for wage increases. But as the situation was highly unfavorable and as pushing restraint to the limit has social and political costs, it would have been in order to call upon direct balance-of-payments controls if only for the benefit of their shock effect.

Use of Controls

However the situation may develop, the inhibition against using direct controls on a temporary basis is a weakness in the U.S. armory of monetary and economic weapons. No doubt caution must be the watchword in the imposition of direct controls because they can mask the need for more basic adjustment measures, invite bureaucratic abuse, and often be effective for only short periods. But cases and times arise when the free play of market forces is subject to obstacles, as it has been with respect to trade, or when a market does not supply its own brakes against excesses, as has occurred in the exchange market. In such instances, rejecting direct controls can frustrate the attainment of more essential objectives.

The U.S. balance of payments, for example, has been in substantial deficit on both capital and current account. Given the tremendous need for oil imports, the capital account should have been in surplus rather than in deficit, and allowing the free export of funds by the capital market and the banking system was not justified. The extremes to which such movements can go were shown in the fourth quarter of 1978, when the net foreign assets of the banks increased by over $14 billion. While it was an exceptional period, to aim at shifting the capital-account balance entirely by restrictive monetary policy can involve undue restriction of domestic economic activity. It would be expedient to impose temporary controls on capital exports to allow a more reasonable trade-off.

The U.S. position in the monetary system has sometimes been likened to that of a bank.[1] This designation is inappropriate if it is meant to suggest that an excess of total foreign assets over total foreign liabilities of the United States should be sufficient to ensure a sound external position of the currency. The market knows that private net foreign assets cannot be used to offset net official liabilities, especially liquid liabilities, and changing the statistical presentation of the balance of payments does not bolster confidence in the dollar in the face of rapidly rising official liabilities. Accordingly, the option of direct control over capital exports must be considered.

The lagging response of the trade deficit to the depreciation of the dollar has been another example of a difficulty which could be eased by temporary direct controls. Voluntary and legal controls have been used to limit imports of various individual products in the interest of protecting domestic industries. But a broader imposition of controls as a balance-of-payments protection is needed when competitive prices fail to influence the channels of trade sufficiently. In this instance, hesitating to take effective action cannot be accounted for strictly by unfailing faith in market freedom; the United States is quite prepared to have Japan impose export restrictions on itself. This U.S. attitude recalls the situation in the late 1960s, when revaluation was urged upon surplus countries while the par value of the dollar was to be rigidly maintained.

All too often it appears that the question of whether to impose controls as an exception to the general reliance on free markets is decided on political grounds. The price of oil in the United States was held down by controls for political reasons, even though the low price was an obstacle to adjustment to the new energy situation. On the other hand, the government backed away from wage controls because of political considerations even though wage demands were highly exaggerated by inflationary psychology, and the dominant power of strong labor organizations compromised the process of what is called free collective bargaining. Hence, the appeal both to a free market philosophy and to the imposition of controls is often determined by political expediency, with the result being governmental weakness and a failure to face realities.

I want to emphasize that I am not advocating direct controls when free market forces are perfectly capable of bringing about essential adjustments, but the case is quite different when there are obstacles to adjustment that the market cannot overcome or when distortions of market forces are themselves a cause of disequilibrium. To reject any use of direct controls in such circumstances is to confuse ends with means.

The Need to Curb Inflation

None of this, however, diminishes the need for the United States to bring its inflation under control if the balance of payments is to be successfully managed and reasonable stability achieved both in the dollar's exchange rate and in the monetary system at large. Inflation weakens confidence in the currency, besides attracting imports and limiting exports at any given exchange rate; indeed, it is the classic scenario for balance-of-payments difficulties. While dominance over cost-push inflation is to a significant extent an exercise in the art of government and the molding of public opinion, the imposition of adequate fiscal and monetary restraint is much more a matter of political will. Yet like many other countries, the United States has become more tolerant of inflation; it has accepted a higher rate of price increase as normal. And when an acceleration of inflation threatens, the urge to delay restraining measures is justified by the argument over the short-term trade-off between greater price stability and higher unemployment.

The Federal Reserve authorities have not escaped influence by these attitudes. In the late months of 1978 and for most of 1979, monetary policy was far from severely restrictive, although inflation was at a high rate and the declared objectives were to bring it down and to stabilize the dollar. As inflationary expectations had become stronger, money market interest rates at 10-11 percent did not mean the same monetary squeeze that they did ten or even five years earlier. Restraint was, however, sharply intensified after October 1979, and interest rates rose toward the 20 percent level. Whatever short-term peaks interest rates may reach, mastery of inflation will require a somewhat restrictive orientation of policy to be sustained not merely for a brief spell but over a run of years.

Lord O'Brien, in a lecture to the Belgian Royal Economic Society,[2] has made a strong plea for the independence of central banks. The importance of this cannot be stressed too often. It has been apparent that the countries with strong central banks have achieved the best record in the struggle for monetary stability. The United States was among this group of countries for much of the postwar period. But the Federal Reserve has become a target for growing harassment, the need for secrecy in its deliberations and policymaking has been infringed upon and its independence from political pressures weakened. The situation, on the other hand, demands that the Federal Reserve be supported, both officially and by public opinion, in its efforts to limit the growth of credit and to make bolder use of monetary policy instruments. It is also worth reemphasizing that domestic stability and external stability are ultimately indivisible. In the United States, both public and official opinion remain inclined to consider the external sector as the tail which must not be allowed to wag the dog. Yet increased U.S. dependence on imported oil should be evidence enough that a healthy balance of payments is vital to the well-being of the entire economy. And the damaging effects of the fall of the dollar should be evidence enough that monetary disorder in the domestic economy is aggravated by neglect of external imbalance.

Alternatives to the Dollar?

Although a comprehensive new blueprint for the world monetary system is not in prospect, the question arises whether any particular reforms or innovations can be found to alleviate the strain on the dollar and contribute to future stability of the monetary system. Rising gold reserves, for example, formerly financed part of countries' aggregate surpluses without corresponding deficits, and this function of gold could have been considerably augmented by a rise in its official price. The opportunity for this, however, has been substantially lost by the course of events. Speculative forces in the gold market gradually gained momentum during the 1970s, and price movements became larger—until the explosion of 1979, which put all previous developments in the shade. (See Figure 4.) After the U.S. measures of November 1, 1978 (including further expansion of the U.S. Treasury gold sales) had halted the dollar's slide and brought a decline in the gold price to $208, the price began to rise once more in December—this time not only in dollars, but in terms of all major currencies. Demand was boosted by events in Cambodia and Iran and by the OPEC countries' decision in mid-December to raise oil prices progressively in 1979. Gold passed the $250 mark for the first time in early February 1979. It then eased to $232 in mid-April, but a renewed upward movement was triggered by the U.S. Treasury's announcement that it was halving the volume of gold to be sold at its monthly auctions. Further increases in oil prices, exchange-rate uncertainties, and concern about accelerating inflation, particularly in the United States, where the market in gold futures was now playing a significant role, all helped to intensify the demand for gold. Amid sometimes hectic trading conditions, the price

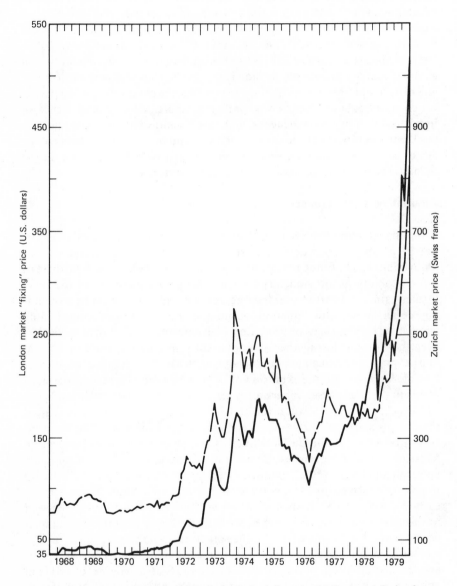

Figure 4. Market prices of gold bars in U.S. dollars (solid line) and Swiss francs (dashed line), 1968-79 (end-of-month, per fine ounce).

reached $300 in July 1979, $400 at the beginning of October, and $500 in the last week of December, when the entry of Soviet troops into Afghanistan added a major new element to anxieties about the international situation. The gold price leaped ahead in the early weeks of 1980, increasing on some single days by as much as $80 and reaching a peak of $850 in late January. At that point, the market price had within little more than a year roughly quadrupled in terms of all major currencies.

To be sure, gold will remain a major element in global reserves for the foreseeable future. The monetary authorities of countries outside the Communist bloc hold between them more than 1 billion ounces of gold, of which over one quarter belongs to the United States. At a price of, say, $525 an ounce, these Western official gold holdings are worth about $600 billion, almost twice as much as all other reserve assets together at end-1979 (that is, foreign exchange, SDRs, and net reserve positions in the IMF). Although the United States has sold some gold in recent years, no other country has been willing to do so (except in conditions of acute economic difficulty), and there is no superior asset for which monetary authorities would be willing to exchange gold. Gold is thus a preferred asset of central banks—as well as of many private individuals. Monetary uses are likely to be found for gold reserves from time to time. In the past, Italy has borrowed foreign exchange against gold collateral, and South Africa made some gold sales under repurchase agreements. Moreover, confidence in the dollar would benefit if the U.S. authorities abandoned their continuing antagonism toward gold. From the standpoint of confidence, the sales of gold to the market out of U.S. reserves should be stopped altogether, not just halved as they were in April 1979, and not just held at erratic intervals rather than regularly; and the published reserves should be revalued nearer the current market price.

Nevertheless, gold has no well defined monetary role at present. For it to regain such a role, monetary authorities would have, as a minimum, to buy and sell gold to one another. It would be a major innovation for the authorities to attempt this without first repegging their currencies to gold, or at least without reasonable assurance that the world price of gold would remain stable over a prolonged period. No such assurance is conceivable with an economic climate of continuing rapid inflation in many countries, and with a gold market dominated by speculation and price volatility. The United States, of course, has had no intention anyhow of reverting to a fixed gold parity for the dollar; but even had it wished to do so, the idea of such a "return to gold" could, in the circumstances of recent years, be no more than a fantasy.

The European Monetary System set up in 1979 to consolidate and extend regional fixed-rate arrangements in Europe calls for member countries to deposit with the European Monetary Co-operation Fund part of their gold reserves (initially 20 percent) valued at market-related prices. In its initial form this commitment means little more than that gold is one element determining the size of mutual swap credits available within the EMS. The swap lines themselves are denominated in the new European Currency Unit (ECU), which is a basket of currencies. The EMS concept could become a first step in restoring the use of gold in transactions between monetary authorities, but only after it had proved possible to keep the price of gold on the free market within a narrow range of fluctuation and without a marked upward trend; this in turn implies that inflation will have abated and exchange rates become reasonably stable. Even then, a political consensus on the restoration of an active monetary role to gold would remain elusive, so long as the United States and also the International Monetary Fund (acting here partly as spokesman for the Third World) were still hostile to it.

Another suggestion for relieving the need for U.S. deficits to supply the growth of reserves has been for evolution toward a multicurrency reserve system. Such relief to the U.S. deficit does not arise from the type of exchange-market support arrangements operated in the later 1970s by Germany, Japan, and Switzerland. These arrangements involve the central banks concerned taking in dollars against the amount of their own currencies that they supply to the market or to the U.S. authorities. They are financing and substitution arrangements rather than adjustment arrangements. For a genuine multicurrency reserve system to arise, the reserves supplied by Germany, Japan, and Switzerland would have to stem from overall balance-of-payments deficits of those countries. Such deficits need not necessarily mean a weak payments position, as these countries could have surpluses on current account, with the deficit emerging from overseas loans and investments in excess of the current-account surplus. The United States ran just such a deficit in 1951-57, when foreign monetary authorities acquired an average of less than $700 million a year in dollar reserves.

Accumulation of official reserves in D-Marks, Swiss francs, and yen had reached a significant level by the end of the 1970s. In addition, sterling reserves were in process of reversing much of the substantial decline that they had undergone in 1976, and some reserves were also placed in French francs. In 1978, dollars still accounted for 76 percent of global foreign-currency reserves. The dollar figure, however, included some $87 billion—more than 40 percent of total reserves in dollars—held by the central banks of Germany, Switzerland, and Japan. These secondary reserve centers are unable in practice to engage in significant diversification out of dollars, not least because part of their dollar holdings comprises the proceeds of support operations, rather than a welcome—and needed—accretion of external reserves. When the secondary reserve centers are excluded from the figures, the share of dollars in exchange reserves at the end of 1978 works out at 65.7

percent, indicating that diversification on the part of those relatively free to pursue it had already gone further than was commonly recognized.

Nevertheless, the extent to which payments deficits in Germany, Japan, and other countries can be looked to as a future source of reserve growth is uncertain. In the first place the scope for these countries to run deficits as reserve centers without jeopardizing the strength of their currencies is smaller than for the United States; and the countries themselves have no desire to test those limits. Second, they have less extensive financial markets than the United States in which other countries can or could place reserves. In addition, a multicurrency reserve system would be likely to generate stability problems of its own. These problems would be lessened insofar as the acquisition of reserves in nondollar currencies reflected an autonomous and lasting wish by monetary authorities to diversify their reserve-asset portfolios in the interest of risk avoidance, and not merely a temporary reaction to weakness of the dollar. Such a lasting change seems quite likely, in view both of the dollar's record of depreciation in the 1970s (which will not be soon forgotten) and of the external borrowing in nondollar currencies undertaken by a considerable number of countries. Even then, however, it may not prove easy to meet increased demand for official holdings of nondollar currencies in an orderly way. A high degree of exchange stability will be required to operate a multicurrency reserve system in which the equal attractiveness of several different currencies as reserves is maintained over time through modest differences in interest rates.

Finally, the amended (post-Jamaica) IMF Articles incorporate the idea that IMF Special Drawing Rights should eventually become the principal element in the creation of monetary reserves. Here too, the distinction between financing or substitution arrangements, on the one hand, and balance-of-payments adjustment, on the other, has to be kept in mind. Under the first heading, a currency substitution account in the IMF began to be seriously negotiated during 1979, the U.S. authorities having dropped their previous opposition and come out in support of the idea. Such an account would allow countries seeking diversification of their reserves to deposit dollars with the Fund against an asset denominated in SDRs. The notion is akin to that of "consolidating the dollar overhang," which was prominent in the monetary reform debates of 1972-74. (See Chapter 8.) If successful, a substitution account would lessen pressure on secondary reserve centers to provide facilities for diversification in terms of their own currencies. It might also be seen by the U.S. authorities as a painless way of helping to strengthen the dollar, although this would depend partly on the extent to which the United States itself carried the exchange risk between dollars and SDRs inherent in the substitution account.

Success of the arrangement is not, however, a foregone conclusion, in either the short run or the long run. The secondary reserve-center countries will not wish the United States to feel it can relax its own efforts to stabilize the dollar. Other countries may be reluctant to acquire and retain substantial amounts of SDRs—a standard basket of, at present, 16 currencies—in preference to ordinary holdings of a smaller number of currencies, for whose prospective value governments and markets alike have more "feel." This applies particularly if some currencies are "felt" to promise continuing relative strength, making them more attractive than a basket containing good, bad, and indifferent currencies together. Moreover, any subsequent switches between SDR claims and currency balances, if not precluded by appropriate limitations on countries' freedom to vary the composition of reserves (which would reduce the scheme's attractions to reserve holders), may bring stability problems similar to those of a multicurrency system.

As regards adjustment mechanisms, any contribution by the SDR must come essentially from new SDR allocations and not from substitution facilities. As was explained in Chapter 8, the idea, or hope, at the outset was that central banks will look upon SDR allocations as equivalent to an earned increase in gold and dollar reserves, and that surplus countries would accordingly strive to reduce their earned increase in reserves to offset the amounts obtained from SDR allocations. This hope is as unrealistic in the 1980s as it had been in the 1960s—partly because SDR allocations do not expand a country's monetary base and so do not generate an automatic incentive to adjust and partly because the reserve needs of the system cannot in any case be specified in advance and in abstraction from the actual pattern of international payments. No such specification was required in the gold-dollar system, which accordingly had much greater flexibility than can be envisaged for an SDR system. In practice, questions about SDR allocations have been embroiled in the general conflict of national interests and outlooks on monetary affairs, with the developing countries seeking more aid through the "link," low-inflation surplus countries wary of being enticed into faster expansion of international credit than they think advisable, and most countries keen to saddle others with responsibility for balance-of-payments adjustment while minimizing any obligations upon themselves. Since the initial allocation of 9.5 billion SDRs in 1970-72, only one further series of allocations has been agreed to—SDR 4 billion a year in 1979-81. As the free world is not united in political and economic objectives, it is idle to imagine the IMF being transformed into a kind of one-world central bank with extensive powers to control the world supply of reserves.

More Active Cooperation

While the monetary system has not come full circle from fixed par values through free floating and back again to fixed exchange rates, the major industrial countries evidently intend to strive for greater exchange stability in the future than they have experienced in the past several years. Not only has the United States abandoned blind faith in the efficacy of free floating, but the EEC countries have sought to strengthen their regional fixed-rate arrangements through the establishment of the EMS. Various factors will continue to make the achievement of greater exchange stability difficult. Cost-push inflation is a persistent threat to competitive prices, and budget pressures of the welfare state are liable to generate excessive money creation. After so much exchange turmoil, it will take time to rebuild confidence, and large flights of money from shaky currencies will remain likely. In short, the monetary system needs to be managed, and the other countries, along with the United States, should be prepared to play their part in managing it. The composition of reserves and the possibilities for supervising the creation of international liquidity are two major issues that call for a cooperative approach by the leading industrial countries. Other monetary questions needing cooperative consideration include exchange rates, the relationship of the new European Monetary System to the dollar, and the sharing of essential international lending by surplus countries.

The United States has been seeking cooperation largely through bilateral discussion, but there is need for an active forum in which the principles of joint management can be worked out. Joint management has been lacking since the early 1970s despite the plethora of international meetings, because the United States, in its resentment at having to devalue in 1971, allowed the Group of Ten to become an empty shell. Meetings of the IMF Interim Committee have given too much time to formal speeches, and the diversity of interests represented in the committee limits its ability to come to grips with the problems of the system.

Under prevailing circumstances, the best solution is for the United States to revitalize the Group of Ten; the Group is composed of the major countries that must form the nucleus of cooperation, which is why it was constituted as a group in the first place. The emergence of major reserve holders in OPEC, and of newly industrializing nations in other parts of the Third World, does not alter this basic fact. The G-10 central-bank governors who meet at the BIS can deal with technical problems, but they need governmental directives to make real headway on the substance of cooperation. Working Party 3 of the OECD serves the function of analyzing current and prospective developments, but the Group of Ten is more suited for preparing policy decisions.

Active cooperation among the leading industrial countries is more urgently needed now than ever because the negative-sum game of the system without gold and with the OPEC surplus is much more difficult to operate than the positive-sum game of the 1950s and the early 1960s. Under the pressure of Western recession and the OPEC surplus, trade and payments restrictions have increased, and the adjustment process has been made more onerous. The amended IMF Articles are relatively permissive on exchange-rate policies and do not provide the clear guidelines that were part of the Bretton Woods conception.

The problem for the monetary authorities in the 1980s and beyond will be how to maintain exchange stability in a fundamentally unstable environment. This task is not one that they can ignore in the hope that markets will resolve it for them. The march of events has often been described as being the result of impersonal and mysterious forces. But as I have seen it, the force and determination of political leadership, or the lack of it, is a key element in the chemical compound of monetary affairs.

Notes

Chapter 1. Balance-of-Payments Adjustment and the Gold-Dollar System

1. In his economic column in the London *Evening News,* February 12, 1973.

2. D. S. L. Cordwell, *Technology, Science and History,* London, 1972, p. 73.

3. For a sophisticated analysis of this phenomenon, see W. D. Nordhaus, "The Political Business Cycle," *Review of Economic Studies,* April 1975, pp. 169-90.

4. Fred Hirsch and J. H. Goldthorpe, eds., *The Political Economy of Inflation,* London, 1978—a broad-gauge inquiry into the causes of contemporary inflation.

5. Stephen V. O. Clarke, *Exchange Rate Stabilization in the Mid-1930s: Negotiating the Tripartite Agreement,* Princeton, N.J., 1977.

6. Armand Van Dormael, *Bretton Woods: Birth of a Monetary System,* London, 1978, p. 88.

7. An arrangement for the reciprocal exchange of national currencies—usually for 90 days.

8. Van Dormael, *Bretton Woods,* p. 84.

9. K. M. Savosnick, "Economic Growth and Balance-of-Payments Problems," in Roy Harrod and D. C. Hague, eds., *International Trade Theory in a Developing World,* London, 1963, sets forth a theoretical analysis of this case.

10. H. G. Johnson, "Toward a General Theory of the Balance of Payments," reprinted in J. A. Frankel and Harry G. Johnson, eds., *The Monetary Approach to the Balance of Payments,* London, 1976, Chapter 2.

11. Made up of the 20 executive directors appointed by the member countries.

12. E. M. Bernstein, "Strategic Factors in Balance-of-Payments Adjustment," *IMF Staff Papers,* August 1956, indicates official thinking about the adjustment problem. Bernstein, as assistant to Harry White, had been an active participant in the creation of the IMF. He subsequently served as director of the IMF economic staff.

13. Printed in the proceedings of the conference *Gespräche der List Gesellschaft,* Stuttgart, 1965.

14. "The Case for Flexible Exchange Rates," in his *Essays in Positive Economics,* Chicago, 1953.

15. The official settlements balance (also called the balance on reserve transactions) was defined as the sum of changes in U.S. reserve assets and in U.S. liabilities (of whatever maturity) to foreign monetary authorities.

16. Reprinted in Herbert G. Grubel, ed., *World Monetary Reform*, Stanford, 1963, p. 71.

17. See, for example, *International Reserves: Needs and Availability*, International Monetary Fund, Washington, D. C., 1970, particularly the papers by Walter S. Salant, "Practical Techniques for Assessing the Need for World Reserves"; Jürg Niehans, "The Need for Reserves of a Single Country"; and the IMF staff, "The Need for Reserves: An Exploratory Paper," and "Reserve Developments, 1951-68."

Chapter 2.   The Pound Sterling

1. *The Economist*, July 18, 1945.

2. Cited by Henry Pelling, *Britain and the Second World War*, London, 1970, p. 233.

3. G. D. N. Worswick and P. H. Ady, *The British Economy, 1945-50*, New York, 1952, p. 10.

4. J. M. Keynes, *How to Pay for the War*, reprinted in 1940 from three articles in *The Times* (London) of November 1939.

5   Richard N. Gardner, *Sterling-Dollar Diplomacy*, Oxford, 1956, pp. 184-87.

6. Ibid., Chapter XI and XII.

7. Christopher Dow, in his outstanding study, states: "The charge that, though necessary now, it was past Government policies that had made it [devaluation in September 1949] so, was perhaps off the mark; a postwar adjustment of the dollar parity . . . would probably have had to be made some time." J. C. R. Dow, *The Management of the British Economy, 1945-60*, New York, 1964, p. 45. Roy Harrod's view that devaluation was due to some sort of speculative accident, combined with inadequate arrangements vis-à-vis the sterling area, ignores the fundamental disequilibrium. See Roy F. Harrod, *The Pound Sterling*, Princeton, 1952, pp. 23-28.

8. Worswick and Ady, *British Economy*, p. 483. Balogh thought that controls were eased too much and that there was an unfair division of the burden between Britain and the United States.

9. André de Lattre, *Politique économique de la France depuis 1945*, Paris, 1966, p. 455.

10. Many details about the 1949 devaluations are given in both Vol. I and II of the informative Fund history, *The International Monetary Fund 1945-65*, Washington, D.C., 1969.

11. Dow, *Management*, p. 41.

12. *The Economist*, September 24, 1949, p. 650.

13. *Hansard,* September 27, 1949.

14. Roy Harrod, *And So It Goes On,* London 1951, p. 139.

15. See R. Nurkse, "The Relation Between Home Investment and External Balance in the Light of British Experience, 1945-55," *Review of Economics and Statistics,* May 1956, pp. 121-54.

16. A group of independent experts of the OEEC, with Professor Lionel Robbins as chairman, stressed the need for restoring an active role to monetary policy. *The International Financial Situation in Member and Associated Countries,* Paris, August 1952; also Robbins, *The Balance of Payments* (Stamp Memorial Lecture), London, November 1951.

17. Andrew Shonfield, *British Economic Policy Since the War,* London, 1958, pp. 216-18.

18. Lord Birkenhead, *The Prof in Two Worlds: The Official Life of Professor F. A. Lindemann,* London, 1961, pp. 203-90.

19. Lord Butler, *The Art of the Possible,* London, 1971, p. 161.

20. Ibid., pp. 157-62.

21. A. W. Phillips, "The Relation Between Unemployment and the Rate of Change of Money Wage Rates in the United Kingdom, 1861-1957," *Economica,* November 1958.

22. *The Diaries of a Cabinet Minister,* London, 1975, Vol. 1, p. 71. Referring to the matter again in August 1965, Crossman says (pp. 289-90): "Devaluation was something Harold Wilson could contemplate as little as George Brown and Callaghan. The division was between, on the one side, these three plus their political advisors and, on the other, the economic advisors. All the economists were urging that the pound should float, while the three politicians were fighting for the pound on the grounds that no Labour Government could survive devaluation in 1965 after the devaluations of 1931 and 1949."

23. *Federal Reserve Bulletin,* March 1969, p. 359.

24. Two views of the size of the effects of the devaluation are given by the National Institute of Economic and Social Research, *Economic Journal,* Special Issue, March 1972 and by Jacques R. Artus, *IMF Staff Papers,* November 1975. I find the views of Artus more realistic and agree with him that the National Institute takes too narrow a view of the effects of the devaluation.

Chapter 3. The French Franc

1. Reprinted in de Gaulle's *Mémoires de guerre,* Vol. III.

2. Ibid.

3. *Le Figaro,* June 29 and July 1, 1973.

4. Wormser has observed that de Gaulle's reputation as a great man and a glory to France is in no way affected by any unsure grasp of monetary problems. The same applies, Wormser added, to Churchill.

5. de Lattre, *Politique économique,* p. 452.

6. After Henri Queuille had become finance minister,

7. E. M. Bernstein, "Some Economic Aspects of Multiple Exchange Rates," *IMF Staff Papers,* 1950-51; also *IMF History,* Vol. II, pp. 120-30.

8. The policy measures in this period are detailed by Warren C. Baum, *The French Economy and the State,* Princeton, N.J., 1958, pp. 92-108. André de Lattre, *Les finances extérieures de la France,* Paris, 1959, covers a longer period.

9. The attention of policymakers and the Assembly was very involved in foreign affairs, such as the intervention in Suez in opposition to Nasser and in support of the Israeli military operation in the Sinai peninsula.

10. "Rapport sur la situation financière," Paris, 1958, reprinted in Jacques Rueff, *Combats pour l'ordre financier,* Paris, 1972.

11. Milita Obradovitch, *Les effets de la dévaluation française de 1958,* Paris, 1970.

12. Raymond Aron, *La révolution introuvable,* Paris, 1968, p. 22.

13. Wormser, *Le Figaro,* July 1, 1973.

14. Jean-Marcel Jenneney, "et Demain?" *Le Figaro,* August 13, 1969.

Chapter 4.   The Deutsche Mark

1. "German Monetary Policy and the Dilemma between Internal and External Equilibrium 1948-75," in the Bundesbank's anniversary volume, *Währung und Wirtschaft in Deutschland 1876-1975,* Frankfurt, 1976. Published in English by the International Finance Section, Department of Economics, Princeton University, 1977.

2. Reprinted in Erhard's book *Deutsche Wirschaftspolitik,* Düsseldorf, 1962, pp. 62-68. Also Hans Moller, "Die westdeutsche Währungsreform von 1948," in the Bundesbank's anniversary volume.

3. An advanced social security system, instituted by Bismarck, had been established in Germany many years before.

4. Alec Cairncross and Per Jacobsson, "Consideration of Germany's Position," OEEC, EPU, Paris, November 20, 1059, mimeograph.

5. OEEC, *10th Annual Report,* p. 34.

6. Emminger, "Germany Monetary Policy."

7. Ibid.

8. To some extent, this increase was the result of flight from the dollar late in 1960, when the price of gold on the London market rose to $40.

9. Charles A. Coombs, *The Arena of International Finance,* New York, 1976, pp. 32-37.

10. M. C. Deppler, "Some Evidence on the Effects of Exchange Rate Changes on Trade," *IMF Staff Papers,* November 1974. An earlier paper by E. Spitäller, *IMF Staff Papers,* March 1970, reached similar results.

11. WP3 is a restricted working party of the OECD Economic Policy Committee dealing mainly with problems of international payments equilibrium.

12. The rate of interest charged by the central bank on the rediscounting of money-market paper.

13. Emminger considers that the real role of the D-Mark and the Swiss franc in the breakdown of the system was not in 1971 but in February-March 1973. See the speech he delivered to the Basel Statistical Society in April 1979, "Wechselkurspolitik und Geldmengensteuerung in der Bundesrepublik Deutschland," mimeograph.

Chapter 5. A Broad View of the Gold-Dollar System

1. The United States had a veto in the IMF, though it never had to use it.

2. *History of the IMF, 1945-65,* Vol. II, p. 191.

Chapter 6. The Defense of the Dollar, 1958-71

1. G. F. Warren and F. A. Pearson, *Interrelationship of Supply and Price,* Ithaca, N.Y. 1927.

2. Sherman J. Maisel, *Managing the Dollar,* New York, 1973, pp. 222-43.

3. Theodore C. Sorensen, *Kennedy,* Harper and Row, 1965.

4. Robert V. Roosa, *The Dollar and World Liquidity,* New York, 1967, p. 13.

5. The substance of the report was put into Kennedy's balance-of-payments message to Congress soon after. Sproul was the former president of the New York Federal Reserve Bank; Blough was a professor of economics at the University of California and former member of the Council of Economic Advisors under President Truman; McCracken, a Michigan University professor, was a member of the Council under President Eisenhower.

6. Triffin's thought was more advanced than mine at that time. In 1960, I knew very little about gold, like most Americans, and did not see the deep significance of gold versus the dollar.

7. Arthur Okun, *The Political Economy of Prosperity,* Washington, D. C., 1969.

8. In answer to a question from the floor at his Moskowitz lecture. "Fiscal Policy and

Inflation," printed in *Inflation,* New York University Press, 1970. This gives a broad discussion of the problems of congressional implementation of fiscal policy.

9.   The paper, updated, was later published in two parts by the Princeton and New York University presses. See the Editors' Introduction to this volume.

10.   Several such schemes are presented by John Parke Young, "United States Gold Policy: The Case for Change," International Finance Section, Princeton University, October 1966. Needless to say, Young had a scheme of his own.

11.   Robert Z. Aliber, "Cost Benefit Analysis of a Rise in the Price of Gold," Washington, D.C., 1962, unpublished.

12.   Coombs, *International Finance,* p. 171.

13.   Robert Solomon, *The International Monetary Sytem 1945-1976,* New York, 1977, Chapter X.

14.   *Federal Reserve Bulletin,* February 1968. Martin said: "To raise the price of gold because the general price level has risen would be like increasing the length of the yardstick because the average height of human beings has increased."

15.   Solomon, *International Monetary System,* Chapter XI.

Chapter 7.   The Smithsonian Agreement

1.   Schweitzer had been fending off suggestions by several executive directors for a Fund study of the gold problem. As a gesture to them, he had invited me about two years earlier to give a talk at the Fund on the significance of the gold price. The audience was in the main hostile to my argument that the system was in fundamental disequilibrium because of the shortage of new gold; the response of Schweitzer and others was that the issuance of SDRs would be a viable remedy for the shortage of gold. Searching for a way to bring home the point, I posed the following question. The IMF staff, I said, will soon have its annual consultations with the United States. After its review of the situation, it will formulate its recommendations for restoring the dollar to equilibrium. Can it, in submitting those recommendations, guarantee that their implementation will stop U.S. gold losses and reestablish a strong dollar, unless the proposals include a considerable rise in the price of gold? Such a guarantee must be based on the world and its monetary authorities as they are, which clearly maintain a strong interest in gold regardless of SDRs. Schweitzer and others simply repeated their faith that the SDR would be an effective remedy for the shortage of gold.

2.   The scheme was published subsequently: Jacques Artus and Rudolf Rhomberg, "A Multilateral Exchange Rate Model," *IMF Staff Papers,* November 1973.

3.   The term "central rate" came into use following the Smithsonian Agreement. It referred to exchange parities declared to the Fund by member countries in lieu of a par value in terms of gold. See M. G. de Vries, *The International Monetary Fund 1966-71,* Vol. I, Chapter 27.

4.   See *IMF International Financial News Survey,* 1971, p. 418.

5. Convertibility, of course, was the essential U.S. technical means of supporting exchange stability of the dollar—as the market well understood.

Chapter 8. Monetary Reform

1. Robert Triffin, *Gold and the Dollar Crisis: The Future of Convertibility,* New Haven, 1960.

2. For a review of all of Harrod's writings on the subject, see Harry G. Johnson, "Roy Harrod on the Price of Gold," in W. A. Eltis et al., *Induction, Growth & Trade: Essays in Honour of Sir Roy Harrod,* New York, 1970.

3. Suardus Posthuma, vice-governor of the Netherlands Bank, writing in a personal capacity. His paper, "The International Monetary System" was published in *Banca Nazionale del Lavoro Quarterly Review,* 1963.

4. Maxwell Stamp, "The Stamp Plan—1962 Version," reprinted in Herbert G. Grubel, ed. *World Monetary Reform,* Stanford, 1963,

5. Henry Wallich, "Cooperation to Solve the Gold Problem," *Harvard Business Review,* May-June 1961. The article focused on cooperation in the composition of reserves, arguing that countries other than the United States should not in the aggregate seek to add to their reserves each year more gold than was becoming available to the monetary system from new production.

6. Issued in the EMB (Ltd.) service, June 26, 1963.

7. Ministerial Statement of the Group of Ten and Annex Prepared by Deputies, August 1964.

8. Group of Ten, *Study Group on the Creation of Reserve Assets,* 1965.

9. Group of Ten, *Communiqué of Ministers and Governors and Report of Deputies,* July 1966.

10. John Williamson, *The Failure of International Monetary Reform, 1971-74,* Sunbury-on-Thames, 1977, pp. 33-34, argues the other side.

11. IMF, *International Monetary Reform: Documents of the Committee of Twenty,* Washington, D.C., 1974.

12. The amended Articles of Agreement have been published by the IMF; the Jamaica communiqué is printed in the *IMF Survey,* January 19, 1974.

Chapter 9. The Floating Dollar and the OPEC Surplus System

1. EMB (Ltd.) report of December 27, 1977.

2. Alfred Marshall, *Principles of Economics,* 2 vols., New York, 1961, pp. 346 and 806.

3. *Brookings Papers on Economic Activity,* Washington, D.C., 1975, pp. 675-715.

4. See *IMF Survey,* January 21, 1974, p. 17; also IMF, *International Monetary Reform, Committee of Twenty,* pp. 216-19.

5. *The International Monetary Tangle,* White Plains, N.Y., p 14.

6. At the International Monetary Conference (held annually by an international group of large banks) in the spring of 1974, a question about gold was put by a banker in the audience to the governors on the platform. At the end of his reply, Governor Carli said, "I do not understand why anyone wants to destroy Italy's reserves," a large part of which were in gold. Chairman Burns, also on the platform, did not offer any explanation. As Burns had been in favor of retaining gold in the system, his silence at this point probably reflected disagreement on the matter in Washington.

7. The IMF Annual Report on Exchange Restrictions was thicker than ever.

8. See *Report of the Advisory Committee on the Presentation of Balance of Payments Statistics,* U.S. Department of Commerce, 1976.

9. *International Herald Tribune,* July 22, 1977.

10. Thomas D. Willett, *Floating Exchange Rates and International Monetary Reform,* American Enterprise Institute, Washington, D. C., 1977, for the complete switch to faith in floating.

Chapter 10.   Summary and Conclusion

1. Walter Salant went some way toward this view in contending that the U.S. deficit resulted from financial intermediation furnished by the United States—lending long-term capital and receiving short-term funds. He did not discuss the possibility that without a deficit on capital account the United States would have had a deficit on current account. See Walter Salant, "Capital Markets and the Balance of Payments of a Financial Center," The Brookings Institution, Washington, D. C., 1966. Further implications of this view are given by Emile Despres, Charles Kindleberger, and Walter Salant, "The Dollar and World Liquidity—A Minority View," *The Economist,* February 5, 1966.

2. Lord O'Brien of Lothbury, "The Independence of the Central Bank," Société Royale d'Economie Politique de Belgique, Bruxelles, December 1977.

Index